ROMAN PORTRAIT SCULPTURE
217-260 A.D.

# COLUMBIA STUDIES
# IN THE
# CLASSICAL TRADITION

*under the direction of*

WILLIAM V. HARRIS (Editor) — † W. T. H. JACKSON
PAUL OSKAR KRISTELLER — † STEELE COMMAGER
EUGENE F. RICE, JR. — ALAN CAMERON
JAMES A. COULTER

## VOLUME XII

LEIDEN
E. J. BRILL
1986

# ROMAN PORTRAIT SCULPTURE
## 217-260 A.D.

*The Transformation of an Artistic Tradition*

BY

SUSAN WOOD

LEIDEN
E. J. BRILL
1986

Columbia Studies in the Classical Tradition *publishes monographs by members of the Columbia University faculty and by former Columbia students. Its subjects are the following: Greek and Latin literature, ancient philosophy, Greek and Roman history, classical archaeology, and the classical tradition in its mediaeval, Renaissance and modern manifestations.*

*The publication of this work was aided by the Stanwood Cockey Lodge Foundation and by Harvard University*

ISBN 90 04 07282 9

PRINTED IN THE NETHERLANDS BY E. J. BRILL

To my parents,
Alexander C. Wood III
and Evaline S. Wood,
in love and gratitude.

# CONTENTS

# PREFACE

This monograph is based on a doctoral dissertation which was submitted to Columbia University in 1979. It deals with a period which has long been recognized as a seminal phase in the origins of late-antique and medieval art, and has been of lively interest to modern scholars. As with most doctoral dissertations, however, the chronological parameters of this study have been somewhat arbitrarily determined. If its publication in book form is to be justified, then, an explanation of the choice of topic is required.

The assassination of Caracalla in 217 brought to an end the last reign of a mature man with a dynastic and constitutional claim to power which the Roman empire was to witness for almost a century. The Severan family managed to perpetuate its power until 235 through two young boys whose distant family connections to Caracalla were strengthened by the convenient fiction that they were his natural sons. After the assassination of Alexander Severus and his mother Julia Mammaea in 235, however, the empire entered a period of near-chaos during which a number of short-lived emperors, usually elected by various legions of the army, rapidly replaced one another, either overthrown by rivals or killed in battle in the frequent border-wars which plagued the Roman provinces. Gallienus managed to reestablish a temporary period of relative political stability between 253 and 268, despite severe military setbacks in the eastern empire, and the humiliating capture by the Sassanian Persians of his father Valerian, who had been Gallienus's senior coregent until 260. Under the patronage of the intellectual Gallienus, literature and philosophy were able to enjoy a brief renaissance. After his death, Rome was again ruled by a series of short-lived "soldier emperors," until the drastic reorganization of the empire under Diocletian.

Despite the political and economic upheavals of this era, however, the visual arts not only survived but expressed in a dramatic and compelling manner the social and psychological effects on individuals of the events of their times. Portraiture, which by its very nature seeks to convey information about a human being's personality and psychological state, gives the modern viewer a particularly vivid insight into the society of the Roman empire in the third century. The expressions of anxiety and emotional stress, long since noted as typical of many of these works of art, are only one part of a larger picture: the shift from naturalistic to abstract and symbolic treatment of human faces during this period reveals much about the ways in which people of this time perceived themselves. It will be my goal in this monograph to trace the steps by which the artistic traditions of conventions of portrait sculpture were changed by artists to meet the new needs of their society and their patrons, both imperial and private.

The period of the last Severans, characterized by classicism and elegant restraint in the treatment of emotions (in official portraiture, at least), was followed by the harsh realism and emotional power of portraits from the period of the soldier emperors. This veristic phase (a term to be defined and discussed in more detail elsewhere) in turn develops into a somewhat abstract style, in which contours and volumes tend to become rather geometric, and features to be expressed by harsh patterns of line which symbolize rather than realistically represent facial expressions. This abstract style reached its maturity during the reign of Gallienus, a period when cool and elegant classicism was again favored in imperial portraiture, but a classicism of a very different type from that of the time of Alexander Severus. Some of the most aesthetically pleasing examples of third-century abstraction are datable to the time of Gallienus, due in part to the willingness of artists of that period to seek decorative effects for their own sake. But the roots of the style are traceable to the preceding soldier-emperor period, and can be seen as a logical outgrowth of some experiments with well-established formal traditions of Roman portraiture.

Needless to say, the periods both before and after the one selected for study are of equal importance for the understanding of the development of late-antique art, but the portraiture from both those eras has been the subject of fairly recent studies, including the dissertation of Sheldon Nodelman on Severan portraiture, an enlarged version of which will soon be forthcoming in book form, and a monograph by Marianne Bergmann on portraits from the time of Gallienus through the later third century. Portrait sculpture of the early and middle third century has been of considerable interest to scholars for many years, but most studies have necessarily been concerned with the identification of imperial portrait types. Discussions of the private portraiture and the development of sculptural styles during this period have tended to be cursory.

It is not my intention to add to the many fine studies of imperial iconography of the third century already in print, but to make use of the imperial portraits whose identifications have now been established with reasonable certainty by the work of such scholars as Bianca-Maria Felletti-Maj, Helga von Heintze, Klaus Fittschen, Max Wegner, and Wegner's collaborators on the *Herrscherbild* series. These identified portraits can now provide a chronology for dating the unidentified portraits of the period, and both the public and private works can then be examined for the light which they can shed on the development of sculptural style during this era. An exhaustive listing of all extant portraits datable to this period, an undertaking more appropriate to a dissertation or to a large, collaborative effort such as *Das römische Herrscherbild*, is not my aim, though I have included an appendix listing all the imperial portraits which are identified with reasonable security.

I do, however, hope to discuss a broad, representative sampling of objects, including some masterpieces which, because they represent unidentifiable private individuals, have received relatively little scholarly attention. These works will now be described in the context of the history of the art of their times, rather than in the sort of short catalogue entries to which they have generally been relegated. An effort has been made to provide photographs of all the works discussed at any length, but in the interests of limiting costs, it has often been necessary to dispense with profile and rear views. The reader interested in locating better photographs of any object discussed here should be able to find appropriate references in the notes.

The assistance of many people has enabled me to undertake these studies. My first and most important debt of thanks is to Professor Richard Brilliant, under whose direction I wrote the dissertation on which this book is based; Professor Alfred Frazer, second reader of the dissertation, and to Professors Evelyn Harrison, William Harris, and James Beck. All these members of the defense committee provided me with constructive criticism, the results of which are reflected in the present text, as are the suggestions of the editorial board of *Columbia Studies in the Classical Tradition*. Mrs. E. A. M. Jackson's editing of the dissertation was of immense value, as was the advice offered to me by many scholars. Professors Klaus Fittschen, Marianne Bergmann, Jean-Charles Balty, and Helga von Heintze were all particularly patient and generous with time and expertise; Professors John D'Arms, Christoph Clairmont, Marion Lawrence, Herbert Long, George Hanfmann, and Sheldon Nodelman all offered valuable suggestions and information. Dr. Anne Haeckl of the University of Colorado at Boulder deserves my special gratitude; when she and I were fellows together at the American Academy in Rome, and were writing dissertations on very similar topics, Dr. Haeckl was consistently generous with books, information, and ideas. And I would also like to express my thanks to Gary Ralph for his tireless and good-humored help with the correspondence and photograph orders involved in this project.

I owe thanks to many institutions, as well as many individuals: to the American Academy in Rome and to the Whiting Foundation, which provided the fellowships which supported the research and writing of the dissertation, and to the Andrew W. Mellon Foundation and to Case-Western Reserve University for a post-doctoral fellowship which enabled me to write most of the present version of this monograph. The curators and staff of many museums were also most generous and cooperative in giving me access to storage areas, archives, and objects not on display. The Fogg Museum of Harvard University, the British Museum, the Ny Carlsberg Glyptotek, the Pergamon Museum at Berlin, the Munich Glyptothek, the Vienna Kunsthistorisches Museum, the Louvre, the Museo Archeologico di Venezia, the Museo Nazionale Romano delle Terme in Rome, the antiquarium of Ostia Antica, the Vatican museums, the J. Paul Getty Museum, and the University Museum at Bonn all deserve my special thanks. The Walters Art Gallery and the Musée Cantonale d'Archéologie in Neuchâtel have also been very generous with photographs and information about objects in their collections. The Deutsches Archaeologisches Institut in Rome and the Cleveland Museum of Art facilitated my research greatly by giving me access to their libraries, and I greatly appreciate their cooperation. And finally, thanks are owed to the Stanwood Cockey Lodge Foundation and the Harvard University for grants which made the publication of this monograph possible.

*Susan Wood*
December, 1983

# ABBREVIATIONS

All periodicals and standard reference works have been abbreviated according to the practice of the *American Journal of Archaeology*, as listed in "Notes for Contributors and Abbreviations," *AJA*, 82 (1978), 3-10. Published books will be cited in full in the first reference, and in abbreviated title format thereafter, both in notes and in the appendix. The following are some of the more frequently cited books:

Amelung, *Die Skulpturen des vaticanischen Museums:* Walther Amelung. *Die Skulpturen des vaticanischen Museums*. Vol. I, Berlin: Georg Reimer, 1903. Vol. II, Berlin: Georg Reimer, 1908.

Bergmann, *Studien*: Marianne Bergmann. *Studien zum römischen Porträt des 3. Jahrhunderts n. Chr*. Vol. 18 of *Antiquitas*, 3rd ser. Bonn, 1977.

Bernoulli, *Römische Ikonographie*: Johann Jakob Bernoulli, *Römische Ikonographie*. Stuttgart: W. Spemann, 1882-1894.

Blümel, *Römische Bildnisse*: Carl Blümel. *Römische Bildnisse*. Bd. suppl., *Katalog der Sammlung antiker Skulpturen*. Berlin: Schoetz, 1933.

Bracker, "Bildnisse Gordians III": Jörgen Bracker. "Bestimmung der Bildnisse Gordians III nach einer neuen ikonographischen Methode." Diss., Westfälische Wilhelms Universität zu Münster, 1966.

Breckenridge, *Likeness*: James D. Breckenridge, *Likeness: A Conceptual History of Portraiture*. Evanston: Northwestern University Press, 1968.

Buchholz, *Kaiserinnen*: Käte Buchholz. *Die Bildnisse der Kaiserinnen der Severerzeit nach ihren Frisuren, 193-235 n. Chr*. Frankfurt am Main, 1963.

Charbonneaux, *Sculpture grecque et romaine:* Jean Charbonneaux. *La Sculpture grecque et romaine au Musée du Louvre*. Paris: Ministère d'état, affaires culturelles, 1963.

Felletti-Maj, *Iconografia*: Bianca-Maria Felletti-Maj, *Iconografia romana imperiale*. Rome: L'Erma di Bretschneider, 1958.

——, *Ritratti*: Bianca-Maria Felletti-Maj, *Museo Nazionale Romano: i ritratti*. Rome: Libreria dello Stato, 1953.

Giuliano, *Catalogo*: Antonio Giuliano. *Catalogo dei ritratti romani del museo profano Lateranense*. Vatican: Tipografia poliglotta Vaticana, 1957.

von Heintze, *Römische Porträt-Plastik*: Helga von Heintze. *Römische Porträt-Plastik*. Stuttgart: H. E. Gunter, 1961.

Kluge and Lehmann-Hartleben, *Grossbronzen*: Kurt Kluge and Karl Lehmann-Hartleben. *Grossbronzen der römischen Kaiserzeit*. 2 vols. Berlin-Leipzig: De Gruyter, 1927.

L'Orange, *Studien*: H. P. L'Orange, *Studien zur Geschichte des spätantiken Porträts*. Oslo: H. Aschebourg & Co., 1933.

Mansuelli, *Galleria degli Uffizi*: Guido A. Mansuelli, *Galleria degli Uffizi: le sculture*. 2 vols. Rome: Istituto poligrafico dello stato, 1961.

Meischner, "Frauenporträt": Jutta Meischner. "Das Frauenporträt der Severerzeit." Diss., Freie Universität, Berlin, 1964.

Mustilli, *Il Museo Mussolini*: Domenico Mustilli. *Il Museo Mussolini*. Rome: Libreria dello Stato, 1939.

Nodelman, "Severan Imperial Portraits": Sheldon Nodelman. "Severan Imperial Portraits, A.D. 193-217." Diss., Yale University, 1965.

Pelikàn, *Vom antiken Realismus zur spätantiken Expressivität:* Oldrich Pelikàn. *Vom antiken Realismus zur spätantiken Expressivität*. Prague: Státni Pedag, 1965.

F. Poulsen, *Catalogue*: Frederik Poulsen. *Catalogue of Ancient Sculpture, Ny Carlsberg Glyptotek*. 2nd ed., trans. W. E. Calvert. Copenhagen: Ny Carlsberg Glyptotek, 1951.

——, *English Country Houses*: Frederik Poulsen, *Greek and Roman Portraits in English Country Houses*. Oxford: Clarendon Press, 1923.

V. Poulsen, *Les Portraits romains:* Vagn Poulsen. *Les Portraits romains.* Copenhagen: Munksgaard, for the Ny Carlsberg Glyptotek, 1974, Vol. II.

*RIC:* Harold Mattingly, Edward A. Sydenham, and C. V. H. Sutherland. *The Roman Imperial Coinage.* Vol. IV part 2, London: Spink and Son, Ltd., 1938. Vol. IV part 3, London, Spink and Son, Ltd., 1949.

Stuart-Jones, *Museo Capitolino:* Members of the British School at Rome. *The Sculptures of the Museo Capitolino.* Ed. H. Stuart-Jones. Oxford: Clarendon Press, 1912.

——, *Palazzo dei Conservatori:* Members of the British School at Rome. *The Sculptures of the Palazzo dei Conservatori.* Ed. H. Stuart-Jones. Oxford: Clarendon Press, 1926.

Traversari, *Ritratti:* Gustavo Traversari. *Museo archeologico di Venezia: i ritratti.* Rome: Istituto poligrafico dello stato, 1968.

Visconti, *Museo Torlonia:* Charles Ludovico Visconti. *Les Monuments de sculpture antique du musée Torlonia.* Text and plates. Rome, 1884.

Wegner, Bracker and Real, *Herrscherbild,* III[3]: Max Wegner, Jörgen Bracker, and Willi Real, *Gordianus III bis Carinus.* Vol. III part 3 of *Das römische Herrscherbild.* Ed. Max Wegner. Berlin: Mann, 1979.

Wiggers and Wegner, *Herrscherbild,* III[1]: Heinz Wiggers and Max Wegner, *Caracalla bis Balbinus.* Vol. III, part 1 of *Das römische Herrscherbild.* Ed. Max Wegner. Berlin: Mann, 1971.

# INTRODUCTION

A) *Problems, Methods and Goals*

Of the works of sculpture which have survived from classical antiquity, few intrigue the modern observer as much as those which record the appearances of real individuals of another era. The viewer of ancient portraits is likely to feel both a fascination with the uniqueness of the persons portrayed and a sense of the common humanity which he shares with these people of the past. Yet because of the emotional nature of these responses, perceptions of portraits tend to be affected by a variety of factors. The viewer of a portrait can be manipulated by his own attitudes, in particular by the expectations with which he approaches the work.

What is portraiture, and what functions does it serve? In modern usage, "portrait" is generally taken to mean a work of art which reproduces the appearance of an individual human being in such a way that a viewer familiar with the subject can recognize his image. Concepts of portraiture have varied considerably throughout history, however. For cultures such as that of ancient Egypt, the inscription of the subject's name on a statue was sufficient to convert that statue into an image of that individual.[1] No effort needed to be made to reproduce the person's unique appearance: the goal of making the image recognizable was achieved through verbal, rather than through iconographic, means. Conversely, a very precise study of a nude model may be a likeness of an individual human being, yet is not, strictly speaking, intended as a portrait.[2] An absolute and all-encompassing definition of portraiture is perhaps not possible. However, an important common element among portraits of all times and cultures is the goal of recognition by the viewer of the image of a specific person.

The functions and purposes of portraiture, again, differ considerably from culture to culture. An image of a person may serve a magic or religious function, for example, as did the statues which were placed in the tombs of Egyptians, to serve as surrogates for their mortal bodies. If, however, a portrait was intended to be seen by living audiences, then it seems logical to assume that the work was intended as a visual document concerning its subject. A portrait executed in a durable material such as

---

[1] George M. A. Hanfmann, "Personality and Portraiture in Ancient Art," *ProcPhilSoc*, 117, No. 4 (1973), 259-261; James D. Breckenridge, *Likeness: a Conceptual History of Portraiture* (Evanston: Northwestern University Press, 1968), p. 42.

[2] Breckenridge, *Likeness*, p. 4.

stone or bronze would presumably be expected to outlive its subject, and would therefore be intended for more than one audience. The first audience for a portrait would be the contemporaries of the subject, either his immediate family and friends, or the public at large, depending on whether the work of art was intended for private or public display. The secondary audience would be people who live after the time of the subject, people who are not able to compare the image against the living person, but who instead examine the portrait in order to learn what that person looked like. Therefore, a likeness of a person would not be made unless the creators of the work—both the artist and the client who commissions the portrait—assume that the audience will regard the portrait as a document concerning some person in whom they have a special interest.

What, then, of a portrait the identity of whose subject has been forgotten? How should the viewer respond to such a work of art? Many react with disappointment and boredom, based on the belief that if the subject has no special interest for the modern observer, then his portrait has ceased to serve any useful purpose. This attitude is well expressed by the following passage, from Nathaniel Hawthorne's *Marble Faun*, in which Hawthorne is describing the studio of a fictional American sculptor:

> Other faces there were, too, of men who (if the brevity of their remembrance after death can be augured from their little value in life), should have been represented in snow rather than in marble. Posterity will be puzzled what to do with busts like these, the concretions and petrifactions of a vain self-estimate, but will find, no doubt, that they serve to build into stone walls, or burn into quicklime, as well as if the marble had never been blocked into the guise of human heads.

Hawthorne's viewpoint is shared by layman and scholar alike, particularly in relation to the portraits from classical antiquity. The study of Roman portraiture tends to be dominated by problems of iconography, that is, the identification of the likenesses of known historic persons. This interest is perhaps fostered by the importance in Latin literature of biographies,[3] and by the intriguing record which such literary works have preserved for us of the personalities of various historic figures. We tend to infer, probably correctly, that the importance of portraiture in Roman art reflects a similar interest in analysis of the personality of the individual, and to seek in such works of art visual parallels to the literary accounts of the lives of historic figures.

The study of portraits as documents concerning historic persons is a perfectly valid and proper approach to portraiture, but not the only possi-

---

[3] George M. A. Hanfmann, "Observations on Roman Portraiture," *Latomus*, 11 (1952), 337-338.

ble approach. A portrait is, after all, not only an historic document but also a work of art. The task of capturing a person's appearance is a very subtle and difficult challenge to an artist. In order to convey a convincingly life-like impression of the subject, it is frequently necessary to represent the person with a facial expression which in some way reveals his or her personality.[4] The types of expressions with which artists choose to portray their subjects, the formulae which they use for those purposes, and the emotional responses which they seem to attempt to elicit from the viewer, can tell us much about the cultural milieu in which portraits were created. Specifically, they can reveal much about the ways in which the people of a certain time and place perceived themselves, and the ways in which they wished to be perceived by others. The portrait, in short, is more than an historic document concerning the individual whom it represents; such an image is also a document of the social history and art-history of the time and place in which the work of art was created. It is in this context that Roman portraits of the third century will be considered in the present study.

For these purposes, anonymous portraits can furnish as much information as the identifiable likenesses of known individuals, though the latter must be used to provide chronological guidelines for the dating of the former. Anonymous portraits can be dated partly through the anti-quarian evidence of fashion: the type of coiffure worn by a woman, the length of a man's hair, the length and cut of his beard (if he wears a beard at all); the type of clothing represented. The tool of visual analysis should also be used: the anonymous portraits should be stylistically compared to the portraits of known individuals. Since judgments concerning style tend to be subjective, however, such criteria should not be applied to the dating of an object until the external evidence of fashion and hairstyle has been considered.

Stylistic discussions of both public and private portraits will often be based upon structural analysis, a technique developed for the study of ancient sculpture by Kaschnitz-Weinberg, and applied and refined by many scholars since him.[5] In the analysis of portraiture, which tends to evoke very personal and emotional responses from viewers, the analysis of the concrete form of a sculptured head or bust as though it were a purely abstract solid, prior to a discussion of the effects which it achieves and

---

[4] Ernst H. Gombrich, *Art and Illusion*, Bollingen Series, 35, A. W. Mellon Lectures in the Fine Arts, 5 (Princeton: Princeton University Press, 1956), pp. 330-358.
[5] An excellent study of structural analysis, and a review of its history in twentieth-century scholarship, has been provided by Sheldon Nodelman, "Structural Analysis in Art and Anthropology," *Structuralism*, ed. Jacques Ehrmann (New York: Doubleday-Anchor, 1970, pp. 79-93.

the emotional responses it elicits, is a very useful means of describing the object's actual physical appearance.[6] Nodelman's masterly study of this approach to ancient sculpture should answer and lay to rest any current doubts as to the continuing value and validity of this method of analysis.[7]

The objects which will be studied in this monograph are products of the society of imperial Rome, a cultural milieu in which portraiture played a variety of important functions, both in public and in private life. These works also present a special set of problems for the modern scholar, particularly in the matter of identification. Public portraits of the Roman empire can, for the present purposes, be grouped into two categories: imperial portraits, which comprise both the likenesses of the emperors themselves and of the members of their families; and portraits of non-imperial public figures, such as magistrates, athletes, or prominent men of letters. With rare exceptions, only the imperial portraits can now be securely identified, since iconographic studies must usually rely heavily upon comparison of monumental sculpture with coin portraiture.[8] The coins of the Roman empire are the only artifacts which consistently preserve a likeness of an individual together with an identifying inscription, but since only members of the imperial family generally enjoyed the right of coin portraiture, the numismatic material can furnish us only with information concerning the imperial portraits. In some cases, monumental relief sculpture, for example, the triumphal arches, will preserve an inscription which enables identification of the portrait figures in the relief panels. Again, however, only members of the imperial family are generally represented on such monuments. For the period which will be discussed in the present work, the early and middle third century after Christ, such monuments are in any case almost totally lacking.

How, then, can one recognize a non-imperial but public portrait? A crude but convenient rule of thumb is that if more than one replica of a work exists, most if not all of the replicas were probably intended for public display. A strictly private portrait might, of course, also have existed in more than one replica; one copy might have been displayed in the subject's house, another in his tomb. If an individual had a need for more than one portrait of himself, it would have been cheaper and more convenient for him to have an existing portrait duplicated than to sit for

---

[6] For an application of structural and semiotic techniques to the analysis of Roman portraiture, see Sheldon Nodelman, ''How to Read a Roman Portrait,'' *Art in America*, 63 (1975), pp. 27-33.

[7] Nodelman, *Structuralism*, esp. pp. 80-84.

[8] Klaus Fittschen, ''Zum angeblichen Bildnis des Lucius Verus im Thermenmuseum,'' *JdI*, 86 (1971), 220.

another portrait. On the other hand, given the fact that many works of sculpture have not survived from antiquity, the preservation today of two or more replicas of a given portrait might well imply the original existence of many more.[9] The existence of copies is, in fact, often interpreted as proof of the imperial status of the subject, but this assumption is not always reliable. The philosopher and philanthropist Herodes Atticus had no imperial status, nor did his student Polydeukion,[10] yet portraits of these individuals survive in many replicas.

In these cases, we are fortunate in knowing the names of the subjects of non-imperial portraits, and something about their lives, but for many other public portraits, such information does not survive. One such work, which will be discussed in a later chapter, is a handsome portrait of a man, represented by replicas in the Terme museum (fig. 21), in Vienna and in Smith College. The work has been identified as Gallienus and as Volusian, both of which identifications must be rejected on stylistic grounds, as Fittschen has recently proven.[11] The portrait should probably be dated to the late Severan period, yet the subject resembles no coin portraits of imperial figures from that dynasty. Who, then, was he? Felletti-Maj, has suggested that he may have been a popular athlete, since in the Terme replica, the fragmentary bust appears to wear the uniform of a charioteer.[12] His name, however, and the details of his life must remain unknown, though his portraits were probably displayed in public. In the present study, these public but anonymous portraits must, for practical reasons, be discussed along with the private portraits. Nonetheless, their difference in function and status from the purely private portraits must be borne in mind.

Of the portraits which were displayed in public places, those of imperial figures would probably have been the most widely distributed, hence the most influential, works of their time, as well as being the richest in ideological content. Portraits of the emperors served the highly important function in imperial propaganda of presenting the ruler to the public, and of projecting the personality with which he wished to be perceived. In addition, they played a variety of important religious, social and legal functions, as devotional objects of the imperial cult, as surrogates for the emperor's own presence, in front of which oaths could be taken, or as treasured private possessions which demonstrated the

---

[9] I am indebted for this observation to Professor Richard Brilliant of Columbia University.

[10] Fittschen, *JdI*, 86 (1971), 223.

[11] Klaus Fittschen, "Bemerkungen zu den Porträts des 3. Jahrhunderts nach Christus," *JdI*, 84 (1969), 226-230.

[12] Bianca-Maria Felletti-Maj, *Museo Nazionale Romano: I Ritratti* (Rome: Libreria dello Stato, 1953), pp. 150-151, No. 300.

loyalty and patriotism of their owners.[13] Statuary groups of imperial families afforded opportunities for the communication of a number of messages. For example, the likenesses of the emperor's designated heirs, either his own children or his adoptive sons, could help to promote support for his dynastic aims by presenting the successors in a favorable manner to the public. The imperial couple, furthermore, could be portrayed as a paradigm of virtues such as *concordia*.[14]

That the portraits of imperial figures were copied in great quantity and distributed throughout the empire is amply attested both by finds of the portraits themselves and of inscribed bases which record dedications. The mechanics of the distribution of these objects is not, however, fully understood. Conceivably, the entire process was a fully controlled and calculated program, in which prototypes of the imperial portraits were sent to the various provinces with instructions that the portraits should be copied and publicly displayed.[15] It is more likely, however, that the distribution was at least in part a spontaneous matter; that copies of imperial portraits would be commissioned independently by cities which needed imperial likenesses for display in temples or public places.[16] A recent contribution to the understanding of the reproduction of imperial types has been made by Soechting,[17] who has distinguished among the portraits of Septimius Severus the products of several different ateliers which vary considerably in the style and quality of their work. It is an unfortunate accident of preservation that the replicas which survive today are usually in marble, since bronze and more valuable metals seem to have been the preferred materials for more prestigious statues of the emperors.[18] Such works, naturally, tended to be melted down in later times, and few survive. When dealing with the extant replicas of imperial types, therefore, it must be borne in mind that the marble examples do not give us a complete picture of the type as it was originally displayed around the empire.

Whatever the means of their distribution, such highly visible works of art could not but have influenced the taste of the general public. The private portraits, therefore, would presumably reflect the trends set by

---

[13] Hans Georg Niemeyer, *Studien zur statuarischen Darstellung der römischen Kaiser* (Berlin: Mann, 1968), pp. 20-26.

[14] For a discussion of the "concordia" group of Antoninus Pius and Faustina, see Gerhard Rodenwaldt, "Über den Stilwandel in der antoninischen Kunst," *AbhBerl* (1935), pp. 13-15.

[15] E. H. Swift, "Imagines in Imperial Portraiture," *AJA* 27 (1923), 286-301.

[16] Merriweather Stuart, "How were Imperial Portraits Distributed Throughout the Roman Empire?" *AJA*, 43 (1939), 601-617.

[17] Dirk Soechting, *Die Porträts des Septimius Severus* (Bonn: R. Habelt, 1972), pp. 83-106.

[18] Niemeyer, *Statuarischen Darstellung*, p. 29.

the imperial commissions. It is, furthermore, logical to assume that the sculptors commissioned to create the imperial types would have been among the best artists available. The reproduction of their work in large quantity, and the public display of the types which these men created, would have furnished other artists with information as to the innovations of the masters in the service of the imperial family.

Private portraits, on the other hand, served considerably different functions and different audiences from public portrait sculpture. These works were displayed, generally, in the home and in the tomb of the subject. The custom of keeping "house portraits" of one's self and one's distinguished ancestors appears to have been generally accepted among the aristocratic classes of the Roman empire. The tradition had its roots in the very ancient religious custom of preserving and venerating masks of deceased members of the family. This custom and its importance in the development of Roman portraiture are issues too complex to discuss here;[19] suffice it to observe that by the first century B.C., the custom had become fully secularized, and the perishable masks with their magic function replaced by sculptured portraits of the Hellenistic type in permanent materials. However, during the imperial period, the custom of displaying portraits of ancestors in the atrium of the house remained popular, if only for its snob appeal.[20] The presence of such portraits would furnish concrete proof of noble descent; an individual might commission his own portrait if he expected to take a place among the distinguished representatives of his family. The continuing funerary importance of portraits during the imperial period is illustrated by the archaeological evidence of reliefs such as those from the tomb of the Haterii, [21] and by the occasional survival of busts, such as that of Aurelia Monina,[22] (fig. 87) with inscriptions which explicitly state their funerary function.

Though these works were not as prominently displayed, nor as influential, as the imperial and public portraits, they afford certain opportunities to the scholar which the imperial likenesses do not. Most importantly, they are generally original works, made by artists who had seen and studied their subject in person, rather than mechanical copies of a pro-

---

[19] Annie N. Zadoks-Josephus Jitta, *Ancestral Portraiture in Rome* (Amsterdam: Allard Pierson, 1932), pp. 22-40.

[20] Ibid., p. 40.

[21] Antonio Giuliano, *Catalogo dei Ritratti Romani del Museo Profano Lateranense* (Vatican: Tipografia poliglotta Vaticana, 1957), pp. 47-48, Nos. 51, 52. Helbig⁴, Nos. 1071, 1075 (E. Simon).

[22] Carl Blümel, *Römische Bildnisse*, bd. suppl. of *Katalog der Sammlung antiker Skulpturen* (Berlin: Staatliche Museen, Antiken-Sammlung, 1933), p. 49, No. R118, pl. 75. Inscription: *CIL* VI, 13360.

totype. They thus enable us to observe the artist's composition, and his personal stylistic idiom, at first hand. Second, they can often give a fuller picture of the style of an era than is afforded by the imperial portraits alone. During the reigns of Elagabalus and of Alexander Severus, for example, there is no imperial type for a mature man. Anonymous portraits from those years illustrate the formulae through which artists presented adult males.

The imperial portraits, with their special burden of propaganda, cannot be analyzed in entirely the same context as private portraits, and so the first chapter of this work will deal specifically with portraits of emperors. The traditions for presentation of the ruler during the period under study will be analyzed, with attention to the qualities of character which artists sought to convey, and the devices which they used to achieve those goals. The following chapters will begin with discussions of the imperial types, both male and female, which give us our chronological guidelines, and then proceed to a discussion of private and unidentified portraits which can be roughly grouped with those imperial images. This monograph does not attempt to give a comprehensive listing of all private portraits datable to the early and middle third century, nor of all replicas of each imperial type, but to analyze a selection of those works of higher quality and better preservation which represent well the artistic movements of their times.

For practical reasons, the works to be considered will be limited to the products of the artistic capital of the western empire, that is, the area of Rome. Issues of provincialism, though they are highly important in the study of Roman art, are not within the scope of this work. The portraits discussed will also, with a few exceptions, be sculptures in the round. Many sarcophagi from the third century bear portraits in relief, but in the great majority of cases these portraits are so crude and sketchy as to contribute very little to a study of sculptural style. Therefore, sarcophagi will be discussed here only when they have some special significance for the study of imperial iconography—the sarcophagus of Balbinus, for example—or when their relief portraits are of exceptionally high quality, and can bear valid comparison with contemporary sculpture in the round.

It is important to bear in mind throughout this study that in virtually no case are we fortunate enough to be able to deal with a complete work of art. Even the best preserved busts and statues have lost their original paint, but it is unfortunately more common for portraits to survive as disembodied heads. Worse, these heads are often mounted on Renaissance or baroque busts which can wildly distort their original position in relation to the body, or on ancient busts and statues to which they do not belong.

There is some justification for dealing with these portrait heads as though they were self-contained works of art, since they were often carved as separate pieces, with plug-like neck bases which were inserted into stock body types. It is likely that the parts of such a statue would be worked by different sculptors and that the portraitist would have been comparatively unconcerned with the type of body for which the head was destined. Even in the case of statues carved in one piece, furthermore, which have since been broken, the bodies would frequently have been designed to standard types—either pastiches of classical Greek originals or formulaic figures in contemporary dress—while only the portrait heads would have received individualizing attention. Nonetheless, the rows of portrait heads preserved only from the neck up, which are such a common sight in the more modern European and American museums, would have seemed to a Roman viewer decidedly bizarre.

Wegner's exhaustive study of bust-types of the third century[23] has collected most of the available evidence for the sorts of compositions to which many of the portrait heads under study would have belonged. Busts, with their traditionally funerary associations, seem to have been more common for private portraiture, and statuary for public and imperial likenesses;[24] again, a thorough catalogue of extant statues of emperors, and a categorization of their types, has been undertaken by Niemeyer.[25] Not all imperial portraits belonged to such full-length statues, however: for example, two handsome and well-preserved busts to be discussed in the following chapter represent the emperors Pupienus (fig. 4) and Philip the Arab (fig. 9). It is difficult, therefore, to speculate on the complete original composition of a portrait head which does not survive in one piece with its body.

With all these problems in mind, I believe that it is possible to trace the stylistic evolution of portrait sculpture during the first half of the third century. In addition, wherever possible, the issue of artistic personality will be addressed. In the case of the imperial portraits, we must not forget that we are dealing with the work of the most prominent and influential artists of their day, men whose work would have enjoyed great public exposure. Therefore, the innovations and experiments which can be observed in their work should be given considerable attention; such innovations must have played some role in the shaping of general trends in portrait sculpture.

---

[23] Max Wegner, "Bildnisbüsten im 3. Jahrhundert n. Chr.," *Festschrift für Gerhard Kleiner* (Tübingen, 1973), pp. 105-132 and pls. 23-27.

[24] Niemeyer, *Statuarischen Darstellung*, pp. 14-15.

[25] Ibid., pp. 38-64 and 82-114.

The private portraits were not such influential works and were frequently not the products of artists as good as those who fulfilled imperial
commissions. On the other hand, these anonymous works have the ad-
vantage, as mentioned above, of being originals, of presenting us with an
artist's composition as executed by his own atelier, rather than filtered
through the medium of a copyist. In a few cases, it has been possible to
recognize the personal idioms of an individual artist, or the
characteristics of a certain atelier, in several different works. These
groups of works are of great interest, especially when they span a period
of years, since they illustrate the ways in which an artist or group of artists adapted and used in their works the innovations which were taking
place in sculpture at the time.

The personality and role of the individual artist, long regarded as a
highly important aspect of the study of ancient Greek art and of European art from the renaissance onward, has been largely neglected in the
study of the sculpture of the Roman empire. In this respect, the attitude
of the modern scholar tends to reflect that of the Romans themselves,
who appear to have held the artists of their own culture in relatively low
esteem. The ancient literary sources provide us with names and
biographies for many Greek and Hellenistic artists, but virtually no comparable information about the masters who worked during the period of
the Roman empire.[26] Yet these artists were responsible for many highly
original achievements, some of which have had a far-reaching effect upon
the history of European art. The development of portraiture as we know
it was one of the most important contributions made by these sculptors.

In recent years, a need has been felt by some scholars for a better
understanding of the artistic personalities of Roman sculptors, with the
result that several valuable studies have been undertaken of the styles of
various court portrait masters. Sheldon Nodelman, for example, has
analyzed the *oeuvres* of several portraitists in the sevice of the Severan
dynasty,[27] while Vagn Poulsen has made a comparable study of the
master who created the portrait types of Marcus Aurelius and Lucius
Verus.[28] It is my hope that such studies, including the present one, will
point the way for more extensive research into the *oeuvres* of Roman artists, not only in portraiture, but in all forms and media. If we wish to
understand the art of a given culture, we neglect at our peril the fact that
works of art must be executed by individual artists.

---

[26] Hanfmann, *Latomus*, 11 (1952), 339.

[27] Sheldon Nodelman, "Severan Imperial Portraits, A.D. 193-217," Diss., Yale
University, 1965, pp. 392-418.

[28] Vagn Poulsen, *Les Portraits romains*, Vol. II (Copenhagen: Ny Carlsberg Glyptotek,
1974), 18-20.

Thus far, the problems which have been discussed, and the methodology which has been proposed for dealing with them, have involved portraiture in general, and Roman portraiture in particular. No mention has been made of the special problems involved in the period which has been selected for this study, the end of the Severan dynasty through the age of the "soldier emperors". The years from 217 until 260 were characterized by political and social upheavals which create a variety of difficulties for a study of the social history or art history of that era. Before the portraits from those years can be studied productively, some theories concerning third-century sculpture must be considered.

## B) *A Review of the Literature on Third-Century Art*

The third century has long been recognized as one of the most important phases in the history of Roman imperial art, yet also one of the most difficult to study. The era presents a variety of special problems for scholarship, not least of which is the comparative scarcity of surviving material. The nature of the anarchy and revolution of the years after Caracalla's death, and the influence of those social upheavals on art, are complex issues, but one of their effects is unquestionable. The brevity of the reigns of most emperors, and the economic difficulties of the empire, prevented the creation of major public monuments such as the triumphal arches, sculptured columns, and other types of reliefs which provide so much of our knowledge of the development of Roman art during the first and second centuries. The original creations of the art of the third century (as opposed to copies of earlier originals), are represented for the modern observer only by sarcophagi, by some fragmentary paintings from tombs and houses, and by portrait sculpture. From the realm of public art, of works designed for display to the general public, we have virtually nothing but the portraits of emperors, members of imperial families, and of other public figures.

Yet what does survive illustrates clearly that the third century was a time of revolutionary change in art, of radical shifts in aesthetic goals and in the technical means used to achieve them. At one end of the century, for example, are the portraits of Septimius Severus, still allied to the hellenistic traditions of the portraiture of the Antonines, in which an elegant and idealized treatment of the subject is accompanied by supple modeling and an obvious understanding of the organic nature of the human face. At the other end, we have the portraits of Constantine: hard, stereometric, the features stiffened into a highly abstract pattern which suggests trance-like meditation rather than a life-like moment of emotion. The works datable between these boundaries show a bewildering profusion of styles, which, in the official portraits, seem to replace one another abruptly with each change of reign, and sometimes to coexist in the portraits of coregents. The differences in style between the portraits of Maximinus Thrax and his son Maximus, of Pupienus and Balbinus, and of Valerian and Gallienus, are examples which will be discussed in the following chapters. This rich variety of style has produced a correspondingly great profusion of theories from modern scholars attempting to analyze the development of those years.

Prior to the epoch-making work of Alois Riegl, it was conventional to regard the third century, as well as the following centuries, as a period of decline in technical and artistic ability, occasioned partly by social and economic chaos, and partly by the influx into the empire of "barbarian" peoples who had no understanding of Greco-Roman artistic traditions. The theory of a decline has by no means been abandoned, but most scholars now agree with Riegl that many of the ultimate results of the developments of late-antique art were positive. It is generally acknowledged that the shift in aesthetic goals which took place during those years enabled the creation of masterpieces of Medieval art, and that an understanding of the nature and causes of the changes of art in late-antiquity are necessary for a fuller understanding of the cultural heritage of our own society.

Central to any understanding of third century art is the question to what extent sculpture at this period developed according to its own internal logic and necessity, and how much sculpture was affected by external forces, such as the propaganda aims of any given emperor. Any work of art produced in a cultural milieu such as that of imperial Rome must of course be explained both in terms of the tradition in which the artist was working and of the wishes of the patron which were necessarily imposed upon him. In the case of the third century, the problem is whether a significant continuity of artistic tradition still existed, or whether art was predominantly "other-directed" rather than "inner directed."[29]

One major school of thought sees the styles of this era not as evolutionary but as cyclical, the products of several coexisting cultural traditions, each of which came to the fore at various different times depending upon the sympathies of the emperor in power. Gervase Mathew[30] briefly described three currents in imperial portraiture, the "militaristic" style traceable through the portraits of Decius, Aurelian, and Diocletian; the "senatorial" or "Gordianic" represented by the portraits of Pupienus,

---

[29] Ernst Kitzinger, *Byzantine Art in the Making* (London: Faber and Faber, 1977), pp. 13-14.

[30] Gervase Mathew, "The Character of the Gallienic Renaissance," *JRS*, 33 (1943), 66-67.

Balbinus, the Gordians, Tacitus, Florian, Claudius II, and Quintillus; and the "Augustan," found in the portraits of Alexander Severus, Gallienus, and Probus.

Bernard Schweitzer, several years later, advanced a similar theory, though he identified only two coexistant styles: the "Augustan" and the "veristic."[31] The latter term, a very useful one for any study of third-century portraiture, may be defined as the use of details and asymmetries contrary to traditional ideals of beauty, such as the facial lines produced by advancing age, physical fatigue or emotional stress. Such details serve the purpose of producing an unflatteringly realistic likeness of an individual, but can also be used for expressive purposes, as the means to convey the subject's personality or emotional state. Schweitzer elaborates on the nature of both the "Augustan" and the "veristic" trends as revivals of earlier styles, the one (as the name implies) of Augustus' classicizing austerity, the other of Republican and Flavian realism.[32] The influence of these earlier works is seen as direct, and the references to them in third-century art intentional: Schweitzer postulates the survival in Rome of public monuments[33] from all these periods, works which could have served as inspirations and prototypes for sculptors. The "Augustan" and "veristic" styles of the third century would have arisen concurrently as reactions against the so-called Antonine baroque style, which was characterized by a smooth, fluid treatment of the face, set off by masses of curly hair in which the drill was used to produce complex patterns of shadow. All the portrait sculpture of the early third century, in Schweitzer's view, shows a "regeneration of plastic form,"[34] and an avoidance of decorative contrasts of light and shadow in hair and beards.

Though the two trends, according to this theory, arose in part from similar stylistic motivations, they never fully merged. "Veristic" portraiture was favored throughout the third century by the "soldier emperors," the men who owed their power primarily to election by the army, since that style was well suited to convey soldier-like qualities of strength and toughness, traits which had enabled those individuals to get power, and would presumably enable them to exercise it.[35] The "Augustan" style, on the other hand, was used for portraits of emperors who came to power through dynastic succession: Alexander Severus,

---

[31] Bernard Schweitzer, "Altrömische Traditionselemente in der Bildniskunst des 3. nachchristlichen Jahrhunderts," *Zur Kunst der Antike, Ausgewählte Schriften* (Tübingen: Ulrich Hausmann, 1963), II, 267. Article originally published in *Nederlands Kunsthistorische Jaarboeck*, 5 (1954), 173-190.

[32] Schweitzer, *Zur Kunst der Antike*, II, 266-267.

[33] Ibid.

[34] Ibid., pp. 265 and 276-278.

[35] Ibid., p. 273.

Gordian III, and Gallienus. These portraits would have demonstrated sympathy with the ideals of orderly, constitutional monarchy and a nostalgia for Augustus's "golden age."[36] Since these styles never achieved a synthesis with one another,[37] the third century is seen as a period of uncertainty and lack of direction, unable to find a coherent form of expression of its own, and relying instead on constant retrospection.[38]

Zinserling accepts this image of the third century as an era lacking in direction, and characterized by abrupt schisms in artistic styles. He disagrees however with Schweitzer's theory that the "realism" of Maximinus Thrax's portrait is an intentional revival of the style of the republic, a past which after all had nothing to do with Maximinus's own origins.[39] Instead, the realism which appears both in republican portraits and in Maximinus's likenesses is seen as the product of somewhat comparable circumstances: a need in both cases to assert the personality of the individual as strongly as possible.[40] The portraits of the republic were privately commissioned works which played a role in the cult of ancestors, a function for which good and recognizable likenesses of individuals would have been desirable. Maximinus's portraits were publicly displayed, but they represented a man who had no link with the dynastic traditions of his predecessors, and who owed his power solely to his own military prowess. The propaganda goal of asserting Maximinus's authority over the empire could, according to Zinserling, best be served by a complete break with the artistic traditions of earlier dynastic portraits, in favor of a direct and forceful expression of the power of Maximinus's personality.

The following chapters will attempt to demonstrate, however, that the change in style of imperial portraiture between the reigns of Alexander Severus and Maximinus did not constitute a complete or abrupt break such as that described by Zinserling. As Fittschen has rightly observed,[41] the portraits of Maximinus show unmistakable formal relationships to those of Caracalla; in addition, they also demonstrate continuity with some private portraits datable to the intervening years, during which the style of Caracalla's portraits was never fully abandoned.

---

[36] Ibid., p. 277.

[37] Ibid., p. 267.

[38] Ibid., pp. 277-278.

[39] Gerhard Zinserling, "Altrömische Traditionselemente in Porträtkunst und Historienmalerei der ersten Hälfte des 3. Jahrhunderts u.z.," Klio, 41 (1963), 200-201.

[40] Ibid., pp. 202-203.

[41] Klaus Fittschen, "Ein Bildnis in Privatbesitz — Zum Realismus römischer Porträts der mittleren und späteren Prinzipätszeit," Eikones: Festschrift Hans Jucker, 12th Beiheft of Antike Kunst (Bern: Francke Verlag, 1980), 111-112.

One more proponent of the "revival" theory is Donald Strong, who points out that retrospective elements can also be found in the portraits of Septimius Severus and Caracalla.[42] The lack of a legitimate base of power for their dynasty would presumably have prevented these emperors from using earlier artistic traditions with any confidence. Both during the Severan dynasty and during the anarchic years that followed, according to Strong, styles which were revived were chosen erratically, in a manner that reveals lack of direction.[43]

In any study of revivals during the third century, the reign of Gallienus occupies a special position. Mathew and Schweitzer both observed that Gallienus's portraits, and the contemporary private portraits, enrich the "Augustan" style with elements derived from Trajanic[44] and Antonine[45] sculpture. The borrowings from these periods can be most clearly seen in the treatment of hair in male portraits: the close-clipped, military hairstyle fashionable from the time of Caracalla until about 250 is abandoned in favor of longer hair, which is represented as being combed forward around the face, in a pattern strongly reminiscent of Trajanic portraits.[46] Later in the Gallienic period, the fuller hair of male portraits, which is sometimes detailed with drill work, recalls Antonine portraiture.[47]

The self-conscious revivals and references to earlier imperial portraits in the likenesses of Gallienus are a securely established fact, and will be discussed in more detail later. On the other hand, the use of these visual quotations should not be allowed to obscure the fact that Gallienus's portraits are harmonious and stylistically coherent works which do not merely borrow but intelligently incorporate into a new style some elements of earlier styles. These works find their closest parallels not in imperial portraiture of the first and second centuries but in that of Gallienus's recent predecessors such as Gordian III, portraits which experiment with forms of abstraction and patternization which are developed further under Gallienus's patronage.

Furthermore, in light of the recent work of Fittschen,[48] caution must be used toward the conventional view that art under Gallienus was heavi-

---

[42] D. E. Strong, *Roman Art*, ed. J. M. C. Toynbee, Pelican History of Art (Harmondsworth: Penguin, 1976), pp. 122-123. 2nd ed., 1980, p. 228.

[43] Ibid., pp. 122-123 and 136-137. 2nd ed., pp. 228, 250-255.

[44] Schweitzer, *Zur Kunst der Antike*, II, 272.

[45] Mathew, *JRS*, 33 (1943), 68.

[46] Schweitzer, *Zur Kunst der Antike*, II, 272.

[47] See Mathew, *JRS*, 33 (1943), 68, on the Antonine references in the portraits of Gallienus.

[48] Klaus Fittschen, "Zwei römische Bildnisse in Kassel," *RömMitt*, 77 (1970), 132-143, and *JdI*, 84 (1969), 197-236.

ly retrospective. Fittschen has convincingly redated to the early Severan period many portraits of young men which had been believed on the basis of their long hair to be Gallienic.[49] The resulting picture of art under Gallienus is of a style far less reactionary than previously supposed. As early as 1943, of course, Mathew had already rightly observed that even if the revivals apparent in Gallienus's portraiture were reactionary in intention, they were progressive in effect. Gallienus's portraits, like other aspects of art and thought of his time, incorporated—perhaps unconsciously and unintentionally—new elements of spirituality, new expressions of mystic contemplation and transcendancy, that were to have a long life in Byzantine and Medieval art.[50]

These, then, are what might be classified as the "revival" theories which have frequently been adduced to explain the variety of styles represented among portraits of the third century. Most of these theories involve the notion of several different but coexisting cultural traditions, one or another of which might be selected as the source for the style of official propaganda. The nature and origin of those differing traditions, however, are open to many interpretations. Kaschnitz-Weinberg first developed the influential theory that the realism which periodically appears in Roman portraiture of the imperial period belonged to a native Italic artistic tradition, which had been suppressed but never completely destroyed by the Hellenistic style sometimes adopted in official art.[51] Simple, firmly closed contours, and intense facial expressions which are concentrated into a few features, are described as hallmarks of this Italic style,[52] traits which can be observed in the "veristic" portraits of the era of the soldier emperors.

Schweitzer essentially followed this theory in his explanation of why republican and Flavian works should have been chosen as prototypes for the "veristic" works of the third century.[53] This style, according to Schweitzer, was not so much a reaction against the "Augustan" style as an older tradition which had been kept alive in popular art even at times when a more classical style was favored in official art. Rodenwaldt adopted a similar point of view in accounting for the "*Stilwandel*" between the art of the second and third centuries.[54] Rodenwaldt's study concentrates on relief rather than on portraiture, and on the treatment of the human body as a whole rather than of the face, but clear relationships

---

[49] Fittschen, *JdI*, 86 (1971), 226-228.
[50] Mathew, *JRS*, 33 (1943), 68.
[51] Guido Kaschnitz-Weinberg, "Spätrömische Porträts," *Die Antike*, 2 (1926), 42.
[52] Ibid, p. 40.
[53] Schweitzer, *Zur Kunst der Antike*, II, 277.
[54] Rodenwaldt, *AbhBerl* (1935), pp. 25-26.

exist between these reliefs and portraits of the "veristic" style. In the series of sarcophagi in which he traces the emergence of a native Italic style, the increasing distortion of the proportions of the body, and the use of dramatically expressive but inorganic gestures, are comparable to the rejection in portraiture of classical ideals of beauty in favor of expressive harshness and asymmetry.

Bianchi-Bandinelli's analysis of Roman art in light of social history has added a new dimension to our understanding of the roles of the realistic and the classicizing currents of style. The cold and academic classicism of the Augustan period was, as Bianchi-Bandinelli demonstrates, a somewhat artificial creation, an arbitrary break with the traditions of both Hellenistic and Italian art.[55] This style might be used in official art, and in the art commissioned by the aristocratic elite who followed the trends set by imperial taste, but could not replace the more animated and expressive style which thrived at all times in more humble, privately commissioned works and frequently made its way into imperial monuments as well.[56] For the native Italian-Hellenistic style, which involved among other things a strong taste for verism in portraiture,[57] he coined the term "plebeian," pointing out, however, that this trend should not be regarded as a conscious opposition to the "high" style of official art.[58] Nor should "plebeian" art be strictly equated with the social class of its patrons.

In discussing the styles of the third century, Byvanck adopts the term "plebeian art," but redefines it as the product of a certain school of sculptors.[59] These artists, he argues, specialized in the production of sculpture as quickly and as cheaply as possible. For this purpose, they relied on the easiest technical means available, for example, the use of the drill rather than the chisel wherever possible. This school of artists would have evolved traditions and conventions of its own, many of which were highly expressive.

Oldrich Pelikàn, on the other hand, regards this increasing reliance on primitive techniques as an involuntary process.[60] According to his analysis, the classical ideals of organic volumes and of faithful reproduction of the tactile form of the human anatomy were dealt a blow from

---

[55] Ranuccio Bianchi-Bandinelli, *Rome: the Center of Power*, trans. Peter Green (New York: Braziller, 1970), pp. 86, 177-202.

[56] Ibid., pp. 212-221.

[57] Ibid., pp. 71-105.

[58] Ibid., p. 64.

[59] Alexander Wilhelm Byvanck, "Les Origines de l'art du bas-empire," *BABesch*, 39 (1964), 5.

[60] Oldrich Pelikàn, *Vom antiken Realismus zur spätantiken Expressivität* (Prague: Státni Pedag, 1965), pp. 33 and 76-77.

which they never recovered by the Antonine baroque style. Works of the Antonine period employed optical effects achieved through extensive use of negative carving. From the reign of Caracalla onward, the overly refined and decorative effects of this style were rejected, but the impressionistic use of light and shadow was not forgotten. Many portraits of the "veristic" style show a comparable play of shadow in the deeply carved furrows and creases of the faces.

Thus, unlike Schweitzer, Pelikàn believes that there was no true return to plastic form in the third century; classical organic modeling had been irrevocably lost, and the void it left was filled by stereometric treatment of the human form, a less technically demanding approach. Little anatomic knowledge or spatial perception is, after all, required of a sculptor who produced the form of a human body or head simply by minimal modification of his block of stone.[61] Thus, after the traditions of classical art had destroyed themselves, sculptors were thrown back upon the naive devices of folk-art. This "decline" in technical ability is not seen, however, as an entirely negative development, since it allowed Roman art to be reinvigorated by the powerful simplicity inherent in any naive style.[62]

Another issue of great importance for the understanding of third century sculpture is the role of various provinces in shaping the development of art as well as of other aspects of culture. Many of the emperors from the end of the Antonine dynasty onward came from the east[63] or from the Danube areas, and their origins might well have affected the nature of their official monuments.

In a highly influential study, Alföldi elaborated on the role of the emperors of Balkan origin, and of their provinces, in third-century religion, thought, and art. Alföldi's argument is too complex and broad in scope to summarize adequately here. Suffice it for the present purposes to say that he describes the ever-increasing importance in the Roman empire of the Danube region as a source of leadership and political initiative.[64] Septimius Severus and many of the soldier-emperors were elected by the Pannonian legions; Trajan Decius was himself a Pannonian. The Danube area cannot, of course, be regarded as in any way a "barbarian" region, but a thoroughly Romanized province with great respect for Roman traditions, combined, in Alföldi's view, with a hardy

[61] Kitzinger, *Byzantine Art in the Making*, pp. 8-9.
[62] See also Kaschnitz-Weinberg, *Die Antike*, 2 (1926), 54.
[63] Ibid., pp. 51-53.
[64] Andreas Alföldi, "Die Vorrherrschaft der Pannonier und die Reaktion des Hellenentums unter Gallienus," *Fünfundzwanzig Jahre römisch-germanische Kommission* (Berlin-Leipzig, 1930), pp. 11-13.

frontier spirit. Nonetheless, the provinces were beginning to preempt the traditional centers of political power, just as socially revolutionary religions like Christianity were gradually encroaching upon the old state cults.[65] Gallienus, according to Alföldi, sought to combat these trends by promoting as an alternative to the oriental mystery cults a cult long since integrated into the state religion, the Eleusinian mysteries, and the intimately related philosophy of Plotinus.[66] This religious policy was accompanied by pointed displays of philhellenism. Though Alföldi does not undertake a complete study of third-century art, he does discuss the reappearance of longer hair in Gallienic male portraits, and its wealth of romantic associations with the Greek past.[67]

Art of the soldier-emperor period may, by the same token, reflect the provincial origins of leaders such as Maximinus Thrax,[68] Philip the Arab, and Trajan Decius. Areas like these would have been strongholds of the less pretentious and more expressive "plebeian" style at times when a more classicizing manner was favored in official art. Products of provincial sculptural centers, like Aquileia,[69] demonstrate a definite preference for verism in portraiture, and it is therefore not surprising that emperors whose origins lay in such areas would tend to favor an unflatteringly realistic style in official art.[70] The Danube provinces were, however, as thoroughly Romanized in art as in other aspects of life, and though sculpture from provincial centers might have a distinctive local character, it tended to follow the lead of the cultural capitals of the empire. The contribution of such areas would have consisted in shaping the tastes of the men whose choices as artistic patrons influenced the directions taken by artists of the period.

The sculpture of the provinces of the east cannot, of course, be described as "provincial" in the same sense as that of areas like Pannonia or cities like Aquileia. The cities of Asia Minor were in many cases the heirs to Hellenistic sculptural traditions which predated Roman control of the region, and these cities and areas continued to be major artistic centers.

---

[65] Ibid., pp. 14-20.

[66] Ibid., pp. 21-23.

[67] Ibid., pp. 44-46.

[68] See Jutta Meischner, "Zwei Stilrichtungen in der Porträtkunst des 3. Jahrhunderts n. Chr.," *AA* 82 (1967), 34-46. Unfortunately, Meischner's argument for an identifiably provincial style in the portraits of Maximinus Thrax is based on a portrait type which cannot be accepted as a portrait of Maximinus. See Marianne Bergmann, *Studien zum römischen Porträt des 3. Jahrhunderts n. Chr.*, Vol. 18 of *Antiquitas*, r. 3 (Bonn, 1977), p. 31.

[69] Valnea Santa-Maria Scrinari, *Museo Archeologico di Aquileia: Catalogo delle Sculture Romane* (Rome: Istituto Poligrafico dello Stato, 1972), pp. 67-71, Nos. 196-210, and pp. 82-85, Nos. 250-262, on portraits from the third century.

[70] I am indebted for this observation to Professor Anne Haeckl of the University of Colorado at Boulder.

The magnificent recent finds from Aphrodisias,[71] which still await full publication, include portrait sculptures of the third century which demonstrate a level of technical and artistic sophistication perhaps higher than that of works from the area of Rome. These works, however, like the published examples of portrait sculpture from Asia Minor,[72] appear in general to have followed the same trends of fashion and style as those of the artistic centers of the west.

Late in the third century, at the period of the Tetrarchs, and early in the fourth century, it is possible that, as Kitzinger has argued, sculptors of provincial origin may actually have been chosen over city-Roman artists for the execution of public monuments.[73] It is unlikely, however, that if provincial artists were employed that they significantly altered artistic movements already in progress at the capital; their work merely reflects an extreme example of taste for a certain type of abstraction which had already been developing in Rome for years. Kitzinger rightly defines provincial and folk-art styles as ''subantique,''[74] traditions which could be used in official art at certain times for political reasons but which could not play a dominant role in the shaping of Roman art.

All the theories discussed so far regard third-century art of Rome as ''other-directed,'' its course of development determined primarily by official policy. Most of them also see the art of this period as characterized by schisms, between ''Augustan'' and ''veristic,'' ''Hellenistic'' and ''Italic,'' ''plebeian'' and ''patrician,'' or provincial and city-Roman styles. There is some truth in all these theories, and the existence of multiple styles at this period as in all phases of Roman art is an incontrovertible fact. It is also possible, however, to recognize some spontaneity in the development of art at this period, when sculptural style was being shaped not only by artificially imposed policy but by the same forces which were altering other aspects of society. A masterly study of this kind was undertaken by L'Orange,[75] in a monograph in which he traces the parallels between the changing role of the individual in society and the portrayal of the human form in art.

Gradual and largely unintentional changes in organization of the empire which had been in progress since the time of Trajan had, in

---

[71] Presented by Kenan T. Erim at the 83rd general meeting of the Archaeological Institute of America. Abstract published in *AJA* 86 (1983), p. 233.

[72] See Jale Inan and Elizabeth Rosenbaum, *Roman and Early Byzantine Portrait Sculpture in Asia Minor* (London: Oxford University Press, 1966), passim. Third-century portraits discussed include cat. nos. 58-65, 84-89, 101-104, 113, 114, 125, 126, 130, 131, 156-188, 234-239, 266-274, 290-296, 302-304, 306, 307, 310.

[73] Kitzinger, *Byzantine Art in the Making*, p. 13.

[74] Ibid., pp. 10-11.

[75] H. P. L'Orange, *Art Forms and Civic Life in the Late Roman Empire* (Princeton: Princeton University Press, 1965).

L'Orange's view, the effect of gradually immobilizing the individual, and of depriving the provinces of their autonomy,[76] while fostering a concept of divine kingship which denied the humanity and individuality of the ruler.[77] In contemporary art, the inorganic treatment of body and face, the frequent reduction of people to rows of identical figures, and the hieratic presentation of the emperor must reflect the way in which individuals perceived themselves in this new society.[78] It is difficult to imagine that all such changes in art were deliberately and consciously chosen.

The writings of Plotinus provide certain insights into the intellectual climate in which third-century portraits were produced. A detailed discussion of the aesthetic philosophy expressed in the *Enneads* is not within the scope of this study. For the present purposes, the ideas of greatest importance are Plotinus's definitions of beauty, and his analysis of the role of the artist. The traditional definition of beauty as a symmetry of parts is rejected by Plotinus as inadequate, since it does not account for the beauty of things which are unities without parts. He cites the examples of light, color, single musical tones, and abstract thoughts. Symmetry also can exist, he argues, between things that are ugly or false. He then goes on to redefine beauty as an idea or form (*eidos*) imposed on matter by the Principle, or Supreme Being.[79] If such aesthetic principles were to be applied to the practise of art, one might expect to find artists attempting to express spiritual inner realities about their subjects, at the expense of personal likeness or anatomic accuracy. This seems to be precisely what was happening in art at the time of Gallienus, when Plotinus was writing:[80] the portraits of this period show increasingly abstract patterns of features.

Later in the *Enneads*, Plotinus elaborates upon the role of the artist as one who does not merely imitate nature, but who conceives form in his mind, then introduces that form into rough material, and whose activities therefore imitate those of the Creator.[81] Plotinus thus differs from Plato in regarding art not as a sterile process of imitation, but as an activity that is partly one of original creation. Art must of course remain partly imitative, since pure creation can be achieved only by God.[82]

---

[76] Ibid., pp. 4-8.

[77] Ibid., pp. 46-53.

[78] Ibid., pp. 85-104.

[79] Plotinus, *Enneads*, trans. Stephen MacKenna, 3rd ed., rev. B. S. Page (London: Faber, 1962), I, 6, 1-2.

[80] Breckenridge, *Likeness*, p. 211.

[81] Plotinus, *Enneads*, V, 8, 1.

[82] John P. Anton, "Plotinus's Conception of the Functions of the Artist," *Journal of Aesthetics and Art Criticism*, 26 (1967), 94-97.

Nonetheless, according to such a philosophy, an artist would be expected to give primary importance to preconceived patterns and forms of his own invention, and only secondary attention to the production of recognizable likenesses of things. This, again, appears to be what is happening in the increasingly abstract art of the mid-third century.

It is not inconceivable that the thought of Plotinus and his contemporary neoplatonists could have had some impact upon art of their time; Plotinus was a member of Gallienus's court circle, and as such could have influenced the thought of the emperor, whose taste in turn would have influenced official art.[83] Plotinus, however, did not write in a vacuum; he was a product of his times, of the same society which produced the artists whose work we are studying. Ferri has rightly pointed out that Plotinus's principles can be applied not only to art under Gallienus, but to the "veristic" style of the preceding years.[84] A passage of enormous interest to students of portraiture is the following:[85]

> Why else is there more of the glory of beauty upon the living and only some faint trace of it upon the dead though the face yet retains all its fullness and symmetry? Why are the most living portraits the most beautiful, even though the other happen to be the more symmetric? Why is the living ugly more attractive than the sculptured handsome? It is that the one is more nearly what we are looking for, and this because there is soul there, because there is more of the Idea of The Good . . . .

Plotinus almost seems to have before his mind's eye one of the fine portraits of the veristic style of the 240's or 250's such as the Capitoline portrait of Trajan Decius (fig. 10).

Portraiture of the third century, in short, can be regarded as one aspect of general trends in art, literature and thought. As such, the development of portrait sculpture would be primarily "inner-directed," and only secondarily shaped by the demands of official policy. Perhaps for this reason, for many years scholars such as L'Orange have been conscious of the need to seek logical connections and continuities of tradition between the successive styles which appear in the third century, rather than to explain them in terms of dichotomies. L'Orange,[86] like Schweitzer, recognized the existence both of "classical" or "Augustan" styles and of more realistic stylistic currents, but he saw the alternating appearances of these styles as reactions against, and logical developments from one

---

[83] Breckenridge, *Likeness*, pp. 211-214.

[84] Silvio Ferri, "Plotino e l'arte del III secolo," *Critica d'Arte*, I, No. 4, pp. 166-171.

[85] Plotinus, *Enneads* VI, 7, 22.

[86] H. P. L'Orange, *Studien zur Geschichte des spätantiken Porträts* (Oslo: H. Aschebourg & Co., 1933), pp. 1-9. See also H. P. L'Orange, "The Antique Origin of Medieval Portraiture," *Likeness and Icon* (Odense: Odense University Press, 1973), pp. 91-102, and *Art Forms and Civic Life*, pp. 105-125.

another.[87] He described the portraits of Alexander Severus as the extreme result of a trend in which volumes were simplified, surfaces made fluid and indefinite, and borders between parts of the face minimized. The viewer's eye is thus invited to travel over the whole, rather than to focus on any one feature. The "verism" of the soldier-emperor period would have been a deliberate reaction against this slick and somewhat vapid style; the irregularities and details of the human face were now not only recognized but used as formal means to achieve a new effect of life and energy. The asymmetries of the patterns of line, and the flicker of highlight and shadow produced by the deep carving of facial furrows were most effective devices for conveying a momentary facial expression in which the character of the subject could be vividly revealed. This "impressionistic" phase of third-century portraiture was defined in greatest detail in L'Orange's studies of a portrait type which he identifies as Plotinus[88] (fig. 50).

L'Orange described the so-called "renaissance" at the time of Gallienus as a reaction against both these styles, both of which involved a dissolution of plastic anatomic forms. But the classical understanding of the organic structure of the human head and face had by then been irrevocably lost; what the Gallienic style achieved, instead of a reassertion of the tectonic nature of the human anatomy, was a new type of geometric abstraction. This evolution from impressionism, which sought to capture a lifelike moment of emotion, to expressive abstraction, he paralleled to a similar development in nineteenth- and twentieth-century painting, in which the dissolution of tectonic form in the one style prepared the way for the abstraction of the next.[89]

L'Orange is of course not the only scholar to see third-century styles as the products of the organic development of a tradition. Kaschnitz-Weinberg, for example, traces a continuous process of development in art of the "realistic" style, which he regards as natively Italic.[90] Rodenwaldt, as mentioned above, describes the "*Stilwandel*" of the third century as a gradual process with roots traceable to the Antonine period,[91] and in this point of view, he is largely followed by von Heintze,[92] Pelikàn,[93] and Kitzinger.[94]

---

[87] L'Orange, *Studien*, pp. 1-4.

[88] H. P. L'Orange, "Plotinus—Paul," *Likeness and Icon* (Odense: Odense University Press, 1973), pp. 32-42, originally published in *Byzantion*, 25-27 (1955-57), 473-485.

[89] L'Orange, "Antique Origin of Medieval Portraiture," *Likeness and Icon*, p. 94.

[90] Kaschnitz-Weinberg, *Die Antike*, 2 (1926), 40-42.

[91] Rodenwaldt, *AbhBerl* (1935), pp. 19-25.

[92] Helga von Heintze, *Römische Porträt-Plastik* (Stuttgart: H. E. Gunter, 1961), pp. 13-15.

[93] Pelikàn *Vom antiken Realismus zur spätantiken Expressivität*, pp. 76-77.

[94] Kitzinger, *Byzantine Art in the Making*, pp. 14-16.

A recent contribution to the understanding of development of style within the third century has been provided by Marianne Bergmann, in an excellent study of the portraiture of the second half of the century. She argues very convincingly that the impression of a dramatic change in style under Gallienus is partly the deceptive result of comparisons of only certain replicas of each of Gallienus's portrait types.[95] Bergmann's more comprehensive survey of the imperial and private portraits from the time of Gallienus shows that the transition from an emotionally turbulent and realistic style to an elegantly abstract one was in fact a gradual process, and not the result of an artificial imposition by Gallienus of his own tastes upon art. Sheldon Nodelman[96] has also cast an interesting light on the development of style during the soldier-emperor period by pointing out the importance of individual artists and their contributions to a continuous and living artistic tradition. The artist whom he calls the ''Caracalla master'' played an important role, according to Nodelman, in the acceptance of simple, compact volumes, clear planes and geometric patterns of line for the representation of emotional expressions.

Many theories have been advanced to explain the rapidity of changes in sculptural style in the third century. The art of this period has been explained in terms of the policies of imperial propaganda; such a point of view regards the art of this time as primarily ''other-directed.'' Conflicts of native and Hellenic traditions, of the coexisting currents of plebeian and patrician art, and of the intruding art of provincial areas have all been analyzed as having an impact on sculptural style. The present discussion will concentrate primarily upon the ''inner-directed'' aspect of art at this period, however, and on the process by which imperial portraits of the years 217-260 build upon the traditions of their predecessors. The third century, like any other period in the history of art, was an era both of change and of continuity, and it would be both distorting and overly simplistic to attempt to deny the stylistic schisms and revivals which do characterize this period, or to deny the importance of patronage and taste in dictating to artists their stylistic choices. I wish to demonstrate, however, that the elements of abrupt change in third century portraiture have received somewhat exaggerated emphasis, at the expense of our understanding of the workshop traditions within which new styles had to be developed to meet the new demands of a changing society. Artists could not create new schemata and stylistic devices from thin air, but had to proceed by altering techniques which they had learned from older artists, and by observing, learning from and vying with one

---

[95] Bergmann, *Studien*, pp. 57-72, 89-103.
[96] Nodelman, ''Severan Imperial Portraits,'' pp. 392-418.

another's work. Nonetheless, all the theories which have been discussed in this section cast some light on the period under study. They should therefore be borne in mind as we proceed to an examination of the portraits themselves.

# CHAPTER ONE

# THE HERITAGE OF CARACALLA:
## TRADITIONS IN PORTRAITS OF EMPERORS

No matter how complex and varied the sculptural styles of the third century may seem, there is one connecting thread which can be traced throughout the period under study, particularly in male portraiture, and this is the influence of the images of Caracalla. The career of this emperor as described by the ancient sources hardly seems today to recommend him as a model worthy of emulation, yet the portraits of many later emperors of the third century seem to show a deliberate suggestion of physical resemblance to him. There are a variety of reasons for this phenomenon: first, whatever his other faults, Caracalla did manage to maintain popularity with the army, by following his father's deathbed advice to "enrich the soldiers and scorn all other men."[1] After Caracalla's assassination, the women of the Severan dynasty were able to rally the support of the troops at Antioch to their cause by playing upon the loyalty which the majority of soldiers still felt for him.[2]

The portraits representing Caracalla as a child played a significant role during these events, since they were displayed beside Caracalla's young cousin Elagabalus to demonstrate a family resemblance and to encourage the false rumor that Elagabalus was Caracalla's natural son.[3] It is very likely that Caracalla's adult portrait types continued to be reproduced and displayed long after his death,[4] since the tenuous family connections of Elagabalus and Alexander Severus to him were the only basis of legitimacy for their reigns. Later soldier-emperors such as Maximinus Thrax and Philip the Arab had no dynastic claim to imperial power at all; their position rested solely on the support of the army. The portraitists responsible for presenting these men to the public seem to have turned for inspiration to the images of Caracalla, perhaps because the soldierly qualities of toughness and determination were extraordinarily well conveyed by these portraits.

All Caracalla's portraits, from his childhood onward, reveal the work of a strong and innovative artistic personality whose style and career have

---

[1] Dio Cassius, LXXVII 15.2.
[2] Dio Cassius, LXXIX, 30-32.
[3] Dio Cassius, LXXIX, 32, 2-3.
[4] See Heintz Wiggers and Max Wegner, *Caracalla bis Balbinus*, Vol. III, part 1 of *Das römische Herrscherbild* (Berlin: Mann, 1971), 10.

been analyzed by Sheldon Nodelman.[5] These works are characterized by simple, compact volumes, firm enclosing contours and planes, and the use of subtle geometric patterns of line for the expression of emotion. The portraits which represent Caracalla as a child and adolescent,[6] though they follow Antonine traditions in the smoothness of the skin areas and the rich use of the drill for detailing in the long, full hair, still convey a new air of intensity through the blocky form of the head and the strong horizontals of eyebrows and mouth. The full hair tends to lie smoothly along the scalp in long waves, leading the eye back inward toward the face, rather than to expand the form of the head with an aureole of curls, as had been done in Antonine portraiture. This shift from an open to a compactly closed form, though subtle, is most significant.[7]

The sculptures which were made later in the lifetime of Septimius Severus to portray Caracalla as a young adult show a rejection of that hairstyle, however, and a preference for a short-cropped, military haircut which allows the contour of the skull to become even more compact.[8] In the portrait types which show the prince with a fully developed beard, the beard too is cropped short, the small curls lying close to the skin. The heaviness of Caracalla's features, in particular the broad ridge of his nose and the V-shaped bulge of his forehead muscle, are increasingly emphasized in these portraits.[9] His final portrait type, made for the period of his sole rule after the execution of his brother Geta, show the fullest and most dramatic exploitation of these elements for emotional effect.

These portraits, of which the bust in Berlin[10] (fig. 1) is a good example, give the head a strong, spiraling turn to the left, as though Caracalla had suddenly whirled to look behind him. This pose lends immediacy to the

[5] Nodelman, "Severan Imperial Portraits," pp. 392-418.

[6] For a fuller discussion of the type and a review of extant examples, see Wiggers and Wegner, Herrscherbild, III¹, 17-22; Ludwig Budde, Jugendbildnisse des Caracalla und Geta (Münster Westf.: Aschendorffsche Verlagsbuchhandlung, 1951), pp. 21-33, pls. 1, 10-19; Nodelman, "Severan Imperial Portraits," pp.140-160.

[7] James D. Breckenridge, "Imperial Portraiture: Augustus to Gallienus," Aufstieg und Niedergang der Römischen Welt, II, 12, 2 (Berlin and New York: De Gruyter, 1981), 504.

[8] Wiggers and Wegner, Herrscherbild, III¹, 22; Nodelman, "Severan Imperial Portraits," pp. 160-185; Budde, Jugendbildnisse, pp. 8-9 and pls. 4, 6.

[9] Wiggers and Wegner, Herrscherbild, III¹, 23, 27. Nodelman, "Severan Imperial Portraits," pp. 185-203.

[10] Berlin, Staatliche Museen, Antiken-Sammlung, cat. R96, inv. SK 384. Marble bust, h. 0.57. The bust shows chest and upper arms, nude except for sword belt and paludamentum. Restored: foot of bust, chips from paludamentum and lower rim of bust. Preservation excellent except for minor chips and scratches.

Published: Johann Jakob Bernoulli, Römische Ikonographie, Vol. II part 3 (Stuttgart, Berlin, Leipzig: W. Spemann, 1894), 54, No. 56, pl. 20. Carl Blümel, Römische Bildnisse, bd. suppl. of Katalog der Sammlung antiker Skulpturen (Berlin: Schoetz, 1933), pp. 39-40, No. R96. Wiggers and Wegner, Herrscherbild, III¹, 57.

facial expression, which has now become an emphatic scowl: the tense facial muscles are modeled in strong relief, and the furrows across the contracted forehead and around the taut mouth deeply carved out, so that the surfaces of the face have a strong undulation which allows a complex play of light and shadow. The pattern created by these creases has been brilliantly analyzed by Nodelman,[11] who has pointed out how the V-shaped forehead muscle, together with the triangle formed by the furrows around the mouth, build a large X which slashes across the face, knotting the heavy features into an intense moment of emotion. This X is superimposed on the severely rectilinear pattern of heavy, horizontal eyebrows, taut horizontal lips, and the strong vertical of the ridge of the fleshy nose. In this latest type, the creases which set off the forehead muscle on either side are no longer simple diagonal lines, but have a jagged, slightly irregular form, almost like bolts of lightning.[12]

The spiraling turn of the head may have been indirectly inspired by the portraits of Alexander the Great, whom Caracalla admired and emulated,[13] but the more immediate prototype was evidently a statue of Diomedes, whirling upon Odysseus who was about to betray him.[14] Since Caracalla had executed his own brother on charges of treason and was conducting bloody purges against his alleged enemies, the visual reference would have been unmistakable to an educated Roman audience. Even without the allusion to Diomedes, the effect of brute strength and intimidating anger which these portraits seek to convey would be communicated most effectively. Observer after observer[15] has remarked that though these portraits represent a repellant character, they are superb and compelling works of art.

A head in the Metropolitan Museum of Art[16] (fig. 2) seems to follow the same prototype as the Berlin bust, and is one of the technically better and more artistically effective replicas, yet it differs from most other members of the type in stylistic details. Here, the hair on the scalp has some volume, rising in relief to form a cap-like mass, yet the individual curls are not modeled with the same care as in other examples. Instead,

---

[11] Nodelman, "Severan Imperial Portraits," pp. 197, 354.

[12] Wiggers and Wegner, *Herrscherbild*, III[1], 29.

[13] See Bernoulli, *Römische Ikonographie*, II[3], 48, 59 and Herodian, IV.7 and IV.9.

[14] Blümel, *Römische Bildnisse*, p. 40; Nodelman, "Severan Imperial Portraits," pp. 367-369; Adolf Furtwängler, *Meisterwerke der griechischen Plastik* (Leipzig and Berlin: Giesecke and Devrient, 1893), p. 325.

[15] E.g., Bernoulli, *Römische Ikonographie*, II[3], 59; Blümel, *Römische Bildnisse*, p. 40.

[16] New York, Metropolitan Museum of Art, accession no. 40.11.1. Marble head, h. 0.362. Parts of nose, ears, neck broken away, left eyebrow and cheek chipped. Published: Gisela M. A. Richter, "A Portrait of Caracalla," *BMMA*, 35 (1940), 139-142; "Four Notable Acquisitions of the Metropolitan Museum," *AJA*, 44 (1940), 428-442; Wiggers and Wegner, *Herrscherbild*, III[1], 41-42, 71.

the texture of the hair is represented through a very sketchy and impressionistic pattern of chisel strokes. The beard is sketched directly onto the surface of the face as a pattern of stubble; the curls are not modeled in relief at all. The suggestion has been made that this head is an earlier work than the dramatic, scowling portrait made for Caracalla's sole rule, and that the smoothness of the cap of hair is consistent with the general elegance and restraint of the young prince's portraits, while his youth presumably accounts for the immature form of the beard.[17] Other scholars have questioned the authenticity of the head altogether.[18] All technical features of the Metropolitan head, however, find good parallels in sculpture of the early to mid third century. The treatment of the hair shows a movement toward the purely linear representation of feather-like tufts which can be seen in portraits of Alexander Severus and Maximinus Thrax. These works also demonstrate the technique of representing the beard solely through incision on the face.

The stylistic differences of the New York head from other replicas of Caracalla's final type, therefore, can perhaps be also be explained by Miss Richter's hypothesis that this work is a posthumous portrait,[19] executed at some time during the reign of Alexander Severus. If this dating is correct, then the New York head serves as evidence that the images of Caracalla continued not only to be visible and influential works but also perhaps to act as direct sources of inspiration to the artists called upon to examine and duplicate them.

The portraits of Caracalla's immediate successor, Macrinus, who briefly usurped power in 217 after Caracalla's assassination but who was himself overthrown and killed a little over a year later, can be tentatively identified, though they still present certain problems. Even within his one-year reign, this short-lived emperor appears to have been represented in at least two different portrait types, and possibly four, which are reflected in his widely differing coin profiles.[20] These numismatic portraits range from a type with a very short, military-style beard, to one with long, hanging curls, reminiscent of the beards worn by the Antonine emperors. A bronze head discovered near Belgrade in 1969[21] is the best preserved and most securely identified portrait of

---

[17] Nodelman, "Severan Imperial Portraits," pp. 179-183.

[18] See Wiggers and Wegner, *Herrscherbild*, III[1], 71.

[19] Richter, *AJA*, 44 (1940), 441; Wiggers and Wegner, *Herrscherbild*, III[1], 41-42, 71.

[20] Wiggers and Wegner, *Herrscherbild*, III[1], 132-134; Vladimir Kondić, "Two Recent Acquisitions in Belgrade Museums," *JRS*, 63 (1973), 47; Dieter Salzmann, "Die Bildnisse des Macrinus", *JdI*, 98 (1983), 353-360. Salzmann here convincingly disproves the common assumption that the different coin types are the products of different mints.

[21] Kondić, *JRS*, 63 (1973), 47-48, pls. V, VI, VII; Salzmann, *JdI*, 98 (1983), 371-376, figs. 13, 17, 21, 28-30. I am greatly indebted to Prof. George M. A. Hanfmann for calling to my attention the existence of this portrait and the evidence in favor of its identification as Macrinus.

Macrinus in existence. It is a work apparently of eastern provincial manufacture, and conforms most closely to the long-bearded coin portraits. Here, too, the beard forms long, parallel corkscrew curls, and in this overlife-sized work, the intentional visual allusion to Antonine imperial portraiture is even clearer than on the coins. Macrinus no doubt affected this rather old-fashioned style in order to present himself as a philosopher-king on the model of Marcus Aurelius.[22]

Nonetheless, the close relationship to Caracalla's portraits is unmistakable in the X pattern formed by the musculature of the frowning face. Here, the eyebrows are not horizontal, as in Caracalla's portraits, but flare upward to sharp arches toward the outer corners. The diagonals of the brow ridges parallel and complement the diagonals of the triangular forehead muscle. A renewed interest in unflattering realism can also be observed in the emphasis on the pouches under the eyes and the broad, rather irregular shape of the nose.

Another group of portraits in marble, which appear to follow a common prototype, has also been identified as Macrinus. These works,[23] in the Palazzo dei Conservatori (fig. 36), the Fogg Art Museum (fig. 37), and the Museo Capitolino do clearly represent the same individual, who bears certain physical resemblances to the bronze Macrinus in Belgrade such as the deep pouches under the eyes and the prominent bulge of the forehead muscle. They differ from that head, however, in the forms of the beards and of the hairline. The latter builds sharper angles over the temples and has a more pronounced central peak, where the locks of hair spring upward in an "anastole" rather than falling smoothly forward. Despite these differences, Salzmann has recently argued that all four heads represent Macrinus,[24] attributing their differences in part to the provincial workmanship of the Belgrade bronze and in part to the differences of prototype attested by the variety of portraits on Macrinus's

---

[22] Bergmann, *Studien*, pp. 19-22; Salzmann, *JdI*, 98 (1983), 380-381; Herodian, V.2.3-4.

[23] All three heads are mutilated in such a way as to suggest that their subject suffered a *damnatio memoriae.*

A) Rome, Palazzo dei Conservatori, Museo Nuovo, inv. 1757. Recent publications: Wiggers and Wegner, *Herrscherbild*, III[1], 139, pl. 32, with full literature; Bergmann, *Studien*, p. 19; Salzmann, *JdI*, 98 (1983), 361-371, figs. 12, 16, 20.

B) Cambridge, Mass., Fogg Art Museum, Harvard University, inv. 1949.47.138. Published: Hanfmann, *Latomus*, 11 (1952), 209-215, figs. 5-6. Wiggers and Wegner, *Herrscherbild*, III[1], 137; Bergmann, *Studien*, pp.123, 128, pl. 37, figs. 3-4: Salzmann, *JdI*, 98 (1983), 361-371, figs. 11, 15, 19.

C) Rome, Museo Capitolino, Stanza degli Imperatori, No. 48, inv. 460. Recent publications: Helbig[4], No. 1307. Wiggers and Wegner, *Herrscherbild*, III[1], 138-139; Bergmann, *Studien*, p. 19; Fittschen, *JdI*, 84 (1969), 223, figs. 53-54; Salzmann, *JdI*, 98 (1983), 361-371, figs. 14, 18, 22.

[24] Salzmann, *JdI*, 98 (1983), 351-381.

coins. The arguments presented by Salzman are quite persuasive, though the severe damage to the faces of all three of the marble heads makes difficulties for the comparison of them not only to the Belgrade head but to the coin profiles. The identification of this group can therefore be accepted a little more tentatively than that of the Yugoslavian bronze.[25]

The three marbles appear to have been made in or near the city of Rome, where two of them were definitely found (the provenance of the Fogg head, unfortunately, is unknown), and therefore, as might be expected, are far more sophisticated in style than the provincial head. Within the simple, compact ovoid of the head, the forms of the face have a complex, sensitive modeling which gives the skin surfaces a lively undulation. In the Fogg head, this quality is enhanced by the luminous polish of the marble. The X pattern created by the triangular bulge of the forehead muscle and the nasolabial folds is once again evident, and has been carried somewhat further: here, the V of the hairline and the creases across the forehead form a series of parallel chevrons which repeat and reinforce the pattern of triangles in the upper face. Already, a movement toward abstraction and patternization of the formula is evident: this quality is most clearly represented in the magnificent head in the Fogg (fig. 37). In this head, too, the pattern of the hair has been most completely reduced to an almost linear pattern: the short-cropped hair has a shallow, cap-like volume, but the little "a penna" tufts are represented by purely linear means.

Elagabalus, and Alexander Severus, at the time of his accession, were both too young to have developed the facial creases and bulging musculature which was so effectively exploited in the portraits of Caracalla and Macrinus. The one portrait which can be identified with reasonable certainty as Elagabalus[26] (fig. 14) shows some family resemblance to Caracalla in the blockiness of the head and strong horizontal accents of the mouth and the large eyes. During the reign of Alexander Severus, however, there seems to have been something of a reaction against the intensity of expression seen in the portraiture of his

---

[25] My own opinion concerning these works has changed twice: in my 1979 doctoral dissertation, I accepted the heads as portraits of Macrinus, but retracted this opinion in an article entitled "A Too-Successful *Damnatio Memoriae*: Problems in Third Century Portraiture," *AJA*, 87, 1983. In the latter work, I proceeded on the premise that the identification of the Belgrade head as Macrinus ruled out that of the Fogg-Conservatori-Capitoline type. In light of Salzmann's article, however, and his superb analysis of the numismatic evidence (*JdI*, 98, 1983, pp. 353-360 and 372), I am prepared to concede that this conclusion was far too hasty, and that the four heads may indeed all represent the same man, who can be identified as Macrinus.

[26] Rome, Museo Capitolino, Stanza degli Imperatori, No. 55. Recent publications: Wiggers and Wegner, *Herrscherbild*, III¹, 151, and Bergmann, *Studien*, p. 22. See next chapter for more complete discussion and full references.

immediate predecessors. The portraits of Alexander, which will be discussed in more detail in the following chapter, are characterized by oval forms and graceful, fluid curvilinears. With the reign of Maximinus Thrax, the angry scowl of Caracalla's final portraits reappears with, if possible, greater intensity.

The two best-preserved portraits of Maximinus, in Copenhagen[27] (fig. 3) and in the Capitoline Museum in Rome[28] show a coarse-featured man of massive, powerful bone structure, whose leathery skin is deeply creased and furrowed. We cannot know, of course, how faithfully the portrait reproduced the appearance of its subject, but the heavy, protruding jaw and bulging, ape-like brow ridge seem to be emphasized almost to the point of caricature. Once again, the artistic aim seems to be to impress, perhaps even to intimidate the viewer with a display of brute strength and grimly energetic character. The basic schema of Caracalla's last portraits can be recognized in the X pattern of the triangular forehead muscle and the furrows around the mouth. Here, too, the X traverses a pattern of rectilinears formed by the broad horizontal of the grimacing mouth, the level line of the heavy eyebrows, and the vertical emphasis of the thick nose. Where the portraits of Caracalla had a compact and square face, those of Maximinus take the form of a long, heavy rectangle, the geometric outlines of which are emphasized by the sharp corners of the jaw and of the hairline. Across the top of the forehead, the hairline curves very slightly downward toward a central peak, so that the shallow V of the hairline parallels the V of the forehead muscle, but the forehead is still basically rectangular.

Despite the uses of diagonals in the hairline and forehead muscle, the X pattern is no longer the most conspicuous element of the face. The surfaces of the skin are now broken up into a far more complex pattern of line, highlight and shadow than was the case in Caracalla's portraits: the

---

[27] Copenhagen, Ny Carlsberg Glyptotek, Cat. 744. Marble head, h. 0.43. Restorations now removed: nose, chin, ears. Major publications: Bernoulli, *Römische Ikonographie*, II³, 117, No. 1; Frederik Poulsen, *Catalogue of Ancient Sculpture, Ny Carlsberg Glyptotek*, 2nd ed., trans. W. E. Calvert (Copenhagen: Ny Carlsberg Glyptotek, 1951), No. 744. L'Orange, *Studien*, p. 3. Schweitzer, *Zur Kunst der Antike*, II, 273. Bianca Maria Felletti-Maj, *Iconografia Romana Imperiale* (Rome: Bretschneider, 1958), pp. 117-118, No. 77, pl. IX, fig. 29. Helga von Heintze, "Aspekte römischer Porträtkunst," *Gymnasium Beiheft*, 4 (1964), 161-162, pl. XIVa. Wiggers and Wegner, *Herrscherbild*, III¹, 226-227, pl. 69a. Bergmann, *Studien*, pp. 30-31. Vagn Poulsen, *Les Portraits romains*, II, 161-162, No. 164.

[28] Rome, Museo Capitolino, Stanza degli Imperatori, No. 62. Head set on a bust to which it does not belong. Marble, h. 0.30. Restored: nose, part of chin, ears, left eyebrow. Major publications: Bernoulli, *Römische Ikonographie*, II³, 117, No. 6, pl. 33. H. Stuart-Jones and members of the British School in Rome, *The Sculptures of the Museo Capitolino* (Oxford: Clarendon Press, 1912), p. 207, No. 62, pl. 49. Felletti-Maj, *Iconografia*, pp. 116-117, No. 76. Helbig⁴, No. 1314. Wiggers and Wegner, *Herrscherbild*, III¹, 227-228. Bergmann, *Studien*, pp. 30-31.

furrows across the forehead have become not only broader but more jagged and asymmetrical, canting slightly upward toward the left, while the
pattern of the eyes is elaborated by deep pouches, fine creases below the
rims of the lower lids, crow's-feet at the corners of the eyes, and heavy
rolls of flesh which overhang the upper lids. The flesh of the cheeks sags
somewhat toward the jawline, thus not only allowing the strong
cheekbones to project in higher relief, but giving the surfaces of the face
an additional undulation which allows for a still more varied play of light.

The tendency to elaborate the skin wherever possible with creases
results in the creation of a web of line across every available surface.
There is a remarkable detail in the Copenhagen portrait of Maximinus
(fig. 3), which cannot be anatomically explained: the beard, which ex-
tends far down onto the throat, is outlined at its lower border with a deeply chiseled line. This delight in articulation and demarcation of parts, in
the use of a linear boundary to separate an area of hair from an area of
bare skin, seems consistent with the use of deeply and sharply carved furrows to articulate the face.

An equally elaborate network of creases, again radiating outward from
around a rectilinear structure of features, can be observed in the portraits
of Pupienus, of which the best examples are those in the Vatican[29] (fig. 4)
and the Louvre.[30] The facial type represented here is quite different from
that of either Caracalla or Maximinus: the head is rather long and narrow, the cheeks gaunt, and the bone structure somewhat more delicate.
Furthermore, Pupienus wore a full beard, which tends to lengthen his
face, though he kept the close-cropped, military haircut fashionable during this period. Nonetheless, the similarities in treatment to the portraits
of Maximinus are striking, particularly in the series of jagged, asymmetrical creases which traverse the forehead, the cluster of vertical
creases above the root of the nose where the eyebrows are contracted, the

---

[29] Vatican, Braccio Nuovo, No. 54. Marble bust, h. in toto 0.69. Restored: left
eyebrow, tips of curls of beard, some folds of drapery. Tip of nose and rims of ears chipped. Head and bust preserved in one piece; foot and inscription tablet modern. Major
publications: Bernoulli, *Römische Ikonographie*, II³, 125-126, No. 1, pl. 36. Walther
Amelung, *Die Skulpturen des Vaticanischen Museums*, Vol. I (Berlin: Georg Reimer, 1903),
74, No. 54, pl. 8. Giuseppe Bovini, "Osservazione sulla ritrattistica romana da Treboniano Gallo a Probo," *MonAnt*, 39 (1943), 185, fig. 2. Max Wegner, "Bildnisbüste im 3.
Jahrhunderts n. Chr.," *Festschrift für Gerhard Kleiner* (Tübingen: Wasmuth, 1973), 106.
Felletti-Maj, *Iconografia*, pp. 135-136, No. 119, pl. XII, figs. 42-43. Helbig⁴, No. 428.
Wiggers and Wegner, *Herrscherbild*, III¹, 245, pls. 65b and 77.

[30] Paris, Louvre, MA 1020. Marble head made for insertion into statue, h. 0.35.
Restored: nose, parts of ears, rear part of bust, shoulders, part of breast. Major publications: Bernoulli, *Römische Ikonographie*, II³, 126, No. 3; Jean Charbonneaux, *La Sculpture
grecque et romaine au Musée du Louvre* (Paris: Ministère d'état, affaires culturelles, 1963), p.
179. Felletti-Maj, *Iconografia*, p. 136, No. 122. Wiggers and Wegner, *Herrscherbild*, III¹,
244, pl. 76a.

pouches and crow's-feet of the eyes, the rippling flesh of the cheeks, and the grim tautness of the lips.

The forehead muscle does not bulge as prominently as that of Caracalla or Maximinus, though the forehead cants outward toward a heavy, level brow ridge. Therefore the X pattern which could be traced from the portraits of Caracalla to those of Maximinus is not noticable here. However, the effect which the portraits of Pupienus seem to attempt to achieve is also somewhat different: dourness and energy are certainly suggested, but anger and intimidating strength of will are not. Pupienus glances sharply to his right and seems to have just turned his head in that direction, since the long locks of his beard form a swirl of S-curves across the chin, as though they had been swung by a sudden movement. This glance, together with the tension of the eyebrows and mouth, suggests not only alertness but haunted apprehension. Pupienus was a military man,[31] the general in command of the army which opposed the hated usurper Maximinus, but unlike his opponent, he seems not to try to inspire fear through his public portraits. These images could conceivably suggest that in his role of protector of the state, he himself feels anxiety. These portraits, however, obviously belong to the same formal tradition as those of Maximinus.

Some of the likenesses of Pupienus's coregent Balbinus and of their young successor Gordian III show a strikingly novel reinterpretation of that tradition. The frown of Caracalla's portraits, the schema of plunging diagonals and V's in the forehead and eyebrows, are still present but are carved in a hard and stiffly geometric manner. This style is more evident in some of Balbinus's portraits than in others, most notably the relief faces on his sarcophagus[32] (fig. 5) and a bronze head in the Vatican.[33]

---

[31] SHA, "Maximus et Balbinus," V.5.11; Herodian, VII.10.4.

[32] Marble sarcophagus, Rome, Museum of the Catacomb of the Praetextatus, h. 1.17, 1. 2.32, d. 1.31. Lid: 1. 2.32, h. 0.83, d. 1.17. Figures reclining on the cover are about life-sized, those in relief on box about half life-sized. Pieced together from fragments discovered near Via Appia during excavation of the catacomb of the Praetextatus. Major publications: Margarete Gütschow, Das Museum der Praetextatkatakombe, Vol. IV of Mem-PontAcc, 3rd ser., 1938, 77-106, pls. X-XII. Schweitzer, Zur Kunst der Antike, II, 277. Felletti-Maj, Iconografia, 142-143, No. 136, pl. 15, fig. 50, and pl. 16, figs. 51-52. L'Orange, Studien, p. 97. Hans Jucker, "Drei ergänzte Sarkophage," AA, 70 (1955), 31-32; "Die Behauptung des Balbinus," AA, 81 (1966), 501-514; "A Portrait Head of the Emperor Balbinus," Cleveland Museum of Art Bulletin, 54 (1967), 11-16. Wiggers and Wegner, Herrscherbild, III¹, 247-248, pl. 79.

[33] Vatican library, bronze head, h. 0.38. Provenance: Porta San Sebastiano, Rome. Inner surfaces of eyes and small part of bust restored in gesso. Published: Bernoulli, Römische Ikonographie, II³, 128-129, pl. 35. Kurt Kluge and Karl Lehmann-Hartleben, Grossbronzen der römischen Kaiserzeit (Berlin and Leipzig: De Gruyter, 1927), Vol. II, 43, fig. 1, pl. 14. Gütschow, MemPontAcc, 4 (1938), 85 No. 1, fig. 17. Anna Gräfin von Schlieffen (R. West), "Eine römische Kaiserstatue im Piraeus Museum," ÖJh, 29 (1935), 105-106. Felletti-Maj, Iconografia, p. 140, No. 133, pl. 14, fis. 47-48. Helbig⁴ I, No. 472. Jucker,

His other likenesses, which remain to be discussed in a later chapter, recognizably represent the same face as these works, but are modeled in a more curvilinear and organic style.[34] The life-sized portrait figure of Balbinus which reclines on the cover of the sarcophagus (fig. 6) also shows Balbinus with a more relaxed and meditative facial expression than that of the smaller portraits which appear on the relief of the same monument.

The latter employ the now familiar schema of plunging diagonals in the upper face and rising diagonals around the mouth. The forehead muscle, however, hardly swells at all, though its triangular form is indicated by sharply carved creases alongside it. Instead, the most conspicuous V's are formed by the linear pattern of the peaked hairline, and the lines of the eyebrow ridges as they plunge toward the root of the nose. The long, narrow eyes too are set on a slight slant, and the V pattern is repeated once more in the lower face by the dip at the center of the pursed mouth. The creases across the forehead, the deep vertical notches which rise above the root of the nose, and the furrows around the mouth are all treated as linear designs incised into the smooth, neutral surface of the marble, rather than as furrows between rounded forms, a significant difference from the manner in which facial line is modeled in the portraits of Pupienus or the life-sized figure on the cover of this same sarcophagus. The volumes and surfaces of the relief portraits are kept simple, smooth and compact, the facial features articulated by abrupt angles between planes rather than rounded transitions: note in particular the sharp ridges of the eyebrows and the prism-like form of the nose. The eyes, which are outlined by a narrow but dark and deep crease above the upper lid, and the mouth, which is delineated mainly by the deep furrow between the lips, become primarily linear designs.

All these stylistic elements might be dismissed as reflecting the limitations of reduced scale if they did not also appear in the life-sized bronze head in the Vatican, and in all the portraits of Gordian III. Though this boy, who became emperor at the age of twelve or thirteen, reigned for only six years, his portraits survive in remarkable quantity.[35] Two examples

---

*AA*, 81 (1966), 509. Wiggers and Wegner, *Herrscherbild*, III[1], 248, pl. 78a. Janine and Jean-Charles Balty, "Notes d'iconographie romain," *Bulletin de l'Institut Historique Belge de Rome*, 44 (1974), 31, 35.

[34] For a fuller discussion of the stylistic differences between Balbinus's portraits, see J. and J. Ch. Balty, *Bull. de l'Inst. Hist. Belge de Rome*, 44 (1974), 36.

[35] For a thorough list of extant portraits of Gordian III, see Jörgen Bracker, "Bestimmung der Bildnisse Gordians III nach einer neuen ikonographischen Methode," Dissertation, Westfälische Wilhelms-Universität zu Münster, 1966, passim; Felletti-Maj, *Iconografia*, pp. 147-163, pls. XVII-XXI; Max Wegner, Jörgen Bracker and Willi Real, *Gordian III bis Carinus*, Vol. III part 3 of *Das römische Herrscherbild* (Berlin: Mann, 1979), 13-29.

of especially good quality and preservation can be singled out for discussion here: a bust in Berlin,[36] (fig. 7), which was presumably made in the first half of his reign, since it shows Gordian still as a boy without facial hair, and a colossal head from Ostia,[37] (fig. 8), now in the Terme museum, which represents Gordian not only with a moustache and sideburns, but also with a heavier and more mature bone structure. Both these works, however, display a skillful and imaginative adaptation for a very young face of the devices which were originally developed for Caracalla, when he was a grown man in his late twenties, and subsequently applied in imperial portraiture mainly to the images of older men.

Gordian is represented in all his portraits as having a triangular face which tapers from a broad, flat cranium to a narrow chin. In the earlier portrait type,[38] exemplified by the Berlin bust (fig. 7), the geometric form of the face is very severely outlined and enclosed, while the later one, because it must show a heavier and more developed jaw, gives the cheeks a somewhat freer curvature which plays against the swelling form of the cranium. In both types, however, it is the triangle from forehead to chin which dominates the form of the head. Within this geometric outer contour, the features are carved in a crisp, dry manner and outlined in such a way as to give them the quality of discrete units of an abstract pattern rather than parts of an organic whole. The almond-shaped eyes, for example, are outlined above and below by deeply carved creases, the lips separated by a narrow, deep line of shadow, and—in the Terme head (fig. 8)—outlined by a shallow groove which cannot be explained anatomically.

---

[36] Berlin, Staatliche Museen, Antiken-Sammlung, R102. Marble bust, h. 0.56. Restored: left ear. Bust belongs to head, though neck broken through. Major publications: Bernoulli, *Römische Ikonographie*, II³, 133, No. 14; Blümel, *Römische Bildnisse*, pp. 42-43, No. R102, pl. 66; Felletti-Maj, *Iconografia*, pp. 149-150, No. 148, pl. 18, fig. 59. Helga von Heintze, "Studien zu den Porträts des 3. Jahrhunderts n. Chr. I: Gordian III," *RömMitt*, 62 (1955), 182. Bracker, "Bestimmung der Bildnisse Gordians III," pp. 20-21, 70-72; Wegner, *Festschrift Kleiner*, pp. 106-107. Fittschen, *JdI*, 84 (1969), 200-201, No. 1 and p. 206. Wegner, Bracker and Real, *Herrscherbild*, III³, 16, 21, pl. 7.

[37] Rome, Museo Nazionale delle Terme, inv. 326. Marble head, h. 0.63. No restorations. Ears gone (formerly attached separately); nose broken, face battered. Provenance: Ostia. Major publications: Felletti-Maj, *Ritratti*, pp. 141-142, No. 281; *Iconografia*, p. 155, No. 161, pl. XX, fig. 65; von Heintze, *RömMitt*, 62 (1955), 182; Bracker, "Bestimmung der Bildnisse Gordians III," pp. 34-35 and 103-104. Fittschen, *JdI*, 84 (1969), No. 16, and p. 206. Wegner, Bracker, and Real, *Herrscherbild*, III¹, 19, 27, pl. 9; *Museo Nazionale Romano: le sculture*, ed. Antonio Giuliano (Rome: De Luca, 1979), Vol. I, part 1, 310-312, No. 186.

[38] For a more extensive discussion of Gordian's portrait types, see below, chapter IV and appendix. Relevant literature: Bracker, "Bestimmung der Bildnisse Gordians III," 52-55; Fittschen, *JdI*, 84 (1969), 204; Wegner, Bracker and Real, *Herrscherbild*, III³, 13-20.

Just as in the relief portraits on Balbinus's sarcophagus, the conventional pattern of V's in the upper face is established by the peaked hairline and the sharp plunge of the eyebrow ridges rather than by the form of the forehead muscle. The forehead does have a pronounced convexity which widens from the root of the nose toward the hairline, but now the form is created not by the forehead muscle but by the roundness of the cranium itself. The curvature of the forehead, like that of the cheeks, is smooth, regular, and somewhat inorganic. Another point of resemblance to the relief portraits of Balbinus can be observed in the repetition of the V pattern by the angular dip of the center of the upper lip.

In the portraits of Gordian, the entire pattern of features is more symmetrical, and the central axis of the face far more strongly emphasized, than in any of the portraits of Balbinus. The alignment of the peak of the hairline, the two notches which rise at abrupt angles from the inner corners of the eyebrows, the center of the mouth and the cleft of the small but firm chin makes a strong impression on the observer, though the turn and tilt of the head prevents the symmetry from rendering the face lifelessly stiff. Nonetheless, this new geometric severity has the effect of freezing and immobilizing the contraction of the face which has now become such a standard device for expressing energy, and converting it to a sort of symbol or ideogram of a frown. The abstraction of these portraits, which contrasts so strongly with the elaborate and organic naturalism of the nearly-contemporary likenesses of Maximinus (fig. 3) and Pupienus (fig. 4), may reflect a particular artistic personality, whose style is also clearly evident in the portraits of Gordian's wife Tranquillina (fig. 57), which will be discussed in a later chapter.

We are unusually fortunate to have two examples of these portraits in the context of their complete, or nearly complete, original compositions: the earlier type, as represented by the Berlin bust (fig. 7), which shows him wearing the trabeated toga, and an overlifesized half-body bust in the Louvre[39] which portrays the later, more mature type of Gordian in the cuirass and paludamentum of a general. It has been suggested that this change in costume reflects the shift from senatorial to military control of Gordian's government during the ascendancy of his father-in-law Timesitheus,[40] and the powerful, muscular treatment of the chest and

---

[39] Paris, Louvre, MA 1063, bust (possibly a recut statue), h. 0.75. Restored: tip of nose, fragment of sword, part of left hand, chips of drapery. Right arm broken away at elbow, restored arm now removed. Major publications: Bernoulli, *Römische Ikonographie*, II[3], 131, No. 1, p. 134, pl. 38; Felletti-Maj, *Iconografia*, pp. 151-152, No. 152, pl. XIX, figs. 61-62; Bracker, "Bildnisse Gordians III," pp. 35-50 and 91-93; Wegner, *Festschrift Kleiner*, p. 122; Wegner, Bracker and Real, *Herrscherbild*, III[3], 19, 26, pl. 8. See appendix.

[40] Bracker, "Bestimmung der Bildnisse Gordians III," pp. 36-44.

arms in the Paris bust seems to support such a theory. The Berlin bust, in contrast, displays a slim neck and sloping shoulders which suggest not only a youthful but a delicate physique. It is important to remember, on the other hand, that at least twenty portraits of Gordian survive, of which only these two still belong to busts, and that they hardly constitute sufficient basis for generalization about the prevalence of one bust type or another for the earlier and later portrait type. It is more to the point to observe how both busts complement the style of their portrait heads. The Berlin portrait (fig. 7) shows a dry and linear treatment of the drapery comparable to the linear patterning of the features, while the diagonal edge of the paludamentum of the Louvre figure neatly bisects the rectangular chest into two right triangles, consistent with the taste for oblique lines and triangular patterns in the face.

In the years immediately following Gordian's reign, the "Gordian master" appears not to have been patronized for official portraiture, since the abstract style no longer dominates imperial portraits. Instead, the images of Philip the Arab and of Trajan Decius display a renewed experimentation with emotional intensity, this time expressed through dramatic effects of movement. The most securely identified portrait of Philip the Arab, the handsome bust in the Vatican[41] (fig. 9), demonstrates a return to emphasis on sheer physical strength and bulk in the massive bone structure, leathery, furrowed skin, and coarse features. Philip has a long, rectangular face with a low, sloping forehead, heavy eyebrows, and fleshy lips and nose. His head turns sharply to his right, a conventional mannerism, but instead of turning his gaze downward to the observer, as the portraits of Caracalla did, his glance is directed upwards.

This spiraling upward movement is a very old device in portraiture, traceable to the images of Alexander the Great,[42] and probably intended to show the leader as a heroically inspired man looking to the gods for

---

[41] Vatican, Braccio Nuovo, inv. 2216, marble bust, h. 0.71. Restored: tip of nose, rim of left ear. Foot and inscription tablet are ancient but do not belong to bust. Major publications: Bernoulli, *Römische Ikonographie*, II³, 144, No. 1, pl. 40; Amelung, *Skulpturen*, I, 149, No. 124, pl. 20. L'Orange, *Studien*, p. 3, fig. 5; *Art Forms and Civic Life*, p. 110; Felletti-Maj, *Iconografia*, p. 170, No. 193, pl. 23, fig. 75; Helbig⁴ I, No. 456; Wegner, *Festschrift Kleiner*, p. 106, pl. 23, fig. 1. Wegner, Bracker and Real, *Herrscherbild*, III³, 32, 40, pls. 11a, 12a. Dawson Kiang, "The Metropolitan Antiochus and the Vatican Philip," *Acta ad Archaeologiam et Artium Historiam Pertinentia*, VIII (1978), 75-84, pls. III, IV. Kiang raises the suggestion that the Vatican bust may be an eighteenth-century work, based on a prototype of the Hellenistic period. This theory is easily refuted, however, by the comparisons discussed here with other third-century imperial portraits.

[42] H. P. L'Orange, *Apotheosis in Ancient Portraiture*, Institutet for Sammenlignende Kultursforskning, Serv. B., Vol. XLIV (Oslo, 1947), 19-27. See also Antonio Minto, "Nuovo ritratto in bronzo di Filippo l'Arabo," *Rivista d'Arte*, 29 (1954), 5-6.

favor and guidance. The pose is reinterpreted here with great freshness and imagination, since the movement of the head and eyes has been enriched by the pattern of facial line. The X pattern formed by the V-shaped forehead muscle (here complemented by the V-shaped peak of the hairline) and the upright triangle of creases around the mouth is still present, but now it is the downward-pointing diagonals of the forehead which have been greatly reduced in emphasis, while the strong, curving sweep upward of the furrows around the mouth has gained greatly in importance. The direction of these lines is picked up by the shallower "tired lines" alongside the nose at the corners of the eyes, and again by the three vertical creases which rise from the inner corners of the eyebrows and above the root of the nose.

The eyebrows, furthermore, do not plunge toward the nose, as did Gordian's, but slope gradually upward. The ridges of the eyebrows twist upward at their inner corners into the vertical creases of the forehead, so that the two elements form continuous, rising lines, which are paralleled by the creases of the upper eyelids. The eyes are deeply hooded at their outer corners, so that each orbital fold rises sharply toward the nose, providing still another element in an overall pattern of upward diagonals. The dominant impression created by this portrait is of a single unified movement.[43] All lines are swept inward and upward along the central axis, in the direction of the upturned gaze, so that the entire face quivers with tension and concentration.

Once again, as in the portraits of Pupienus, we seem to see an effort to portray the burden of the emperor's power, and the anxiety which results from his awareness of the magnitude of his responsibility. The emotion is captured here with far greater immediacy than in any preceding imperial portraits. This bust and related works have aptly been described as "impressionistic"[44] in that they employ effects of movement and strong contrasts of highlight and shadow to suggest that the artist has captured a fleeting but emotionally revealing configuration of features. If the portraits of Gordian III used a stiff and abstract pattern of line to create an "ideogram" of a frown, here we seem on the contrary to see a vivid and realistic facial expression, though one which is actually based on a fully rational and calculated design. The artist of this portrait thus differs fundamentally in his approach from the "Gordian master," though he shares with him a few important stylistic devices, most notably an avoidance of any line and detail except that which is most necessary to convey the facial expression. The skin here is not broken up by crow's

---

[43] L'Orange, *Art Forms and Civic Life*, p. 110.

[44] See Kaschnitz-Weinberg, *Die Antike*, 2 (1926), 41; L'Orange, "The Antique Origins of Medieval Portraiture," *Likeness and Icon*, pp. 92-93.

feet or other small creases, while compared to the portraits of Maximinus (fig. 3) and Pupienus (fig. 4), the furrows of the forehead are fewer and less complicated. It is also significant that the hair is no longer represented *"a penna,"* but instead, as in many portraits of Gordian III, by a pattern of isolated chisel marks which are used with particular skill in the Vatican bust to create an impression of the texture of stubbly hair.

One feature which the Vatican bust of Philip (fig. 9), as well as another less well preserved bust of Philip in Leningrad[45] share with the Vatican bust of Pupienus (fig. 4) is the fact that the emperor is represented dressed in a contabulate toga—that is, a civilian garment which reminds the viewer of the legal and constitutional rank of the leader. The two Vatican busts, furthermore, are among the precious few which have survived with heads and bodies intact, so that there can be no question in either case that the head and bust belong together, or that the overall composition survives as it was originally designed. It may be significant that a "soldier emperor" like Philip appears to have been at pains to present himself in a manner emphasizing his consular rank, just as the senatorial emperor Pupienus (fig. 4), the young Gordian III (fig. 7), and the last legitimate heir of the Severans[46] were presented. Philip appears to have been particularly concerned with constitutional observances and with creating a show of legitimacy, a fact reflected by his lavish celebra-

---

[45] Leningrad, Hermitage Museum, marble bust, H. 0.70, of head, 0.27. Restored: nose, rims of ears, chips of drapery. Pieced together from several fragments, and probably heavily reworked. Major publications: Bernoulli, *Römische Ikonographie* II³, 142, No. 10; Felletti-Maj, *Iconografia*, p. 171, No. 194; Bergmann, *Studien*, p. 34, No. 2; Aleksandra Vostchinina, *Le Portrait Romain*, trans. T. Gourevich (Leningrad: Aurore, for the Hermitage Museum, 1974), No. 66, pls. 90-91, p. 184; Wegner, *Festschrift Kleiner*, pp. 106-107; Wegner, Bracker and Real, *Herrscherbild* III³, pp. 32-33, 36, pls. 11b, 12b, 14b. The antiquity of this bust has been challenged on many occasions, most recently by Dawson Kiang, "The Iconography of Philip the Arab," *AJA*, 85 (1981), p. 201.

[46] Two togate busts of Alexander Severus survive intact, both representing him in the trabeated toga like that worn by the Vatican busts of Pupienus and Philip the Arab.

A) Rome, Museo Capitolino, inv. 480, marble bust, H. 0.76, of head 0.215. Well preserved except for chips from hair and eyebrows. Inscription tablet of bust restored. Major publications: Bernoulli, *Römische Ikonographie*, II³, 147, No. 1; Stuart-Jones, *Museo Capitolino*, p. 209, No. 69, pl. 50; L'Orange, *Studien*, p. 94, No. 1; Felletti-Maj, *Iconografia*, pp. 85-86, No. 2, and p. 185, pl. 2, fig. 5; Wiggers and Wegner, *Herrscherbild*, III¹, pp. 191-192; Wegner, Bracker and Real, *Herrscherbild*, III³, pp. 43, 46-47, pls. 17a, 18a. This bust belongs to the type sometimes identified as Philip II, but which I believe to represent Alexander Severus (see next chapter, and appendix).

B) Florence, Uffizi Gallery 198 inv. 1914.245, bust, H. 0.70. Restored: lower part of nose, ears, parts of drapery, foot of bust. Surface harshly cleaned in modern times. Major publications: Bernoulli, *Römische Ikonographie*, II³, No. 8, p. 100, pl. 29; Guido Mansuelli, *Galleria degli Uffizi: le sculture* (Rome: Istituto Poligrafico dello Stato, 1961), Vol. II, 116-117, No. 147; Felletti-Maj, *Iconografia*, p. 93, No. 18, pl. 2, fig. 10; Wiggers and Wegner, *Herrscherbild*, III¹, p. 186, pls. 53 and 65a; Bergmann, *Studien*, p. 27, No. 12.

tion of the millenial games[47] and his emphasis of that historic anniversary on his coinage. But it is probably safe to assume that all emperors were automatically represented in the toga,[48] regardless of their means of attaining power, and that accidents of preservation, rather than any calculated official policy, account for the absence of such representations for other soldier emperors.

Stylistically, these togate busts are generally characterized by a painstaking and accurate reproduction of the volumes of the heavy garment with its broad pleated and clamped folds across the chest and over the left shoulder. The folds, however, tend to be rather drily carved, in sharply cut, linear grooves, consistent with the growing taste for use of linear pattern in portrait faces at this period. The actual fashion of the trabeated toga[49] contributes of course to the stiffness and inflexibility of the drapery, but at this period tastes in clothing and tastes in sculptural style seem to have been compatible.

A still more sophisticated use of impressionistic devices can be observed in the portraits of Trajan Decius, of which the best preserved and most securely identified ancient example is a head in the Capitoline museum (fig. 10).[50] Here, not only the facial lines, which once again tend to converge inward and upward along the central axis of the face, but even the outer contours of the head participate in an effect of sweeping, undulating movement. The long curves of the cheeks sink deeply inward above the cheekbones into the hollow temples, from which the contour swells out again into the broad dome of the cranium. The locks of hair along the temples follow the curves of the surface so that in frontal view

[47] Mattingly, Sydenham and Sutherland, *RIC*, Vol. IV, part 3, pp. 59, 63-64, 70-71, pl. 6, figs. 6-12. The principal evidence for the celebration of Rome's thousandth anniversary comes from the coins.

[48] See Niemeyer, *Statuarischen Darstellung*, pp. 40-43 and 82-90.

[49] Lillian Wilson, *The Roman Toga* (Baltimore: Johns Hopkins Press, 1924), 75-86, figs. 38-46, and pp. 94-101.

[50] Rome, Museo Capitolino, Stanza degli Imperatori No. 70, head in marble, h. 0.24. Restored: tip of nose, ears, part of upper lip, most of neck. Set on bust to which it does not belong. Major publications: Bernoulli, *Römische Ikonographie*, II³, 153, pl. XLVI; Alois Riegl, *Die spätrömische Kunstindustrie nach den Funden in Österreich-Ungarn*, I (Vienna, 1901), 122, fig. 19; Kaschnitz-Weinberg, *Die Antike*, 2 (1926), 44, pl. 6; Stuart-Jones, *Museo Capitolino*, p. 209, No. 70, pls. 50-51; Gerhard Rodenwaldt, "Zur Kunstgeschichte der Jahre 220 bis 270," *JdI*, 51 (1936), 99; L'Orange, *Studien*, p. 3, fig. 2; Helga von Heintze, "Studien zu den Porträts des 3. Jahrhunderts n. Chr. II, Trebonianus Gallus—Trajan Decius; III, Gordians I-II," *RömMitt*, 63 (1956), 59, pl. 24, fig. 1, and pl. 26, fig. 1; Felletti-Maj, *Iconografia*, p. 189, No. 235, pl. 29, fig. 95. Helbig⁴, No. 1320; Schweitzer, *Zur Kunst der Antike*, II, 275, pl. 65, fig. 4; J. and J. Ch. Balty, *Bull. de l'Inst. Hist. Belge de Rome*, 44 (1974), 45-54, pl. 6, fig. 1, and pl. 8, fig. 1; Janine and Jean-Charles Balty, "Notes d'iconographie romain II," *RömMitt*, 83 (1976), 177-178, pl. 43, fig. 1, pl. 44, fig. 2, and pl. 46, fig. 2; Bergmann, *Studien*, pp. 42-43, pl. 6, figs. 3-4; Wegner, Bracker and Real, *Herrscherbild*, III³, 63-64, 66, pl. 26.

they tend to parallel the contours, leading the eye inward toward the temples and outward along the swelling curves of the skull.

Within this restless outline, individual forms are also vigorously modeled: the eyes, for example, are set very deeply into their sockets and have a strong three-dimensional curvature from inner to outer corner. More important for the effect of emotion, however, is the way in which the movement of the facial line complements that of the outer contours. The furrows around the mouth, which now extend to well below the lower lip, pick up the parallel lines of the slack tendons of the throat, broaden outward, and then contract inward again toward the nose, forming tall parentheses within the long curves of the cheeks. Just as in the portraits of Philip (fig. 9), the ridges of the eyebrows slope upward and twist into the furrows above the root of the nose; thus, the pattern of line is drawn most tightly inward at the level of the face where the contour sinks inward at the temples. And finally, the notches which rise from the eyebrows twist outward again into the horizontal creases of the forehead. Thus, the upward sweep of facial line resolves itself into an expanding, fountain-like movement within the broad, expanding contour of the cranium.

The pattern of line is rendered still more complex in this portrait because though the dominant movement follows the upturned gaze of the eyes, some elements create a counter-tension by pulling downward. The pouches under the eyes, for example, and the tendons of the throat, both conspicuously obey the law of gravity, while in profile view the curve of the nose (of which only the very tip is restored) and the corners of the lips both pull downward against the rising arch of the eyebrows. Thus, not only anxious tension but also weariness are most effectively conveyed.

This portrait was one of the finest expressions of the impressionistic style of the mid-third century, and one of the last. Unfortunately, the development of style in the years immediately following the death of Decius in 251 cannot be easily traced, since no portrait of his successor, Trebonianus Gallus, has yet been identified with any security. Of the various works generally suggested as portraits of him,[51] no two even resemble one another closely enough to represent the same man, let alone to reproduce a common prototype. A colossal bronze statue in the Metropolitan Museum in New York[52] (fig. 11) has at least the strongest

---

[51] For thorough discussions of the problem, see Wegner, Bracker and Real, *Herrscherbild*, III³, 83-91; Felletti-Maj, *Iconografia*, pp. 201-207; von Heintze, *RömMitt*, 63 (1956), 56-65.

[52] New York, Metropolitan Museum of Art, bronze statue, h. 2.406, of head, 0.248. Reconstructed from fragments, but only one part of back is missing. Provenance: area of S. Giovanni in Laterano, found in early nineteenth century. Major publications: C. M. Fitzgerald, *BMMA*, 1 (1905), 12-13; Bernoulli, *Römische Ikonographie*, I, 165; Kluge and

claim of any of the candidates to represent an imperial figure; though private funerary portraits are sometimes slightly greater than life-sized, this work is so conspicuously large and creates such an imposing impression of authority that it is difficult to imagine that the work could represent a private individual.

It is ironic that this statue cannot be identified with more certainty, since it is the only bronze statue, and one of the few complete statues of an emperor, to survive from this period. There are several other examples in marble of imperial statues with ideal bodies adapted from Greek prototypes, sometimes endowed with divine attributes: a nude figure of Alexander Severus,[53] a half-draped statue of Balbinus as Zeus from the Piraeus harbor,[54] and a nude figure with a helmet and sword[55] which is most likely to represent Decius as Mars (fig. 46). In all these cases, as with deified imperial portrait statues throughout the period of the Roman empire,[56] the bodies are never literal copies of any identifiable prototype but free adaptations inspired by classical and Hellenistic models. The portrait of Decius as Mars shares with the New York bronze a dramatically expansive pose which complements well the

---

Lehmann-Hartleben, *Grossbronzen*, II, 45, 100, pl. 31; Gisela M. A. Richter, *Greek, Etruscan and Roman Bronzes* (New York: Metropolitan Museum of Art, 1915), pp. 154-156, No. 350; *Handbook of the Classical Collection* (New York: Metropolitan Museum of Art, 1930), p. 304; L'Orange, *Studien*, p. 97; Antonio Minto, ''Un Nuovo ritratto di C. Vibius Trebonianus Gallus,'' *Critica d'Arte*, II (1937), 50, figs. 5, 6, 13, pls. 43-45; Bonini, *Mon-Ant*, 39 (1943), 192, fig. 7; von Heintze, *RömMitt*, 63 (1956), 58, pl. 23, fig. 1 and pl. 25, fig. 2; Niemeyer, *Statuarischen Darstellung*, p. 113, No. 128, pl. 48, fig. 1; Felletti-Maj, *Iconografia*, p. 204, No. 260, pl. 36, fig. 113; J. and J. Ch. Balty, *Bull. de l'Inst. Hist. Belge de Rome*, 44 (1974), 48-49; Bergmann, *Studien*, pp. 44-45; Wegner, Bracker and Real, *Herrscherbild*, III³, 65, 84-86, 89-90; Anna Marguerite McCann, ''Beyond the Classical in Third Century Portraiture,'' *Aufstieg und Niedergang der römischen Welt*, II, 12, 2 (Berlin: de Gruyter, 1981), 630-632, pls. V, VI.

[53] Naples, Museo Nazionale inv. 5993, colossal statue, h. 3.79, marble. Restored: most of lips and ears, both forearms, part of left leg and foot. Face ancient, but carved in a separate piece from the head. May be a recut portrait of Elagabalus. Recent publications: Niemeyer, *Statuarischen Darstellung*, pp. 62, 112, No. 124, pl. 44, fig. 2; Klaus Fittschen and Paul Zanker, ''Die Kolossalstatue des Severus Alexander in Neapel—eine wiederverwendete Statue des Elagabal,'' *AA* 85 (1970), 248-253; Wiggers and Wegner, *Herrscherbild*, III¹, 189, pls. 50, 56a; Bergmann, *Studien*, pp. 26-27. See appendix for fuller references.

[54] Piraeus Museum, marble statue, H. 2.02. Surface corroded, right hand and part of left missing. Basic publications: Gräfin von Schlieffen (R. West), *ÖJh*, 29 (1935), 97-108. Recent publications: Niemeyer, *Statuarischen Darstellung*, p. 112, No. 125, pl. 46; Wiggers and Wegner, *Herrscherbild*, III¹, 248; J. and J. Ch. Balty, *Bull. de l'Inst. Hist. Belge de Rome*, 44 (1974), 40-42, pls. 4-5.

[55] Rome, Palazzo dei Conservatori, statue in marble, h. 2.17. Head broken off and reset, but belongs to statue. Extensive restorations (see appendix). Recent publications with earlier literature: Niemeyer, *Statuarischen Darstellung*, p. 113, No. 127, pl. 48, fig. 2; Helbig⁴, No. 1494; Wegner, Bracker and Real, *Herrscherbild*, III³, 67.

[56] Niemeyer, *Statuarischen Darstellung*, pp. 59-63.

emotion expressed in the face. The former is probably based on the Ares of Alkamenes,[57] the latter a free adaptation of Lysippos's "Alexander with the Lance."[58] In the statue of Decius, however, a feeling of movement, in the spiraling turn of the body away from the weight leg, the toss of the head, upward gaze, and outstretched left hand, is more pronounced than in the bronze statue in New York. (fig. 11).

The latter, with its massive, almost unarticulated torso, its more stably balanced weight, and the vertical emphasis of the lance once held in the upraised left hand, is a far more static composition. If the head is the one originally destined for this body,[59] then the statue also displays a rather cavalier attitude toward uniformity of bodily proportions— features consistent with the stiff and somewhat non-naturalistic treatment of the face.

If this work can be tentatively accepted as a portrait of Gallus, then perhaps it indicates a beginning of the return to favor of the  stylistic devices which characterized the portraits of Gordian III, since here too the eyebrows plunge sharply toward the nose in a stiffly symmetrical V which is repeated by the angular dip at the center of the pursed lips. In addition, the conventional X pattern of Caracalla's portraits is repeated here with an almost mechanical geometry and regularity. Since the identification of this statue is at best tentative, however, it cannot be stated here with any certainty that the abstract and geometric style of Gordian's portraiture reappears in imperial images until Valerian and Gallienus had come to power in 253.

The only surviving portrait of Valerian[60] belongs to the traditions of the images of soldier-emperors like Maximinus and Philip the Arab in its harshly realistic representation of coarse features and furrowed skin. Valerian, like his predecessors, owed his position solely to his military ability, and presumably needed for that reason to be portrayed in a manner which emphasized his toughness and experience. His son and coregent Gallienus, on the other hand, was designated as dynastic heir to Valerian's power, and as such had to be presented to the public in a somewhat different style. It was customary for young men in such a situation to be portrayed in a classically elegant and aristocratic

---

[57] Ibid., p. 63.

[58] Ibid., p. 113.

[59] See McCann, *Aufstieg und Niedergang*, II, 12.2 (1981), p. 631.

[60] Copenhagen, Ny Carlsberg Glytotek, cat. 766c. Marble head, h. 0.425. Provincial work, probably from Asia Minor. Nose missing, surface chipped and flecked, rear of head battered. Major publications: Cornelius Vermeule, *Roman Imperial Art in Greece and Asia Minor* (Cambridge, Mass.: Harvard University Press, 1968), pp. 312, 404; Leslie McCoull, "Two New Third-Century Imperial Portraits in the Ny Carlsberg Glyptotek," *Berytus*, 17 (1967-68), 66-71, pls. 18-19. V. Poulsen, *Les Portraits romains*, II, 169-170, No. 174, pls. 279-280; Bergmann, *Studien*, pp. 51, 59-60, 93, pl. 15, fig. 1. Breckenridge, *Likeness*, p. 205, fig. 108. Wegner, Bracker and Real, *Herrscherbild*, III³, 101-102, 103.

manner,[61] and for these purposes, the stiffly immobile and abstract style of Gordian's portraits was far better suited than the dramatic and emotional impressionism of the imperial portraits from the years following his rule.

The type now generally accepted as the first portrait of Gallienus,[62] the image dating from his coregency with his father, is best represented by a fine head in the Pergamon Museum at Berlin[63] (fig. 12). The dominant mood of this work, in striking contrast to the imperial portraits of Gallienus's recent predecessors, is one of meditative calm, conveyed through the cleanly geometric contours of the face, the regularity and symmetry of features, and the decorative elegance of the patterns of hair and beard. Though the hair is still worn very short, in good soldierly manner, it is no longer clipped to a stubble but allowed to lie in smooth strands along the scalp, and is carved with some volume in relief. The beard, likewise, is not represented merely by a pattern of chisel strokes; small, tight curls are carved in low relief on the cheeks and throat. In both the hair and the beard, however, the chisel work is remarkably crisp and dry, forming sharp little ridges and furrows rather than rounded volumes which would suggest the softness of human hair.[64] The primary objective here seems to be the creation of decorative textures to frame the face and set off some of the features.

The locks of hair which fall forward in a short fringe along the forehead seem to serve the additional purpose of creating a visual allusion to the portraits of Augustus. The little bifurcation of the hair at the center, and the hook-shaped curves of the locks on either side of it, which curl back toward the middle of the forehead, bear an unmistakable resemblance to the characteristic hairstyle of Augustus,[65] the emperor who had not only

---

[61] Helga von Heintze, "Studien zu den Porträts des 3. Jahrhunderts n. Chr. V: Der Knabe des Acilia Sarkophags," *RömMitt*, 66 (1959), 179-180.

[62] See Wegner, Bracker and Real, *Herrscherbild*, III³, 107-108, pls. 40-43; Bergmann, *Studien*, pp. 51-53; Felletti-Maj, *Iconografia*, pp. 222-224; McCoull *Berytus*, 17 (1967-68), 71-74.

[63] Berlin, Staatliche Museen, Antiken-Sammlung, R114, marble head, h. 0.37. Restored: tip of nose, fragment of right ear. Published: Blümel, *Römische Bildnisse*, p. 47, No. R114, pl. 74. L'Orange, *Studien*, p. 5, fig. 7. Giuseppe Bovini, "Gallieno, la sua iconografia e i riflessi in essa delle vicende storiche e culturali del tempo." *MemLinc*. 7th ser., 2 (1941), 148, fig. 13; Bovini, *MonAnt*, 39 (1943), 255, figs. 57-58. Felletti-Maj, *Iconografia*, p. 223, No. 292, pl. 41, figs. 135-136. McCoull, *Berytus*, 17 (1967-68), 71, No. 2. Fittschen, *JdI*, 84 (1969), 227, fig. 48. Bergmann, *Studien*, p. 51, No. 4, and pp. 57-58, pl. 12, figs. 5-6. Wegner, Bracker and Real, *Herrscherbild*, III³, 108, 111, pl. 42.

[64] See Fittschen, *JdI*, 84 (1969), 218-221, 225-230.

[65] On the Primaporta type, which seems to have been the standard official portrait of Augustus from the time when he received that title, see Ulrich Hausmann, "Zur Typologie und Ideologie des Augustusporträts," *Aufstieg und Niedergang der römischen Welt*, II, 12.2 (1981), pp. 565-605, pls. XVIII-XXVII, and Paul Zanker, "Studien zu den Augustusporträts," *Abhandlungen Göttingen*, Phil.-Hist. Klasse, 3rd ser., 85 (1973), 44-46.

long been worshipped as a god but whose calm and classically elegant images had become a symbol of the ideals of order and constitutional monarchy.[66] The borrowing is not a mechanical one; the pattern of Augustus's fork-and-pincer locks[67] is mirror-reversed and slightly altered, but it is unlikely that the allusion could have been lost on Roman viewers familiar with portraits of the divine Augustus.

The traditions which dominate the treatment of Gallienus's face, however, are of more recent origin. Striking resemblances to the portraits of Gordian III (figs. 7 and 8) can be observed in the forms of the eyebrows and mouth, and in the use of outlining to isolate the patterns of certain features. Once again, the eyebrows have a very symmetrical slant downward toward the root of the nose, where vertical notches rise from them at abrupt angles, and again, the long, almond-shaped eyes are outlined above and below by crisply carved folds. There is a sharp, angular dip at the center of the mouth, here further emphasized by the way in which the stubbly strands of the moustache are brushed inward toward the center, and a final accent on the middle axis of the face in the cleft of the chin.

The jaw in this case is longer and broader than that of Gordian, giving the lower face the shape of a half-hexagon rather than of a triangle, while the forehead takes the shape of a broad rectangle. Within the angular lower face, the beard is used to create another sort of geometric pattern, as it curves forward on the cheeks and downward around the chin, thus forming a trefoil frame which helps to articulate the shapes of the cheekbones and jaw. The actual modeling of the volumes of the bone structure is rather inorganic: there is a subtle tendency to give the head a prismatic structure, a fact which is not so evident in the Berlin head illustrated here but which is clearly visible in another replica in the Palazzo Braschi.[68] In that work, the planes of the cheeks meet the front of the face in abrupt angles. The profile view of Gallienus's portraits, like the profiles of Gordian's portraits, shows a similar taste for angularity and isolated form rather than continuous contours: in both works, the root of

---

[66] See Schweitzer, *Zur Kunst der Antike*, II, 267, 277; Mathew, *JRS*, 33 (1943), 66-67.

[67] This pattern was analyzed and described by Otto Brendel, *Zur Ikonographie des Kaiser Augustus* (Nuremberg: Keller, 1931), pp. 11, 21, 32, 53. For a more recent discussion, see Zanker, *Abhandlungen Göttingen*, 85 (1973), pp. 13-14 and passim, esp. p. 45.

[68] Rome, Palazzo Braschi. Marble bust, H. in toto 0.66. Restored: nose, upper lip, left ear, part of hair, parts of cuirass and paludamentum. Major publications: Stuart-Jones, *Museo Capitolino*, p. 211, No. 76, pl. 52. Bernoulli, *Römische Ikonographie*, II³, 167, No. 1. L'Orange, *Studien*, 5. Bovini, *MemLinc*, 7th ser., 2 (1941), 147, figs. 11-12. Bovini, *Mon-Ant.*, 39 (1943), 256-257, figs. 59-60. Felletti-Maj, *Iconografia*, p. 222, No. 289, pl. 40, fig. 134. McCoull, *Berytus*, 17 (1967-68), 71, No. 1, pl. 22, fig. 1. Bergmann, *Studien*, pp. 51, 57-58, pl. 12, figs. 5-6. Wegner, Bracker and Real, *Herrscherbild*, III³, 108.

the nose and the fold under the lower lip form sharp angles, while the upper lip has a strong, beak-like projection.

Upon close examination, it can be seen that much of the traditional schema of Caracalla's portraits is still present in those of Gallienus. The bulging forehead muscle, and the pattern of plunging diagonals in the forehead area, are still used to suggest emotional tension. But what an extraordinary change these devices have undergone! It is difficult to imagine two works more different in style and spirit than the formidable, scowling bust of Caracalla in Berlin (fig. 1), with its vigorously modeled musculature, and its rich play of light and shadow, and the coldly elegant, subtly abstract head of Gallienus in the same museum (fig. 12), yet these works are separated chronologically by only about fifty years.

Nonetheless, an unbroken chain of descent can be traced from one to the other, in the process of experimentation and alteration of the schemata of Caracalla's portraits in the images of the emperors who followed him. This continuity suggests that though this period was one of rapid and radical innovation, we are not dealing with an era of artistic chaos. Schweitzer has already convincingly demonstrated[69] the continuing strength of traditions from much earlier periods in the realism of many portraits of the third century; it seems, furthermore, that these artists were not merely reviving older styles but developing, refining and adapting formal devices of their own. The portraits of the young Gallienus, by refining the scowling expression of Caracalla's portraits to an elegant formula, prepare the way in turn for the more overt abstraction of the latter half of the third century. The next logical phase of the trend can be seen in the later portraits of Gallienus (fig. 13).[70] In order to understand these processes more fully, however, we must now examine a broader range of portraits than those discussed so far.

---

[69] Schweitzer, *Zur Kunst der Antike*, II, 266-267. For a differing viewpoint, see Zinserling, *Klio*, 41 (1963), 200-203.

[70] Rome, Museo Nazionale delle Terme, inv. 644. Marble head, made for insertion into a statue. Recent publications: Bergmann, *Studien*, pp. 51-54; Wegner, Bracker, and Real, *Herrscherbild*, III³, 108-110, 117-118, pl. 45. *Museo Nazionale Romano: le sculture*, ed. Giuliano, I¹, 296-297, No. 181 (Silvia Allegra Dayan). To be discussed at more length in Chapter IV.

# CHAPTER TWO

# THE CLASSICISM OF THE LATE SEVERANS

The two decades following the death of Caracalla saw a temporary retreat from the emotional effects which characterized his portraits. The formal devices developed by the ''Caracalla master'' to indicate muscular tension and psychological concentration were not forgotten, but were used with more subtlety and restraint by the next generation of portrait sculptors. Already in the bronze portrait of Macrinus in Belgrade,[1] the long, vertical lines of the beard lend the face a stability and dignity which tend to reduce the impact of the scowling features.

With the return to power of the Severan dynasty, and the elevation to the throne of fourteen-year-old Varius Avitus (known as Elagabalus), official portrait sculptors were confronted with a new challenge: the boy emperor had to be represented with authority and dignity despite the immaturity of his features. This same problem faced the portraitists of Alexander Severus, who was named *caesar* by his cousin Elagabalus at the age of about thirteen, and become emperor the following year. In both cases, artists seem to have relied on a very old tradition in imperial portraiture of representing boys who were designated as heirs to power in an elegantly classicizing style.[2] The calmness and simplicity of such a treatment of a youthful face could suggest both aristocratic birth and precocious seriousness; parallels of almost a century earlier can be seen in the portraits of the young Marcus Aurelius.[3]

The one portrait which can be securely identified as Elagabalus is a head in the Capitoline museum (fig. 14).[4] The dating of this work to the Severan period has been questioned on more than one occasion by scholars who prefer a Gallienic date; von Heintze has proposed instead

---

[1] See Chapter I, note 21.

[2] See von Heintze, *RömMitt*, 66 (1959), 179-180.

[3] See Max Wegner, *Die Herrscherbildnisse in Antoninischer Zeit*, Vol. II, part 4 of *Das römische Herrscherbild*, ed. Max Wegner (Berlin: Mann, 1939), pp. 34-38, pls. 14, 15, 16.

[4] Rome, Museo Capitolino, Stanza degli Imperatori, No. 55, inv. 470. Marble head, h. 0.46. Nose, chips from chin and upper lip restored. Surface damaged by a harsh modern cleaning. Principal publications: Bernoulli, *Römische Ikonographie*, II³, 88, pl. 25; Stuart-Jones, *Museo Capitolino*, p. 160, No. 55, pl. 39; Helga von Heintze, ''Studien zu den Porträts des 3. Jahrhunderts VII: Caracalla, Geta, Elagabal und Alexander Severus,'' *RömMitt*, 73-74 (1966-67), 215-221, pl. 72, fig. 3, and pl. 73, fig. 4; Helbig⁴, No. 1323; Wiggers and Wegner, *Herrscherbild*, III¹, 151, (with complete recent references); Bergmann, *Studien*, p. 22, pl. 1, figs. 3-4.

an identification as a posthumous portrait of Alexander Severus.[5] This portrait has a very close resemblance, however, to the coin profiles[6] of Elagabalus, not only in physical features but in style. The enlargement of the eyes, for example, which could be interpreted as an abstraction typical of portraiture from the time of Gallienus, is also present in the coins of Elagabalus and of his wives.[7] Much of the "Gallienic" appearance of this piece may be deceptive, the result of a harsh modern cleaning which has erased some of the modeling and given the cheeks a blank hardness. The soft and richly naturalistic texture of the full, touseled hair, on the other hand, shows a far closer relationship to portraits of Caracalla than to those of emperors of the mid-century. Another replica of the same prototype, a beautiful head in Oslo,[8] may if it is genuinely ancient, show how the Capitoline head would originally have looked.[9] In the Oslo head, the graceful simplicity of the compact head and round, childlike face is enriched with a subtle modeling of cheeks and eyesockets which creates an animated play of light and diffuse shadow over the face. Unfortunately, however, the authenticity of this head is somewhat suspect.[10] Only the Capitoline head, therefore, can be relied upon for stylistic study of Elagabalus's portraiture.

The compact, ball-like form of the head and broad, slightly plump face display an unmistakable family resemblance to the portraits of Caracalla, particularly to his childhood types.[11] This resemblance was no doubt emphasized and perhaps exaggerated by the portraitist in order to stress the relationship of Elagabalus to his predecessor, a matter of such importance for the legitimacy of his reign. Just as in the childhood portraits of Caracalla,[12] the hair lies smoothly against the scalp in long, swirling

---

[5] Stuart-Jones, *Museo Capitolino*, p. 160, No. 55; von Heintze, *RömMitt*, 73-74 (1966-67), 218-219.

[6] Harold Mattingly, Edward A. Sydenham, and C. V. H. Sutherland, *The Roman Imperial Coinage*, Vol. IV, part 2 (London: Spink and Son, Ltd., 1938), 23-44, Nos. 1-204, pl. II, figs. 2-20, and pl. III, figs. 1-6. Hereafter abbreviated *RIC*.

[7] For excellent photographs of his coin portraits, see *Herrscherbild*, III[1], pls. 38-41.

[8] Oslo, Nasjonalgalleriet, head and neck in marble, h. 0.33, of head alone, 0.22. Published: H. P. L'Orange, "Zur Ikonographie des Kaisers Elagabals," *SymbOslo*, 20 (1940), 152-159, figs. 1, 3, 4. Von Heintze, *RömMitt*, 73-74 (1966-67), 216; Nodelman, "Severan Imperial Portraits," pp. 384-388; Bergmann, *Studien*, p. 22.

[9] Nodelman, "Severan Imperial Portraits," pp. 384-388. Nodelman believes that the Oslo and Capitoline heads follow prototypes by different artists, though they represent the same boy. The close similarity in the pattern of the locks of hair, however, indicates that both must follow the same prototype.

[10] Bergmann, *Studien*, pp. 22-23.

[11] See Wiggers and Wegner, *Herrscherbild*, III[1], 17-22, pls. 1-5a; Nodelman, "Severan Imperial Portraits," pp. 140-160; Budde, *Jugendbildnisse*, pp. 21-33, pls. 1 and 10-19.

[12] Compare in particular the bust in the Museo Nazionale delle Terme, Rome, inv. 641. Major publications: Bernoulli, *Römische Ikonographie*, II[2], 201; Helbig[4], No. 2461;

waves which tend to emphasize the contours of the cranium. Here, too, the fringe of locks across the forehead curves from right to left, as though swept by a breeze or a sudden movement of the head, and just as in the portraits of Caracalla, the hairline is low, tightly framing the large eyes.

In the Capitoline Elagabalus (fig. 14), however, the hair is represented in much lower relief, and the locks differentiated only with the chisel; the long drill channels which enlivened the texture of young Caracalla's hair are gone. The lunette-shaped eyes, moreover, are enlarged almost to the point of exaggeration, and represented with a wide, intense stare. The eyes and eyebrow ridges both have a strongly three-dimensional curve back toward the temples, while the eyes are further emphasized by the creases which outline both upper and lower lid. The horizontal of the eyes is repeated by the broad, full-lipped mouth. Thus, a comparison of the Capitoline Elagabalus with the childhood portraits of Caracalla on which they appear to be modeled illustrates a taste for simpler, more closed contours, a shallower volume for the cap of hair, and a greater concentration of expression into a few features, especially the eyes and mouth.

Strikingly similar formal devices can be observed in the private portrait of a young woman in Naples[13] (fig. 15). The wide-set eyes have the same enlarged, lunette form, and just as in the portrait of Elagabalus, both the eyes and the broad eyebrows sweep boldly around the corner of the face, from the frontal plane toward the plane of the temples. Here, too, the mouth is broad, full-lipped and slightly parted; once again, the deep channel which separates the lips forms a strong horizontal which parallels that of the eyes. The pinched thinness of the lower face, and the pensive dip of the head in this female portrait create an impression of introspection quite different from the mood suggested by Elagabalus's wide-eyed upward gaze, but all the same, the stylistic devices used to suggest spirituality are quite similar.

It is quite possible that the Naples portrait (fig. 15) is a work of the same atelier as the imperial portrait in the Capitoline museum, especially since the lady's coiffure indicates a date not far from the time of

---

Felletti-Maj, *Ritratti*, p. 129, No. 254; Wiggers and Wegner, *Herrscherbild*, III[1], 79-80, pl. 1, figs. a and b., pl. 5, fig. a; *Museo Nazionale Romano: le sculture*, ed. Giuliano, I[1], 332-333, No. 196 (Emilia Talamo).

[13] Naples, Museo Nazionale, head set on an alabaster bust which probably does not belong to it. Exact measurements not available; life-sized. Tip of nose restored, polish of face modern. Tips of curls in front of ears broken. Published: Roberto Paribeni, *Il Ritratto nell'arte antica* (Milan: Fratelli Treves, 1934), pl. 316; Anton Hekler, *Die Bildniskunst der Griechen und Römer* (Stuttgart: W. Heinemann, 1912), pl. 301; A. Ippel, *Römische Porträts*, Vol. 1 of Bilderhefte zur Kunst- und Kulturgeschichte des Altertums (Leipzig: Hans Schaal, 1930), fig. 56; Jutta Meischner, "Das Frauenporträt der Severerzeit," Dissertation, Freie Universität, Berlin, 1964, p. 140, No. 37, fig. 96.

Elagabalus. Most of the coin portraits of that emperor's three wives[14] show the hair parted in the middle, artificially marcelled, drawn back behind the ears and allowed to fall deeply onto the neck before being looped up, bound into braids, and twisted into a large chignon. This basic hairstyle, commonly known as a *Nestfrisur*, was fashionable throughout the late Severan period, but at the time of Elagabalus, as the coin profiles of his wife Julia Paula indicate,[15] it was fashionable to elaborate the coiffure with little curls which were allowed to escape along the hairline and in front of the ears. Since these coiffures were undoubtedly constructed with artificial hairpieces, we can perhaps imagine that these ladies pulled wisps of their own hair out from under their wigs to form decorative fringes of ringlets.

A beautiful and slightly over-life-sized head in Copenhagen[16] (fig. 16) shows a richer use of this coiffure. Here, the entire face and throat are framed with a maze of curls: a neat row of ringlets across the forehead, and a deep vertical cascade of locks below the ears. The suggestion has been made that this portrait may in fact represent Julia Paula,[17] Elagabalus's wife, or perhaps his mother, Julia Soaemias,[18] but though the scale of the head certainly suggests that the work was publicly displayed, there is no decisive evidence for any identification.[19] Of far more importance than the lady's name is the fact that her portrait illustrates some of the same stylistic trends as that of Elagabalus, particularly the striving for effects of intensity concentrated in the eyes. Here, too, the forehead is low, and the hair forms an arch which encloses and sets off the eyes. Again, the eyes are large and strongly three-dimensional; this time, not only do the eyes and eyebrows sweep backward toward the temple, but the orbital folds are deeply carved out so as to emphasize the spherical form of the eyeball. The upper lids have a heavy droop, suggesting dreamy meditation, and their downward pull

---

[14] Wiggers and Wegner, *Herrscherbild* III[1], pp. 168-169; Klaus Wessel, "Römische Frauenfrisuren von der severischen bis zur konstantinischer Zeit," *AA*, 61-62 (1946-47), 63-64; Käte Buchholz, *Die Bildnisse der Kaiserinnen der Severerzeit nach ihren Frisuren, 193-235 n. Chr.* (Frankfurt am Main, 1963), pp. 51-54.

[15] Wiggers and Wegner, *Herrscherbild*, III[1], 168, and pl. 42; *RIC*, IV[2], pp. 44-48, pl. III, figs. 7-10.

[16] Copenhagen, Ny Carlsberg Glyptotek, cat. 755, inv. 825. Marble head, h. 0.45. Tip of nose restored. Published: F. Poulsen, *Catalogue*, No. 755; Hans Weber, "Zu einem Bildnis der Kaiserin Julia Paula," *JdI*, 68 (1953), 124-138, figs. 1-4. Käte Buchholz, *Die Bildnisse der Kaiserinnen der Severerzeit nach ihren Frisuren, 193-235 n. Chr.* (Frankfurt am Main, 1963), p. 52, No. 164, p. 154; Meischner, "Frauenporträt," pp. 97-100, figs. 64-65; V. Poulsen, *Les Portraits romains*, II, No. 145, pp. 145-148, pls. 234-235; Wiggers and Wegner, *Herrscherbild*, III[1], pp. 170-171.

[17] Weber, *JdI*, 68 (1953), 124-138.

[18] V. Poulsen, *Les Portraits romains*, II, 146-148, No. 145, pls. 234-235.

[19] See Wiggers and Wegner, *Herrscherbild*, III[1], pp. 168-169, 170-171.

is emphasized by the mannered dip of the elongated tearducts, but nonetheless the eyes form as strong a focus of attention here as the dramatically widened eyes of the Capitoline Elagabalus.

Without disrupting the aristocratic beauty of the features, the artist of the Copenhagen head (fig. 16) has managed to introduce subtle tensions and dissonances into the lower face which convey extraordinary character and vitality. The cheeks are thin and drawn, revealing an angular bone structure, the sharp ridge of the nose is not quite straight, and the full lips have a slightly irregular flare.[20] All these assymetries seem, on close examination, to be fully intentional, and to be elements of a very sophisticated composition, despite the fact that in some details such as the curls over the forehead, the workmanship is slightly rough and crude-looking. This, too, is probably done intentionally, in order to make the details of the hair legible from a distance; the scale of the head indicates that it was intended for long-distance effect, probably in a large outdoor space.

Not all portraits from this period, of course, demonstrate such an interest in psychological expression: some which wear coiffures similar to that of the Copenhagen head have bland, conventionally pretty faces. A bust in the British Museum[21] (fig. 17), for example, shows a woman with a smooth, symmetrically oval face, the corners of her lips turned upward in a slightly vapid smile. Only the long eyes, with their calligraphically graceful curves, suggest the influence of works like the Capitoline Elagabalus (fig. 14). Here too, however, though the drill is used freely to achieve a play of light and shadow in the locks which "escape" from the coiffure, the curls create a frame which encloses rather than expands the face.

In the British Museum bust, both arms would originally have projected outward from the bust, as indicated by the break at both elbows, and it is difficult to discern just how they would have altered the composition, though the extension of the arms into the viewer's space would probably have given the bust a vivaciously open appearance. The drapery, too, is busily patterned with folds: the fine crinkles of the

---

[20] See the forthcoming book by Sheldon Nodelman, *Severan Imperial Portraits*. In an unpublished, early draft of this work, which I was able to see in the library of the American Academy in Rome, Nodelman sensitively analyzes the uses of asymmetry in the composition of this face.

[21] London, British Museum, cat. 2009, half-body bust, marble, lifesized. Restored: tip of nose, foot of bust. Arms broken off at elbows; forearms were originally included in composition. Published: A. H. Smith, *A Catalogue of Sculpture in the Department of Greek and Roman Antiquities, British Museum*, Vol. III (London, 1904), 190-191, No. 2009, p. 18; R. P. Hinks, *Greek and Roman Portrait Sculpture* (London: British Museum, 1935), p. 33, fig. 45; Meischner, "Frauenporträt," p. 154, No. 76, and pp. 157-158. Wiggers and Wegner, *Herrscherbild*, III¹, 171.

delicate, Greek-style chiton, and the heavier diagonal swirls of the hima-
tion slung around her shoulders. Close examination of the torso and
drapery, however, reveals both to be surprisingly shallow and flat, their
effects of three-dimensionality illusionistically created by the negative
carving of the folds. The rich virtuosity of this bust shows links to Antonine and earlier Severan portraiture, but the shift in technique toward
a more compactly closed form is now well underway.

A number of male portraits which can be dated to about the same time
as the Capitoline Elagabalus, primarily through the treatment of the
hair, show the same preference for closed, simple silhouettes. In these
works, the drill is used discreetly, if at all: a bust in Munich[22] (fig. 18)
shows a few drill channels in the locks over the ears, but the rest of the
hair is worked with the chisel, in wavy strands which are modeled in low
relief, though their soft and naturalistic texture is painstakingly indicated. The beard is almost volumeless, represented by a pattern of little
tufts which are executed more with chisel incisions than through modeling in relief. This man's face is broad and round, like that of Elagabalus,
allowing for a similarly smooth treatment of the convex surfaces. The
features are small and delicate, allowing for a dominant impression of
coolly aristocratic elegance, yet the hair across the forehead has an irregular, touseled arrangement which lends the face a subtle nervous
energy. Muscular tension, though slight, is unmistakably present in the
contraction of the eyebrows, which forms a triangle of creases above the
root of the nose, and in the shallow but firm incision of the diagonal furrows around nose and mouth.

Another bust in Munich[23] (fig. 19) shows that such restraint in the suggestion of emotion was not universal. Both these busts appear to have
been funerary in function, and have a similar format, representing most
of the chest and the shoulder caps, nude except for the fold of a chlamys
over the left shoulder. The second bust in Munich, too, has hair closely
similar in style and technique to that of Elagabalus, but the bombastic
scowl and vigorous relief of the contorted facial muscles seems more or
less directly inspired by the final portraits of Caracalla. The pattern of the
hair is not merely touseled but explosive: short locks spring upward and
outward from the central peak of the hairline, while longer strands sweep

---

[22] Munich, Glyptotek, cat. 396, inv. 184. Marble bust, h. 0.60. Most of nose broken
away, preservation otherwise excellent. Published: Adolph Furtwängler, *Beschreibung der
Glyptotek König Ludwig I zu München* (Munich: A. Buchholz, 1910), p. 396. No. 396. An exact replica, possibly a modern copy, exists in the Palazzo Pitti in Florence.

[23] Munich, Glyptotek, cat. 386, inv. KH 209. Marble bust, h. 0.63. Most of nose,
large part of left eyebrow with part of forehead and eye broken away. Bust pieced together
from several large fragments. Published: Furtwängler, *Beschreibung*, p. 373, No. 386. Bernoulli, *Römische Ikonographie*, II[3], 73. Bergmann, *Studien*, p. 11, pl. 10, figs. 1 and 2.

forward at the temples as though tossed by a breeze. Despite his obvious dependence on the formal devices pioneered by the "Caracalla Master," the artist of this piece has displayed some originality in his use of the X pattern by giving the triangular forehead muscle a wing-like, sweeping curve toward the temples, and by increasing the curvature of the furrows around the mouth. These creases now continue well past the corners of the lips, complementing the curves of the long, heavy lower face.

Probably attributable to the same artist as the second Munich bust (fig. 19) is a head in the Fogg Art Museum[24] (fig. 20). The chisel work in the hair and beard, the shape of the long, narrow eyes and the manner of outlining the lips all seem to reveal the same "handwriting" in both works. In the Fogg head (fig. 20), however, this sculptor has begun to free himself of the influence of the "Caracalla master," and to follow the current trend toward subtler suggestion of emotion. The heavy, prominent brow ridge and swelling forehead muscle demonstrate that the "Caracalla master's" innovations had not been abandoned, but the face no longer scowls. Instead, the eyes glance sharply to the left, while the left-hand corner of the mouth twists upward in a suggestion of an ironic smile. The cheeks, under the overhanging ridge of the forehead, have been reduced almost to flat planes, which converge diagonally toward the front of the face, and the structure of the cheekbones has been understated. Thus, the outline of the head becomes tighter and the details of the face simpler. The pattern of the hair is now centripetal, rather than centrifugal, swirling inward from the temples and across the cranium toward the central peak over the forehead. The attention of the viewer is allowed to focus more directly on the eyes and mouth.

One more noteworthy portrait datable early in the 220's is a strikingly handsome type which exists in three replicas: in the Terme museum (fig. 21),[25] in Vienna,[26] and in the Smith College Museum of Art.[27] Clearly,

---

[24] Cambridge, Mass., Fogg Art Museum, Harvard University, inv. 1949.83. Head and small portion of neck preserved, nose broken away, ears weathered. Published: Hanfmann, *Latomus*, 11 (1952), 206-209, figs. 3, 4. Fogg Art Museum, *Ancient Sculpture* (Cambridge, Mass.: Harvard University Press, 1950), No. 56.

[25] Rome, Museo Nazionale delle Terme, Cat. 300, inv. 124486, h. 0.51. Head and part of shoulders of a draped bust preserved. Ears chipped, preservation of face otherwise excellent. Published: Felletti-Maj, *Ritratti*, p. 150, No. 300; Jutta Meischner, "Ein Porträt des Kaisers Volusianus," *AA*, 82 (1967), 220-228, figs. 6-8. Fittschen, *JdI*, 84 (1969), 225-230, figs. 43, 45. *Museo Nazionale Romano: le sculture*, ed. Giuliano, I¹, 306-307, No. 184 (Emilia Talamo).

[26] Vienna, Kunsthistorisches Museum, head set on a modern bust. Life-sized; exact measurements not available. Part of nose and lower lip restored, surface heavily cleaned and polished. Published: Meischner, *AA*, 82 (1967), 220-228, figs. 4-5; Fittschen, *JdI*, 84 (1969), 225-230, figs. 44-46.

[27] Northampton, Smith College Museum of Art, marble head, h. 0.407. Large part of rear cranium and neck on right broken; surface apparently cut evenly to receive a separate

this was a public portrait, though the subject cannot be identified with any imperial figure; the best replica, in the Terme museum (fig. 21) appears to be wearing the costume of a charioteer,[28] a fact which suggests that the man may have been a celebrated athlete. His identity is of less importance for our purposes, however, than the extraordinarily subtle and sensitive characterization achieved in his portraits. Here, once again, the brow ridge has a strong projection, and the swelling of the contracted forehead muscle is emphasized, but the man's features and bone structure are delicate. The thin-lipped mouth is drawn taut into a severe horizontal, the forehead is lined, and the hollow cheeks traversed by deep, diagonal furrows which suggest weariness, but none of these signs of emotional tension detract from his aristocratic-seeming beauty. If the subject is indeed a professional athlete, it is most revealing of the trends in taste at his time that such a man of action could be portrayed in this manner.

The decorative pattern of the hair and beard, moreover, enhance the elegance of his appearance. The relief of the hair is lower than that of any of the male portraits discussed so far, and has been reduced almost to a linear pattern incised on a shallow cap, though the relief of the hair in the Smith College head is slightly fuller than that of the other two replicas. The tips of the locks over the forehead are rolled together into a sort of molding around the face, rather than forming a jagged fringe, while the curls of the beard, though still soft and naturalistic, are carved in low relief and are supplemented by a pattern of line incised directly on the cheeks. At the back of the head, the hair of the Terme replica (fig. 21) is represented in a pattern of little feather-like tufts.[29]

This technique, generally known as "*a penna*" treatment of the hair,[30] appears in its fully developed form in almost all the portraits of Alexander Severus. Each lock is outlined by two chisel strokes and divided down the center by a shorter but deeper incision which creates the impression of two forking tips. These tufts are arranged in a neatly aligned and densely imbricated pattern over the cap-like surface of the hair, which still has a very slight volume in relief but which is now represented by a primarily linear pattern. This treatment is consistent with the taste for smoothly curvilinear, unbroken contours and surfaces, and for elegant simplicity, which characterize the portraits of Alexander Severus.

---

piece of marble. The restoration, whether ancient or modern, is now removed. Preservation of face excellent. Published: Martha Leeb, "A New Portrait of Gallienus," *Smith College Museum of Art Bulletin*, 28-31 (1951), 8-10, figs. 1-3; Felletti-Maj, *Iconografia*, p. 231, No. 305; Meischner, *AA*, 82 (1967), 220-228, figs. 1-3; Fittschen, *JdI*, 84 (1969), 225-230.

[28] Felletti-Maj, *Ritratti*, 150-151, No. 300.

[29] Fittschen, *JdI*, 84 (1968), 230, figs. 49-50.

[30] See Felletti-Maj, *Iconografia*, p. 85, No. 1; p. 86, No. 2, pp. 87-95, passim.

The identification of the earliest portrait type of this young emperor, unfortunately, remains somewhat controversial. L'Orange[31] attributed to Alexander a group of portraits of a boy in his early teens which had previously been accepted as Philip II, and L'Orange's identification has received the agreement of most scholars.[32] The two most recent volumes of *Das römische Herrscherbild*,[33] however, have revived the older identification as Philip II. While it is true that these portraits bear some similarity to the coin profiles of the young son of Philip the Arab,[34] their similarities to the securely identified likenesses of Alexander Severus as an adult are even more striking. A comparison of the face of this boy, as represented in a bust in the Capitoline Museum[35] (fig. 22), with the colossal head in the Louvre (fig. 23)[36] of a young man generally agreed to be Alexander Severus, leaves little doubt that the works must represent the same individual, though at different ages. The cranium in both cases is broad and somewhat flat, the lower face a broad half-oval, and the shapes of the trapezoidal foreheads and full-lipped, fleshy mouths virtually identical. The hairlines of both types have a characteristic form, sloping slightly upward from the left toward a sort of arching cowlick over the right eye.

The only differences between these portraits, in fact, are the narrow, chin-strap beard which is delicately incised onto the polished "skin" of the Louvre head (fig. 23), and the slightly heavier and more mature jawline of the same work. The Capitoline bust and the other replicas of its type[37] can without further hesitation be accepted as the earliest official portrait of Alexander Severus, a type modified only very slightly a few years later in order to show his increasing maturity.

---

[31] L'Orange, *Studien*, pp. 94-96.

[32] Including Felletti-Maj, *Iconografia*, pp. 85-91, and Bergmann, *Studien*, 26-29.

[33] Wiggers and Wegner, *Herrscherbild*, III[1], 188, 191-192; Wegner, Bracker and Real, *Herrscherbild*, III[3], 42-50, pls. 15-20.

[34] Wegner, Bracker and Real, *Herrscherbild*, III[3], 43.

[35] Rome, Museo Capitolino, Stanza degli Imperatori, No. 69, inv. 480, marble bust of a boy in a trabeated toga, h. 0.76. Foot of bust restored, surface cleaned in modern time, but polish of skin appears to be ancient. Provenance: Città Lavinia. Published: Bernoulli, *Römische Ikonographie*, II[3], 147, No. 1, p. 150, pl. 45; Stuart-Jones, *Museo Capitolino*, p. 209, No. 69, pl. 50. L'Orange, *Studien*, p. 94, No. 1; Helbig[4], No. 1319; Felletti-Maj, *Iconografia*, pp. 85-86, No. 2, pl.II, fig. 5; Wiggers and Wegner, *Herrscherbild*, III[1], 191-192; Bergmann, *Studien*, pp. 26-27, pl. 2, fig. 2. Wegner, Bracker and Real, *Herrscherbild*, III[3], 43, 46-47, pl. 18a.

[36] Paris, Louvre, MA 1051. Marble head, h. 0.39. Restored: tip of nose, most of left ear, part of right ear, small bust at base of neck. Published: Bernoulli, *Römische Ikonographie*, II[3], 101, No. 11, pl. 30; Charbonneaux, *Sculpture grecque et romaine*, p. 178; L'Orange, *Studien*, p. 1, note 1, No. 5; Felletti-Maj, *Iconografia*, pp. 92-93, No. 17, pl. 4, fig. 9; Wiggers and Wegner, *Herrscherbild*, III[1], 182, 190, pl. 52; Bergmann, *Studien*, p. 27.

[37] See Wegner, Bracker and Real, *Herrscherbild*, III[3], 42-51, for a recent list of the members of this type.

Both Alexander's boyhood and his adolescent type show significant changes from the portrait of Elagabalus: the eyes are smaller in proportion to the face, which is no longer a compact form but a shape more approximating a classic oval. All contours have slow, broad, gentle curves, and the surfaces flow smoothly into one another. Borders such as the eyebrow ridges and the edges of the lips are softly rounded, while in the better replicas, such as the Capitoline bust (fig. 22), all skin areas are highly polished so as to emphasize the simple clarity of the convex cheeks and forehead. The strands of hair of the eyebrows are incised as long S-curves, sweeping gracefully from the inner to the outer corner and complementing the rounded, gently arched form of the eyebrow ridge. The effect of these portraits, in short, is one of grace and serenity consistent with the dreamily detached expression of the eyes and the relaxed, undulating line of the drill channel which parts the lips. The creator of these types seems to have aimed to present Alexander in a mood of quiet spirituality which would contrast with the religious intensity of his hated predecessor Elagabalus.

Two of Alexander's portraits, one from his boyhood (fig. 22) and one from his adolescence, in Florence,[38] are preserved in one piece with busts clad in the trabeated toga. Here, the young emperor is presented in a manner which stresses his constitutional and senatorial role. It is very likely, however, that Alexander Severus was also depicted sometimes in military dress, though accidents of preservation have not allowed any to survive. But two full-length statues,[39] both, unfortunately, heavily restored, demonstrate that he definitely was represented in heroic nudity and colossal proportions which suggest deification, though neither has the recognizable attributes of any specific deity. The Naples statue has generally Polykleitan proportions, in its stocky and muscular treatment of the figure, but a more Lysippean stance, with its slight spiralling turn away from the weight leg.[40] The overall effect of the statue is of a quiet stability consistent with the mood of the face.

---

[38] Florence, Galleria degli Uffizi, inv. 1914.245. For information and references, see Chapter 1, note 46, and appendix.

[39] Naples, Museo Nazionale, 5993, colossal statue, and Rome, Museo Torlonia, 365. See appendix for fuller information on both works.

Naples statue, recent publications: Fittschen and Zanker, *AA*, 85 (1970), 248-253; Wiggers and Wegner, *Herrscherbild*, III¹, 189, pls. 50, 56a; Niemeyer, *Statuarischen Darstellung*, p. 112, No. 124, pl. 44, fig. 2; Bergmann, *Studien*, pp. 26-27.

Torlonia statue, marble, h. 2.25, reconstructed from fragments and heavily restored. Provenance: Porto. Recent publications: Wiggers and Wegner, *Herrscherbild*, III¹, 194; Bergmann, *Studien*, pp. 26-27.

[40] Niemeyer, *Statuarischen Darstellung*, p. 62.

Alexander's mother, Julia Mammaea, is the only woman of his family whose portraits can be identified with any security.[41] Her earlier portraits, such as the bust in the British Museum,[42] (fig. 24), reveal much the same style and mood as those of her son: oval forms, fluidly modeled surfaces, and simple but gently curvilinear contours. The low, broad arcs of the eyebrows and relaxed line of the mouth convey a similar mood of serenity. Within the classic oval of the contours, however, Julia Mammaea's rather unattractive features are by no means idealized. The jowly sag of the cheeks, the heavy jaw and the prominence of the mouth area which suggests projecting teeth are all modeled with uncompromising fidelity. The rounded and gentle transitions of the surface prevent hard lines of shadow from calling attention to the signs of age, but they are there nonetheless.

One group of Mammaea's portraits[43] shows a departure from the oval forms and quiet mood characteristic of works such as the British Museum bust (fig. 24). A bust in the Capitoline Museum,[44] (fig. 25), and a particularly fine head in the Louvre,[45] for example, give the face a more angular form. The coiffure outlines the forehead as a severe triangle, rather than a broad arch, while the lower face appears more pinched and thin, causing the cheeks to taper toward the sharp point of the jaw. The pose, too, has changed: where the portraits such as the British Museum bust (fig. 24) showed Mammaea with her chin confidently lifted and thrust forward, the head now inclines slightly downward, though the eyes gaze up and into the distance. Thus, the upper face, and the eye area, are

---

[41] For a fuller discussion of the iconography of Julia Mammaea, see Felletti-Maj, *Iconografia*, 105-114; Wiggers and Wegner, *Herrscherbild*, III[1], 200-217; Bergmann, *Studien*, pp. 29-30.

[42] London, British Museum, cat. 1920. Marble bust, h. 0.60. Restored: tip of nose. Major publications: Bernoulli, *Römische Ikonographie*, II[3], 110, No. 17; Smith, *Catalogue*, III, 167-168, No. 1920, pl. XVIII; Felletti-Maj, *Iconografia*, p. 108, No. 55, pl. VII, fig. 22; Buchholz, *Kaiserinnen*, p. 157; Meischner, "Frauenporträt," p. 105, No. 81, fig. 71; Wiggers and Wegner, *Herrscherbild*, III[1], 208.

[43] Bergmann, *Studien*, p. 30.

[44] Rome, Museo Capitolino, Stanza degli Imperatori, No. 47, inv. 457, bust in marble, h. 0.43. Restored: part of nose and right shoulder. Major publications: Bernoulli, *Römische Ikonographie*, II[3], 14, 109, No. 1, and p. 112; Stuart-Jones, *Museo Capitolino*, p. 201, No. 47, pl. 46; Felletti-Maj, *Iconografia*, p. 109, No. 57, pl. VII, fig. 23; Buchholz, *Kaiserinnen*, pp. 56, 157; Meischner, "Frauenporträt," p. 105, No. 80, fig. 70; Helbig[4], No. 1305; Wiggers and Wegner, *Herrscherbild*, III[1], 212, pls. 59, 64a; Bergmann, *Studien*, p. 30.

[45] Paris, Louvre, MA3552, fragmentary marble bust showing diademed head and part of shoulders. Unrestored. Part of chin, nose, large part of rear of head and of coiffure missing, face and diadem chipped, bust broken diagonally through the shoulders. Published: Jean Charbonneaux, *Bulletin de la Société des Antiquaires de France*, 1960, p. 55; *Sculpture grecque et romaine*, p. 175, No. 3552; Meischner, "Frauenporträt," pp. 112-113, No. 97; Wiggers and Wegner, *Herrscherbild*, III[1], 211, pl. 60.

canted outward toward the viewer, while the slight widening of the eyes and the greater arch of the eyebrow enhances the emphasis on them.

These stylistic features are shared by several portraits of Alexander Severus, including a head in the Vatican,[46] (fig. 26), which represent the young emperor with a mature beard and moustache, and which must therefore date to the later part of his reign, when he would have been a young man in his late twenties. The Vatican portrait of Alexander (fig. 26) likewise shows a lower face with a thinner, more triangular form, so that the contours no longer invite the viewer's gaze to travel over the whole face but form a rising triangle which expands gradually toward a focus of interest at the level of the eyes. The forehead is lower, and slopes more noticeably outward, thus making the eyebrows more prominent, while the hairline is no longer a single, fluid line but a choppy, broken contour, interrupted by a little bifurcation over the left eye and by the backward sweep of locks along each temple.

The eyes themselves, which are clearly meant to hold the viewer's attention, are not overly large in proportion to the face, but the arching upper lids are designed with a bold, gracefully swinging line that plunges down into a dipping tearduct. This calligraphic execution gives the eyes a more compelling expression than the regular, almond-shaped eyes of Alexander's earlier portraits. In the 230's, therefore, it would seem that the official artist or artists began to feel some dissatisfaction with the proportion, balance and calm of Alexander's and Mammaea's earlier public portraits. Though curvilinearity, smoothness, and simplicity of contour still characterize these later works, some of the devices used to achieve spiritual intensity in the portrait of Elagabalus (fig. 13) seem to be enjoying renewed life.

In private portraiture, on the other hand, indications of emotional tension seem never to have been completely abandoned. One of the closest parallels for the style and mood of Alexander's earlier portraits is presented by a head in Venice[47] (fig. 27) of a young man who shares with the emperor a classic, oval face. Here too, a relaxed, meditative expres-

[46] Vatican, Sala dei Busti, No. 361, inv. 632, marble head set on modern bust, h. 0.28. Nose, right ear, part of left ear, fragments of neck restored. Major publications: Bernoulli, *Römische Ikonographie*, II³, 99-100, No. 4, and p. 85, under No. 2, p. 104; Walther Amelung, *Die Skulpturen des vaticanischen Museums*, Vol. II, part 2 (Berlin: Georg Reimer, 1908), 550-551, No. 361, pl. 71; L'Orange, *Studien*, p. 1, fig. 1; Felletti-Maj, *Iconografia*, pp. 94-95, No. 21, pl. 4, fig. 11; Helbig⁴, No. 186; Wiggers and Wegner, *Herrscherbild*, III¹, 197, pl. 54 (with complete bibliography); Bergmann, *Studien*, p. 27, pl. 2, fig. 3.

[47] Venice, Museo Archeologico, inv. 148. Marble head set on modern bust, h. 0.285. Major publications: Bernoulli, *Römische Ikonographie*, II³, 73, 161; Bovini, *MonAnt.* 39 (1943), 198; Felletti-Maj, *Iconografia*, p. 209; Gustavo Traversari, *Museo Archeologico di Venezia: i ritratti* (Rome: Istituto Poligrafico dello Stato, 1968), No. 75, pp. 93-94, with full earlier literature.

sion is conveyed through the faraway gaze of the eyes and gentle, undulating line of the mouth, while the soft modeling of the forms and the
luminous polish of the skin areas allows all surfaces to flow smoothly into
one another. The beard resembles that of Alexander's later type in that it
is confined to a narrow band along the jawline which leaves most of the
surfaces of the cheeks and chin free. On the other hand, neither the hair
nor the beard is as smooth here as in Alexander's portraits. The beard is
not represented by a purely linear design on the cheeks: some curls rise in
slight relief, interrupting the outer contour, while the "*a penna*" hair
forms two jagged rows of fringe across the forehead and left temple. The
bone structure, too, is slightly more angular and more strongly asserted
than in the portraits of Alexander Severus.

Likenesses of more mature men share with those of the young emperor
a taste for regular, closed contours and for elegance and restraint in the
treatment of detail. A group of portraits including heads in the Uffizi
gallery[48] (fig. 28), in the Prado Museum of Madrid,[49] and in the Palazzo
Corsini in Rome[50] all share smooth, close-cropped caps of hair,
represented "*a penna*," and fuller beards which are however clipped to a
neatly rectangular form. Some use is made of the drill to indicate the textures of the curly beards, but the masses of curls tend to have a firmly
controlling contour and to enclose rather than expand the form of the
face, in much the same manner that curly coiffures in female portraiture
of this period were used to frame the skin areas within a strict rectangle.
(See figs. 16 and 17). The delicate smiles which generally characterize
female and juvenile portraits are absent, however: the lips tend to be
taut, thin, and heavily overshadowed by drooping moustaches, while
signs of age such as furrows across the cheeks and a slight sag of the flesh
away from the cheekbones are present, though very subtly modeled. The
foreheads, in all cases, are traversed by fine creases which indicate tension, while the forehead muscles rise in relief in the characteristic

---

[48] Florence, Galleria degli Uffizi, inv. 1914-280. Marble head set on modern bust. H.
of ancient part 0.30. Nose and left ear restored. Published: Bernoulli, *Römische
Ikonographie*, II³, 127; Felletti-Maj, *Iconografia*, p. 135, No. 127; Guido Mansuelli, *Galleria
degli Uffizi: le sculture*, Vol. II (Rome: Istituto Poligrafico dello Stato, 1961), 119, No. 152;
Wiggers and Wegner, *Herrscherbild*, III¹, 243.

[49] Madrid, Prado Museum. Marble head, set on modern herm, h. 0.50. Nose
restored, beard chipped and weathered, left eyebrow chipped. Published: A. Blanco,
*Museo del Prado, Catalogo de la escultura*, I (Madrid, 1957), 20-21, No. 10-E, pl. 2; Cornelius
Vermeule, "A Graeco-Roman Portrait Head of the Third Century," *DOPapers*, 15
(1961), 10, fig. 24.

[50] Rome, Palazzo Corsini, inv. 1208. Head set on modern bust. White marble, h. of
head 0.30. Restored: lower part of nose, chips from forehead and earlobes. Eyebrows
chipped. Published: Gioia de Luca, *I Monumenti antichi di Palazzo Corsini in Roma* (Rome:
Accademia Nazionale dei Lincei, 1976), pp. 85-86, No. 49, pls. LXXIV-LXXV.

V-shape which is complemented by the dip of the hairlines across the foreheads.

The formula originally developed in Caracalla's portraits to convey a scowl can still be traced in these works, though the modeling of the facial musculature is so subtle, the treatment of the skin areas so smooth and elegantly simple, that the mood conveyed by the contraction of the face has been radically changed. The Uffizi head illustrated here (fig. 28) suggests thoughtful concentration, while a stronger sense of anxiety can be observed in the Corsini and Prado heads, but none of these works suggest anger or menace.

Not all private patrons and privately commissioned artists, however, seem to have shared the tastes of Alexander Severus and Mammaea for elegance and subtlety. A fine and remarkably well preserved bust in the Capitoline Museum[51] (fig. 29) has "*a penna*" hair of a type which indicates a date early in Alexander Severus's reign. Here as in most of the portraits of the young emperor (e.g. figs. 22, 23) the pattern is carefully executed in a dense series of rows of tufts, while along the hairline a few locks rise in higher relief to fall softly over the face, indicating that some naturalism in the modeling of the hair has not yet been abandoned. Yet the spirit of this portrait (fig. 29), with its elongated, gaunt face, its severe frown and its conspicuous asymmetries, could not differ more strongly from the calm elegance favored in imperial commissions. Not only does the forehead muscle bulge, but its convex form is interrupted by two deep notches which slant diagonally upward from the inner corners of the eyebrows, emphasizing their contraction.

The mood of agitation is enhanced by slight asymmetries: the contour of the lower face is broken by the irregular, almost untidy clusters of the curls of the beard, while the long, bony ridge of the nose is not a true vertical but slants a little to the right. But it is the vigor of the modeling which lends this face its most dramatic vitality. The high, prominent cheekbones and the thick-lipped mouth are both strongly three-dimensional; the center of the mouth thrusts forward prominently, while the tapering corners draw back sharply into the planes of the cheeks and are tucked inward under the heavy, drooping moustache. The play of light over these forms, and the rising and falling surfaces, lend an effect of movement, and thus of fleeting emotion, to the face, though the vigor of the modeling almost undermines the organic connection of the parts of the face to one another. The sort of veristic detail which was faithfully

---

[51] Rome, Museo Capitolino, Sala delle Colombe, 18, inv. 708. Formerly in Stanza del Fauno, 13. Marble head, set on draped bust to which it may not belong. H. in toto 0.85, of head 0.24. Restored: both ears, a large part of rear of head. Published: Stuart-Jones, *Museo Capitolino*, p. 320, No. 13, pl. 79; Bergmann, *Studien*, p. 13.

represented but carefully understated in the portraits of Julia Mammaea (figs. 24, 25) is here exploited for expressive effect.

Two more portraits of men with close-cropped hair and fuller beards, a head in Copenhagen[52] (fig. 30) and a bust in Berlin[53] likewise show that interest in individuality and character is once again taking precedence over a taste for idealized beauty. In these two works, as in the Capitoline bust (fig. 29), the bone structures are strongly emphasized and the contraction of the eyebrows indicated by the prominent swell of the forehead muscle. In both cases, too, deep vertical notches rise from the inner corners of the eyebrows. These two works are datable somewhat later than the Capitoline portrait (fig. 29), perhaps in the 230's, since the treatment of the hair resembles that of some of Alexander Severus's latest portraits, such as the Vatican head which represents him as a full-grown man (fig. 26), and in the portraits of some of his successors. In the Copenhagen (fig. 30) and Berlin portraits, as in the Vatican Alexander (fig. 26), the "*a penna*" pattern of the hair has become looser and freer, the chisel strokes scattered more sparsely over the calotte of hair. The chronology of the various types of "*a penna*" patterns in sculpture during the 220's and 230's is not entirely clear, since the conventional pattern of neatly imbricated tufts can be found in portraits as late as those of Gordian III, but as a general rule the freer and more perfunctory execution of the technique tends to be later. In the case of the Berlin and Copenhagen portraits, furthermore, the angular, peaked hairlines resemble that of the portraits of Maximinus Thrax (fig. 3).

The Copenhagen head (fig. 30) still shows the influence of the Severan taste for classical elegance in its oval form, the high polish of the skin areas, and the decorative symmetry of the rather dandified curls of the moustache and beard. The beard of the Berlin bust, on the other hand, is more touseled and irregular, the face more rectilinear, the hairline more severely angular. The Berlin and Copenhagen portraits resemble one another, so much so that the suggestion has been raised that they may represent the same man.[54] The Berlin bust, however, has a broader face with a squarer, heavier jaw, as well as more conspicuous signs of age.

---

[52] Copenhagen, Ny Carlsberg Glyptotek, cat. 750, inv. 820. Head made for insertion in statue, marble, h. 0.38. Nose and ears partly broken away. Published: F. Poulsen, *Catalogue*, No. 750; Felletti-Maj, *Iconografia*, pp. 137-138, No. 125; V. Poulsen, *Les Portraits romains*, II, 138, No. 138; Wiggers and Wegner, *Herrscherbild*, III¹, 138, 243-244.

[53] Berlin, Staatliche Museen, Antikensammlung, R101, Marble bust, h. 0.61. Restored: lower half of nose, rims of ears, parts of drapery. Neck broken through and repaired, but head belongs to bust. Published: Blümel, *Römische Bildnisse*, p. 42, No. R101, pl. 65; V. Poulsen, *Les Portraits romains*, II, 138; Wiggers and Wegner, *Herrscherbild*, III¹, 136-137.

[54] V. Poulsen, *Les Portraits romains*, II, 138, No. 138.

This difference seems to indicate that the similarities between these works are more formal and stylistic than physiognomic; perhaps they are the work of the same sculptor.

A number of female portraits survive which wear hairstyles like that of Julia Mammaea, but comparatively few are of any great artistic interest. The tendency toward simplicity in treatment of the coiffure, combined with the Severan taste for classicizing idealization of features, frequently produced rather blandly pretty images which convey little sense of individuality. A head in Boston (fig. 31)[55] and a very similar work in Copenhagen[56] are examples of attractive and technically competent but unexciting work. One or two portraits, however, usually of somewhat older women, manage to convey the same subtle sense of energy and tension observed in male portraiture of the late Severan period. A head in the Galleria dei Candelabri of the Vatican[57] (fig. 32), for example, represents a woman with a rather gaunt and angular face. Her coiffure has the same severe simplicity as Mammaea's; a few wisps of hair still escape in front of the ears, as was fashionable in Elagabalus's time, but the strands are narrow and lank, with only a slight, gentle wave. The curls do not provide an excuse for virtuoso drill work, as in the British Museum bust (fig. 17) and other such works, but are almost anti-decorative, emphasizing the vertical sides of the rectangular face. The thin-lipped mouth is drawn taut into a horizontal line, and the fine eyebrows drawn slightly downward toward the nose. The corners of the lips turn slightly upward in a little smile, a device very common in female portraits of this period, but the eyebrows seem to frown. A peculiar tension in the facial expression is thus created, suggesting perhaps a sudden shift of mood.

A few generalizations can be made about the portraiture from the reigns of the last Severans: most of the extant works from this period display a taste for closed and simple contours, softly rounded modeling of

---

[55] Boston Museum of Fine Arts, 1970.325, marble head, h. 0.22. Nose, tip of chin, hair under right ear broken away. Published: Cornelius Vermeule, "Recent Museum Acquisitions: Greek and Roman Sculptures in Boston," *Burlington Magazine*, 113 (1971), 45, figs. 60-61; Mary Comstock and Cornelius Vermeule, *Sculpture in Stone* (Boston: Museum of Fine Arts, 1976), p. 237, No. 372.

[56] Copenhagen, Ny Carlsberg Glyptotek, cat. 743, inv. 808. Marble head, h. 0.25. Nose, hair below left ear broken away. Published: F. Poulsen, *Catalogue*, No. 743; Buchholz, *Kaiserinnen*, pp. 58, 118, 159; Cesare Saletti, *Ritratti Severiani*, Vol. X of *Studia Archeologica* (Rome: L'Erma di Bretschneider, 1967), pp. 71-73, pl. 22, fig. 2, and pl. 24; Wiggers and Wegner, *Herrscherbild*, III¹, 220; V. Poulsen, *Les Portraits romains*, II, 164, No. 168.

[57] Vatican, Galleria dei Candelabri, No. 22, marble head set on modern bust, h. of ancient part, 0.24. Restored: nose. Published: Georg Lippold, *Die Skulpturen des vaticanischen Museums*, III² (Berlin: De Gruyter, 1956), 121, No. 22, pl. 56; Meischner, "Frauenporträt," p. 143, No. 47, and pp. 144-145.

detail, and a fairly smooth and elegant presentation of the subject. A mood of brooding tension, however, is a very popular effect at this time, more so perhaps in portraits of men than of women, but well attested in portraits of all classifications. With the assassination of Alexander Severus and the beginning of the military anarchy of the mid-century, effects of immediate and intense emotion regained popularity in portraiture.

CHAPTER THREE

# THE SOLDIER-EMPERORS:
# VERISM AND IMPRESSIONISM

The portraits of Maximinus Thrax demonstrate a dramatic change in spirit from those of the young emperor and older empress whom he had overthrown. Though the later portraits of Alexander Severus and Mammaea showed some interest in effects of spiritual intensity, all their images were characterized by a mood of meditation. The portraits of Maximinus, on the other hand (fig. 3), not only revived the intimidating scowl of Caracalla's last portraits but enhanced the grimness of the expression with a deliberately harsh and angular treatment of detail. The hairline, for example, recedes slightly at each temple to form sharp angles, whereas that of Alexander Severus had formed a fluid curve with a slight, organic asymmetry (figs. 22, 23, 26). The signs of age, moreover, are not only represented but strongly emphasized: the furrows of the skin are carved as deep grooves which are V-shaped in section rather than U-shaped, so that they form harsh lines of shadow. Julia Mammaea's portraits had represented her heavy jaw and slightly jowly cheeks without flattery, but the skin surfaces had not been broken by such a pattern of line. Surprisingly, however, the skin surfaces of some portraits of Maximinus, such as the Copenhagen replica (fig. 3), still show a high, glass-like polish similar to that of late Severan portraits. The execution of some details, such as the incision of the strands of the beard on the cheeks, shows a decorative refinement almost incongruous with the brutally realistic treatment of the features. The polish of the skin areas here serves a stylistic purpose almost diametrically opposed to its function in late Severan portraiture, where it served to emphasize the unity of the fluidly modeled surfaces: here, the linear emphasis of the furrows is made all the more conspicuous because of the shimmering smoothness of the surfaces which they interrupt. But the technique is the same.

Clearer continuities with late Severan portraiture can be recognized in the three extant portraits of Maximus, the son and *Caesar* of Maximinus Thrax[1] (fig. 33). This boy's family resemblance to his father is evident in

---

[1] All three replicas of the portrait of Maximus are in the Ny Carlsberg Glyptotek:
A. Marble head, cat. 745, inv. 819, h. 0.42. Restorations now removed: nose, part of upper lip, chin, rims of ears. Provenance: Rome, Villa Ludovisi, reportedly found along with the portrait of Maximinus Thrax, Ny Carlsberg Glytotek 744, and with another

his bone structure, particularly the prominent brow-ridge and heavy, protruding jaw, yet his face is represented with the same gracefully curvilinear contours and surfaces, the same delicate and spiritual smile, as that of Alexander Severus[2] (figs. 22, 23, 26). Here, too, in striking contrast to the portraits of his father, Maximus's lips are softly modeled with rounded and indistinct borders while a luminously polished surface unites the skin areas. The taste for angularity so evident in the portraits of Maximinus has exercised some influence here, too, however, in the sharply rectilinear corners of the hairline and in the emphasis on the strong bone structure under the smooth flesh.

Other claimants to imperial power during the usurpation of Maximinus left portraits which illustrate these same trends: the survival of traditions of late Severan portraiture together with the emergence of a taste for harsher realism. The iconography of the elder and younger Gordian, who were unwillingly elevated to imperial rank by their legions in North Africa, remains somewhat controversial.[3] One possible candidate for identification with Gordian II (fig. 38) will be discussed later in this chapter. Until more replicas of the type are discovered, it cannot be cited with any security as an imperial type, and therefore it will be discussed with the anonymous portraits here. Suffice it for now to observe that the work does show many stylistic similarities to the portraits of Maximinus. On the other hand, the likenesses of Pupienus and Balbinus, two senators acclaimed at Rome after the death of the Gordiani, can be recognized beyond reasonable doubt, the former in several marble busts and heads[4]

---

replica of the portrait of Maximus, inv. 746. Major publications: F. Poulsen, *Catalogue*, No. 745; L'Orange, *Studien*, p. 96, note 5; Felletti-Maj, *Iconografia*, p. 124, No. 93; Zinserling, *Klio*, 41 (1963), 203; von Heintze, *Gymnasium Beiheft*, 4 (1964), 160-162; Wiggers and Wegner, *Herrscherbild*, III¹, 232 and 234, pl. 71; V. Poulsen, *Les Portraits romains*, II, No. 160, pp. 162-163; Bergmann, *Studien*, pp. 32-33.

B. Copenhagen, Ny Carlsberg Glyptotek, cat. 746, inv. 823, marble head, h. 0.42. Restorations now removed: nose, chips from mouth, and parts of ears. Eyes and cheeks chipped. Provenance: same as for above-listed head in Copenhagen. Published: F. Poulsen, *Catalogue*, p. 518, No. 746; Felletti-Maj, *Iconografia*, pp. 123-124, No. 92, pl. X, fig. 34. Wiggers and Wegner, *Herrscherbild*, III¹, 234, pl. 70a; V. Poulsen, *Les Portraits romains*, p. 162, No. 165. Other references as for preceding object.

C. Copenhagen, Ny Carlsberg Glyptotek, cat. 759, inv. 826. Marble head, made for insertion into a statue, h. 0.34. Nose, chin, ears and side of neck damaged. Published: Bernoulli, *Römische Ikonographie*, II³, p. 157. F. Poulsen, *Catalogue*, No. 759; Felletti-Maj, *Iconografia*, p. 125, No. 96; von Heintze, *Gymnasium Beiheft*, 4 (1964), 161, pl. 16a; Wiggers and Wegner, *Herrscherbild*, III¹, 232, 234; Bergmann, *Studien*, pp. 32-34.

[2] Bergmann, *Studien*, pp. 8-10 and pp. 32-33.

[3] On the history of the Gordians, see *SHA*, "Gordiani Tres," XII-XXIII.3. For a discussion of their portraiture, see von Heintze, *RömMitt*, 63 (1956), 62-65.

[4] On the iconography of Pupienus, see Wiggers and Wegner, *Herrscherbild*, III¹, 241-245; Felletti-Maj, *Iconografia*, 135-140; Britt Haarløv, *New Identifications of Third Century Roman Portraits* (Odense: Odense University Press, 1975), pp. 13-14.

of a gaunt, older man with a full beard, (fig. 4), the latter in the portraits on a magnificent sarcophagus (figs. 5, 6) and in a few sculptures in the round which clearly represent the same face.[5]

The portraits of Pupienus show one technical departure from the portraits both of Maximinus and of Alexander Severus: the hair no longer has any volume in relief, but is represented as a purely linear pattern. The "*a penna*" locks are now very loosely sketched and sparsely scattered on the scalp. This technique reflects the trend toward increasingly summary and abstract treatment of the hair which was to become more and more evident in sculpture of the mid-third century. The full beard, on the other hand, the locks of which are elaborately outlined with drill channels, demonstrates close similarities with many unidentified male portraits of the 220's discussed in the last chapter (e.g. figs. 28, 29), works with which it also shares an expression of tense, watchful anxiety. This effect is now greatly enhanced by the complex pattern of sharply carved furrows across the skin of the face. In this respect, at least, there is a close relationship between the portraits of Pupienus (fig. 4) and those of Maximinus Thrax (fig. 3).

Balbinus, the younger colleague of Pupienus, seems not to have had such a deeply lined face; his portraits, at any rate, do not make use of such a pattern of wrinkles. Balbinus's portraits (figs. 5, 6) are equally unflattering and realistic, however, in their presentation of his plump, middle-aged face, with its sagging cheeks and pouchy eyes. In all his portraits, the trend toward abstraction and simplification of the hair is carried even further than in those of his colleague: both the hair and the beard are now not only volumeless, but are no longer even represented "*a penna.*" Isolated chisel strokes, rather than sketched locks, now suggest the texture of the short stubble on the face and scalp.

The life-sized, reclining figures of Balbinus and his wife on the lid of their sarcophagus, as well as a head of Balbinus in Brussels,[6] are rather conservative in style, and display close relationships with the portraits of the late Severans. Balbinus's face (fig. 6) is represented as a long oval with fluid, curvilinear contours, while the sagging flesh of the aging face has been modeled with great subtlety and sensitivity so as to create an undulating surface over which the light can play. Just as in the portraits of

---

[5] For a recent and excellent discussion of the iconography of Balbinus, see J. and J. Ch. Balty, *Bull. de l'Inst. Hist. Belge de Rome*, 44 (1974), 24-45. Additional discussions of the portraits attributed to Balbinus are Wiggers and Wegner, *Herrscherbild*, III¹, 241-243, and 246-249; Felletti-Maj, *Iconografia* pp. 140-146.

[6] Brussels, Musée du Parc du Cinquantenaire, inv. A3753. Marble head, h. 0.246. Badly battered; top and back of head, end of nose, part of chin gone, surface corroded and chipped. Published: J. and J. Ch. Balty, *Bull. de l'Inst. Hist. Belge de Rome*, 44 (1974), 25-45.

Julia Mammaea, signs of advancing age such as creases and pouches under the eyes are represented but are not set off by conspicuous shadows. The wife of Balbinus, whose name is unknown, had a broader and more squarish face than her husband. The life-sized portrait of the lady on the lid of the sarcophagus (fig. 34), however, avoids harsh angles, softens and rounds the corners of the face, and gives the contours and surfaces a similarly curvilinear, undulating form. The hair, which is brushed away from the face and drawn into a soft chignon at the nape of the neck, has been used in the life-sized portrait to form an oval halo around the face. This woman, like her husband, was evidently middle-aged, but though the signs of her age have been indicated, the reclining figure on the cover of this sarcophagus is a work of great beauty, which represents its subject as a beautiful woman.

In the smaller portraits of both Balbinus and his wife (figs. 5 and 35), which appear on the relief of this sarcophagus, the heads are more squarish, compact, and simply modeled. Though the fleshiness of the faces is still indicated, Balbinus's double chin is less pronounced, his cheeks somewhat firmer. In all the relief portraits, moreover, the features are more crisply carved and sharply set off from one another, the eyes and mouths more strongly emphasized by line, and the facial creases more deeply and angularly cut than in the portraits on the cover.

This difference in style,[7] probably reflecting the work of two sculptors carving the separate parts of the monument, is appropriate to the difference in the moods expressed by the portraits, and their different functions. The reclining figures on the cover (figs. 6, 34) represent the deceased couple in a relaxed pose suggestive of the eternal rest of death. Hence, their large and strongly rounded eyes express peaceful but rather melancholy meditation, though the slightly asymmetrical quirk of the wife's mouth conveys a hint of a smile.[8] The relief, on the other hand (figs. 5, 35) shows the couple in life: during their wedding, in the scene to the right, and in the performance of a public sacrifice. Appropriately, their faces convey more worldly energy and concentration. The eyebrows of both husband and wife are contracted, slanting downward toward the nose, the eyes are long, narrow, and likewise set on a slight slant, and the lips firmly pursed. As discussed in the first chapter, these relief heads are far more closely related to the portraits of Gordian III, the successor of Pupienus and Balbinus, than they are to the late Severan portraits which clearly influenced the treatment of the life-sized figures on the cover. The smaller relief portraits, and the related bronze head of Balbinus in the

---

[7] J. and J. Ch. Balty, *Bull. de l'Inst. Hist. Belge de Rome*, 44 (1974), 36.

[8] Gütschow, *MemPontAcc*, 4 (1934-38), 90-91.

Vatican share with the portraits of Gordian a compact and severely simple treatment of volumes and surfaces, and the use of dark line to emphasize a few significant features.

The sarcophagus of Balbinus is remarkable also in preserving three full-length representations of an imperial figure: one, at the center of the relief, in a scaled cuirass and a paludamentum, the other two in the toga, which is of the old-fashioned, softly draped type rather than the trabeated form. Balbinus is thus shown in the two mortal guises standard for imperial portraits: the emperor in his capacity as citizen and political leader, and as *imperator*. That Balbinus could also be represented in an over-life-sized, divinized form is demonstrated by the statue in Piraeus, which represents him as Zeus.[9] Thus, the fact that Balbinus was a senatorial rather than a soldier emperor does not seem to have made any significant difference as to the figure-types with which he was presented to the public: all the standard formats[10] were used, and this is probably equally true of all other emperors from the period under study, regardless of the means by which they attained power. The styles of the faces, and the types of expressions with which they are portrayed, seem to have varied to some extent according to the propaganda needs of each regime, though it has been my effort throughout this study to demonstrate the existence of a continuity of artistic traditions from reign to reign even at times of rapid change and innovation. But the body types used for full-length statuary and relief representations of emperors do not appear to reflect much response to the differing political goals of their different imperial patrons. Granted, far too few complete statues survive to allow generalization, but the existing evidence appears to be negative.

A dichotomy of styles comparable to that of the portrait faces of Balbinus can be observed in replicas of another public portrait type, which has been tentatively accepted here as Macrinus. Heads in the Palazzo dei Conservatori (fig. 36)[11], the Fogg Art Museum (fig. 37)[12] and

---

[9] See Chapter 1, note 54, and appendix, under "Balbinus," No. 4.

[10] Niemeyer, *Statuarischen Darstellung*, pp. 38-64.

[11] Rome, Palazzo dei Conservatori, Museo Nuovo, inv. 1757. Marble head, h. 0.25. Face badly mutilated: both eyebrows, nose, part of left cheek broken away. Discovered in Rome, in 1900, during excavations for the Quirinal tunnel. Major publications: Domenico Mustilli, *Il Museo Mussolini* (Rome: Libreria dello Stato, 1939), p. 111, No. 25, pl. 68, fig. 269; L. Mariani, "Sculture provenienti dalla galleria sotto il Quirinale," *BullCom*, 29 (1901), 173-176, fig. 6. L'Orange, *Studien*, p. 93, fig. 239. Felletti-Maj, *Iconografia*, p. 137, No. 123; Helbig[4], No. 1755; Fittschen, *JdI*, 84 (1969), 223, fig. 34; Wiggers and Wegner, *Herrscherbild*, III[1], 139, pl. 32; Bergmann, *Studien*, p. 19; Salzmann, *JdI* 98 (1983), 361-371, figs. 12, 16, 20.

[12] Cambridge, Mass., Fogg Art Museum, Harvard University, inv. 1949.47.138. Head in white marble, h. 0.28. Face badly mutilated: both eyebrows and much of forehead, along with parts of both eyes, broken away, nose gone, lower lip broken, end of chin and beard broken off. Published: Hanfmann, *Latomus*, 11 (1952), pp. 209-215, figs.

the Capitoline Museum[13] unmistakably represent the same man: the shape of the oval face, the bone structure, the patterns of creases across the forehead and around the eyes, and the long furrows across the cheeks all match too closely to allow for coincidence. A particularly striking individual feature is the "anastole," or tuft of hair at the center of the peaked hairline which springs upward and back against the grain of the rest of the hair. If this man is indeed Macrinus,[14] the heads must be datable to the year 217; therefore, about twenty years earlier than the sarcophagus of Balbinus. As discussed in the first chapter, the identification must remain tentative: the three marbles of Roman origin show significant differences from the Belgrade head in their hairlines and in their somewhat shorter beards, which tend to follow the contours of the cheeks rather than hanging in corkscrew curls. If these marble heads represent the same man as the Belgrade bronze, therefore, they must follow a slightly different prototype. The damage to the faces, the result of apparently deliberate vandalism, unfortunately creates considerable difficulties in the comparison of these heads not only to the Belgrade bronze but also to the coins. It is however, at any rate, quite certain that their subject must have been some prominent public figure of the earlier third century, who suffered a *damnatio memoriae*.

Despite slight differences in the length of the beard, all three marbles appear to follow the same prototype. Yet the two replicas in Rome show softer and more organic modeling, and more fluid, curvilinear treatment of the hair and hairline, than does the Fogg head.[15] In the latter, the facial furrows are V-shaped in section, forming hard lines of shadow all the more conspicuous because of the glassy polish of the face. In this detail, the Fogg replica (fig. 37) is closely comparable to the portrait of Maximinus Thrax in Copenhagen (fig. 3). The hairline of the Fogg replica is also more rigidly symmetrical and angular than that of the heads in Rome (fig. 36), forming crisp angles over the temples and a

---

5-6; V. Poulsen, *Les Portraits romains*, II, 139, under no. 138; Wiggers and Wegner, *Herrscherbild*, III[1], 137; Bergmann, *Studien*, p. 123, pl. 37, figs. 3-4; Salzmann, *JdI*, 98 (1983), 361-371, figs. 11, 15, 19.

[13] Rome, Museo Capitolino, Stanza degli Imperatori, 48, inv. 460. Over-life-sized head on modern cuirassed bust. Eyes, nose, mouth with moustache and part of beard, end of beard, and rear of skull restored in marble. H. of head 0.37. Published: Bernoulli, *Römische Ikonographie*, II[3], 16, pl. 7, pp. 75-76, No. 2, and p. 79; Stuart-Jones, *Museo Capitolino*, pp. 201-202, No. 48, pl. 46; L'Orange, *Studien*, p. 93; Helbig[4], No. 1307; Wiggers and Wegner, *Herrscherbild*, III[1], 138-139, pl. 33; Bergmann, *Studien*, p. 19; Fittschen, *JdI*, 84 (1969), 223, figs. 53-54; Salzmann, *JdI*, 98 (1983), 361-371, figs. 14, 18, 22.

[14] Sheldon Nodelman, in an unpublished manuscript of his forthcoming book *Severan Imperial Portraits*; Salzmann, *JdI*, 98 (1983), 361-376.

[15] I am indebted for these observations to Sheldon Nodelman's unpublished manuscript *Severan Imperial Portraits*.

symmetrically V-shaped peak at the center which is paralleled by the chevrons of the creases across the forehead. The most striking abstraction is the treatment of the eyes, which are etched onto the smooth surface of the face as shallow, linear designs.

These stylistic features have led more than one scholar to date the Fogg head (fig. 37) to the later third century, and it is true that comparisons of this work with portrait of the 270's and 280's reveal certain similarities both in style and in the mentality behind the approach to the human face.[16] On the other hand, the more conservative nature of the other two replicas argues for an earlier date, while the carefully drawn "*a penna*" locks of the hair of the Fogg head,[17] like the sensitive modeling and lustrous polish, find their closest parallels in portraits of Alexander Severus, (figs. 22, 23, 26), Maximinus Thrax (fig. 3), and Gordian III. The relief heads on the sarcophagus of Balbinus, and the portraits of Gordian III, which remain to be discussed in the following chapter, indicate that this trend toward abstraction had already begun in the late 230's and 240's; the Fogg head (fig. 37) can therefore perhaps be taken as another possibly much earlier representative of this movement.

The Macrinus-type represented in the Fogg, Palazzo dei Conservatori, and Capitoline museums shares with the portraits of Maximinus Thrax (fig. 3) the vigorous modeling of the contracted facial musculature and deep carving of the furrows of the skin, as well as a similar dependence on the traditions and formulae of the portraits of Caracalla. The overall effect of the face, however, is more refined and aristocratic, its mood less angry and more meditatively thoughtful than that of Maximinus, perhaps because the man's features are more delicate and his face closer to a classic oval. The coarse and virile aspect of Caracalla's portraits definitely seems to have returned to favor in the 230's however, not only in the public likenesses of Maximinus, but in private and unidentified portraits. A head currently displayed in the Palazzo Braschi,[18] for example (fig. 38), has a massive rectilinear bone structure, large features and a broad, full-lipped mouth. The artist has not concealed signs of age such as the slight balding above the temples, where the hairline runs far backward onto the scalp.

---

[16] Hanfmann, *Latomus*, 11 (1952), pp. 211-212; Bergmann, *Studien*, p. 123, 128. See in particular the photographic comparisons published by Bergmann, pls. 36-37.

[17] I am indebted for this observation to Prof. Dr. Klaus Fittschen.

[18] Rome, Palazzo Braschi, inv. 478, formerly in the Museo Capitolino, Stanza degli Imperatori, No. 67, then in the Palazzo dei Conservatori, Galleria. Marble head set on a modern bust, h. 0.265. Restored: nose, neck. Provenance: Rome, area of Porta Portese. Major publications: Bernoulli, *Römische Ikonographie*, II³, 123; Stuart-Jones, *Museo Capitolino*, p. 208, No. 67, pl. 50; von Heintze, *RömMitt*, 63 (1956), 64, pl. 31; Felletti-Maj, *Iconografia*, p. 133, No. 114, pl. XII, figs. 39-40; Wiggers and Wegner, *Herrscherbild*, III¹, 240.

The subject's face is regular and handsome, but his good looks are of quite a different type from those of portraits from the late Severan period. The skin of the face is fairly smooth, with few lines, but the cheeks have a slight sag, which does not however suggest flabbiness. Instead, the slackness of the cheeks serves to throw the ridges of cheekbones and jaw into higher relief, and to give the surfaces of the face a slight undulation. The large, deep-set eyes have an almost exaggerated three-dimensionality, displaying a comparable interest in a dramatic rise and fall of surfaces and a vibrant play of light over the features. The strength and authority conveyed by this face would be quite appropriate for the image of a ruler, and indeed von Heintze has proposed that this head may represent the short-lived emperor Gordian II[19]. Such an identification is perfectly consistent with the date proposed here at the time of Maximinus Thrax, though until replicas of the work are discovered, its subject's imperial status must remain unproven.

The tendency toward brutal realism is even more obvious in an extraordinarily fine and well-preserved bust in Venice (fig. 39)[20]. The bust, which includes half the upper arms and all of the rib-cage, is nude except for a military paludamentum which falls over the left shoulder and hangs in softly modeled, vertical folds to the lower border of the bust. The subject of this portrait resembles Maximinus not only in his heavy bone structure, but in his coarse, fleshy features. The artist has dwelt on anticlassical details such as the bulbous nose and thick eyelids. The upper lids are deeply hooded, the lower underlined by creases and puffy pouches. In this portrait, too, the furrows of the forehead and around the mouth create a complex web of shadow across the heavy features, while the massive and broad-shouldered torso represented in the bust gives us some idea of this man's sheer physical strength. Unlike the portraits of Maximinus, however, this bust does not convey quite such ferocity or anger. The lips appear taut, but the well-known formula for a scowl is not employed here. It is likely that this man was a soldier, but since his portrait was probably private and funerary in function, rather than a public image of a leader, the artist who portrayed him could imitate the harsh verism of contemporary imperial portraits without using the style to achieve so intimidating an effect.

In details of technique, the Venice bust (fig. 39) resembles the portraits of Pupienus (fig. 4) more than those of Maximinus Thrax. The hair has

---

[19] Von Heintze, *RömMitt*, 63 (1956), p. 64.

[20] Venice, Museo Archeologico, inv. 8. Marble bust, showing chest and upper arms, nude except for drapery over left shoulder, h. 0.61, of head alone 0.25. Preservation almost perfect except for slight scratches on face and hair, possible modern cleaning and polishing. Published: Traversari, *Ritratti*, p. 92, No. 73, with references to earlier catalogues.

no volume at all but is etched directly onto the scalp as a pattern of line. The incisions still have long, flowing and rather calligraphic curves, as in the later portraits of Alexander Severus (fig. 26), but no longer outline "*a penna*" tufts. Thus, the Venice bust illustrates the trend toward simplification and abstraction of detail, in its hair and beard at least, though the supple and organic modeling of the face is rather conservative.

Female portraits of the late 230's and 240's are somewhat difficult to date, since several types of coiffure seem to have been fashionable at the same time. The wife of Balbinus, as portrayed on the couple's sarcophagus (figs. 34, 35) still wore her hair in the full, bouffant style of the earlier Severan *Augustae*,[21] with the hair partly covering the ears and coiled into a soft chignon, even though the more severe coiffure of Julia Mammaea had been more popular during the 220's. Paulina, the wife of Maximinus Thrax, had died by the time her husband became emperor, but was honored on coins as "Diva Paulina." In these coin profiles, her head is veiled, so that the coiffure is partly hidden, but she appears to have worn a small, tight chignon like that of Julia Mammaea.[22] Tranquillina, on the other hand, who became empress probably in 240 or 241, wore what is generally known as a *Scheitelzopffrisur*: again, the hair is parted in the middle, marcelled, looped behind the ears and braided, but the braids, instead of being twisted into a bun, were drawn up the back of the head. The length of the braids evidently could vary at the discretion of the wearer, and is not a reliable criterion of early or late date.[23] A more reliable indication will be stylistic comparison with contemporary male portraits.

One of the finest extant expressions of the realism of the third century is a head of an older woman in the Capitoline museum (fig. 40).[24] Her hair is drawn up from the nape of the neck into a short rectangle of braids, but the smoothness and severity of the shallow waves around the face has close parallels in the fashions worn by Julia Mammaea and other ladies of the late Severan period. As in so many Severan portraits, the smooth, rectangular outline of the coiffure serves to enhance the long, heavy rectangle of the face. The air of dignity and mood of spiritual

---

[21] See Wessel, *AA*, 61-62 (1946-47), 63-64.

[22] See Felletti-Maj, *Iconografia*, p. 122; Wiggers and Wegner, *Herrscherbild*, III[1], 229-230.

[23] Wessel, *AA*, 61-62 (1946-47), 65-69; Bergmann, *Studien*, pp. 90-91.

[24] Rome, Museo Capitolino, Stanza degli Imperatori, 42, marble bust, h. in toto 0.57. (Measurements of ancient part not available; life-sized). Nose, bust and foot restored, surface chipped and scratched. Published: Stuart-Jones, *Museo Capitolino*, pp. 206-207, No. 61, pl. 49; Bernoulli, *Römische Ikonographie*, II[3], 115; Helbig[4], No. 1312; Hekler, *Bildniskunst*, pl. 302, fig. a.

detachment conveyed by the distant gaze of the large, strongly rounded eyes and arched eyebrows likewise demonstrates close continuities with the calm classicism of the portraits of Julia Mammaea and Alexander Severus (figs. 22-26). On the other hand, whereas signs of age in the portraits of Julia Mammaea were subtly indicated, here they are emphasized and exploited. The forehead and cheeks are deeply lined, the tendons of the throat slack, and the eyebrow ridge and cheekbones thrown into high relief by the concavity of the temples and the sag of the flesh of the cheeks. A complex pattern of line and a lifelike play of light over the rising and falling surface connect this head with the portraits of Maximinus and Pupienus, as well as private male portraits such as the bust in Venice (fig. 39).

In the softly rounded carving of the facial furrows, the sensitive observation of the signs of old age, the pattern of the S-shaped lines around the mouth and the furrows running backward under the chin which set off the tendons of the throat, the Capitoline head shows especially close connections with the Venice bust (fig. 39). Conceivably, these two portraits are the work of the same master. Regardless of the identity of the artist, however, it is intriguing to observe how such similar formal devices can be used to achieve such diverse effects: deliberately coarse strength in the one case, (fig. 39), and noble and dignified old age in the other (fig. 40).

A portrait in the Louvre[25] with a coiffure virtually identical to that of the Capitoline head shows comparably harsh realism applied to a very different facial type. The subject this time is a woman of middle age, with a pinched lower face, an angular bone structure and taut, thin lips. Here, too, an element of otherworldly detachment is introduced by the enlarged, rounded eyes. This lady's eyebrows are raised in high, semicircular arches which again enhance the staring gaze. Even pretty and youthful portraits could reflect the prevailing taste for realistic irregularities: a bust in New York[26] (fig. 41), for example, represents a young woman with smooth skin and delicate features. As in the Louvre portrait, the artist has gone to some pains to emphasize the angularity of the bone structure and thinness of the lips, as well as the asymmetries of

---

[25] Paris, Louvre, MA 1034, head set on bust to which it may not belong. H. of head and neck 0.31, of head alone 0.21. Restored: nose. Published: *Catalogue Sommaire des marbres antiques* (Paris: Louvre, 1896), No. 1034; Meischner, "Frauenporträt," p. 164, No. 93, pp. 165-166, fig. 115.

[26] New York, Metropolitan Museum of Art, accession no. 18.145.39. Half-body bust showing all of right arm and upper half of left. H. 0.65. Nose restored. Published: Gisela M. A. Richter, *Roman Portraits* (New York: Metropolitan Museum, 1948), No. 89, *BMMA*, 16 (1921), 228, *Handbook of the Classical Collection*, 6th ed. (New York: Metropolitan Museum of Art, 1930), pp. 304-305, fig. 213; Buchholz, *Kaiserinnen*, pp. 45, 151; Meischner, "Frauenporträt," p. 143, No. 50.

the features. The left side of the mouth is much shorter than the right, which curls upward in the suggestion of an ironic smile. The strands of hair too are incised on the coiffure with jagged, irregular lines which suggest unruly frizziness, while lending vivacity and movement to the face.

As was demonstrated by the portrait figure of the wife on the cover of the sarcophagus of Balbinus (fig. 34), however, women at this period could be represented in a manner which combined subtle observation with sensuous beauty. A head in Copenhagen[27] (fig. 42), evidently broken from a bust, shows a woman with a face rather similar to that of the wife of Balbinus in that it is broad, squarish, and rather fleshy. The unclassical proportions of the face and broad mouth are not flattered away, but the softness and sensitivity of modeling gives both the contours and the surfaces a rich curvilinearity. Here, too, as in the female portrait on the cover of the Balbinus sarcophagus, the eyes are large and rounded, this time with a broad lunette-shape, the eyebrows slightly raised, and the hair swept upward and back from the hairline rather than draped like curtains on either side of the part. Thus the natural curve of the hairline is exposed, while the strands form a dramatically radiating aureole around the face. The upward gaze gains even more in immediacy because of the sinuous curve of the neck, which spirals forward toward the viewer, and the parting of the lips which suggests a sudden catch of breath.

Whereas Balbinus's wife wore her hair in a large bun, this lady sports the more modern *Scheitelzopffrisur*, in which her hair is bound into a broad column of braids up the back of the skull. It is unfortunate that a large piece of the rear of the head, originally attached separately, is now missing, since it is no longer possible to know just how the hair framed the face. The virtuosity of the representation of the hair, however, can still be appreciated: the thick, rippling locks which sweep outward from the part have been worked in elaborate relief with the chisel, the pattern of strands engraved with variety and calligraphic grace on their rising and falling surfaces, while the row of thick corkscrew curls along the nape of the neck demonstrates delight in rich, decorative detail. Few portraits from this period or any other show such care devoted even to details at the back of the head, which was generally not accessible to the viewer. The Copenhagen bust (fig. 42) ranks with the reclining figures on the

---

[27] Copenhagen, Ny Carlsberg Glyptotek, cat. 738, inv. 792. Marble head and neck, broken from bust, h. 0.33. Nose and left ear broken away, surface chipped. Rear of cranium was worked separately and is now lost. Neck, head and fragment of drapery of bust survive in one piece. Published: F. Poulsen, *Catalogue*, No. 738; Buchholz, *Kaiserinnen*, p. 151; Meischner, "Frauenporträt," p. 141, No. 45; Saletti, *Ritratti Severiani*, p. 34, No. 2; Wiggers and Wegner, *Herrscherbild*, III¹, 123, 174; V. Poulsen, *Les Porträts romains*, II, 149-150, No. 147, pl. 238.

cover of the Balbinus sarcophagus (fig. 34) in sensitivity and in technical excellence, as a masterpiece of third-century portraiture.

It is important to recall that at least some artists of the 230's and 240's were capable of producing works like these which combine anatomic accuracy, organic modeling, and idealizing beauty, because at the same time another trend was developing in sculpture toward hard, geometric abstraction and severely linear detail. This style is less readily accessible and pleasing to modern tastes, and is frequently interpreted as evidence of a decline in technical ability,[28] a regression toward the stiff and naive forms of folk art. Yet the two styles appear together on a single monument, the sarcophagus of Balbinus, a work of uniformly high quality and painstaking execution. The lovely Copenhagen portrait (fig. 42), furthermore, is probably the approximate contemporary of works such as a bust in Venice (fig. 63) and a head in the British Museum (fig. 64), which wear coiffures popular in the first half of the third century, but reveal a much more stylized and abstract approach to the face. These works remain to be discussed in more detail in the following chapter.

Two rather different styles seem, therefore, to have coexisted in Roman portraiture of the second quarter of the third century. The precise origin of the more abstract style can perhaps never be known, but as discussed in the first chapter, the formal devices of the portraits of Gordian III (figs. 7, 8) seem to have been derived from those of Caracalla, and to belong to a continuous tradition of the sculptural workshops in and around Rome. Depending upon the image which the current ruler wished to project, either style could be used in official portraiture. The frozen immobility of the abstract style lent an air of dignity to the portraits of the boy emperor Gordian III, but his successor, Philip the Arab, (fig. 9), chose to be presented in the more lifelike and realistic style which was appropriate for expressing soldierly energy.

The portraits of Philip the Arab (fig. 9) and of Trajan Decius (fig. 10), which were discussed at length in the first chapter, provide evidence of a new use for the more realistic style, and for the formal devices which had characterized the representation of men such as Maximinus Thrax and Pupienus. The facial lines of the furrowed skin now create a pattern of strong, unified movement focused in a particular direction, generally accompanying and enhancing an upturned gaze. Expressions of intense emotion in portraits of the harshly realistic style were by now of course quite commonplace; a quarter-century of artistic elaboration on the traditions of Caracalla's adult portraits had resulted in a rich variety of

---

[28] Pelikàn, *Vom antiken Realismus zur spätantiken Expressivität*, pp. 33, 76-77. See also Rodenwaldt, *AbhBerl*, 1935, p. 25, and "Zur Kunstgeschichte der Jahre 220 bis 270," *JdI*, 51 (1936), 110-112.

schemata for the representation of tension in facial musculature. However, the emphasis on an upward sweep of facial line, of which the earliest datable examples are the portraits of the emperors who reigned from 244 until 251, achieves a novel effect of anxiety, sometimes even of sorrow and anguish.

The observation is frequently made that such works of art reflect the psychological impact on individuals of the social and political chaos of the third century.[29] Indeed, the conclusion seems inescapable that if facial expressions of such unhappiness and insecurity were considered acceptable in portraiture for public display, then they must have touched a responsive chord in those who commissioned such portraits and those who observed them. Imperial portraits such as those of Philip the Arab and Trajan Decius sought perhaps to express the ruler's sense of responsibility for his burden of power, and his paternal concern for the wellbeing of those under his control, but the stylistic devices of these portraits were employed with equal enthusiasm and intensity for men who appear not to have been of imperial rank. The formal similarities of a statue in Berlin[30] (figs. 43, 45) and of a head in the Terme Museum[31] (fig. 44) to the portrait of Trajan Decius in the Capitoline Museum (fig. 10) might reflect only a slavish following of fashion, but in works of such high quality it seems likelier that the dramatic emotional effects, even if inspired by publicly displayed imperial portraits, were sought for their own sake.

Both the private portraits (figs. 43, 44, 45) share with the portraits of Decius deep naso-labial furrows which begin well below the corners of the lips, then swing outward to form broad parentheses around the mouth, and eyebrows which are drawn sharply upward toward their inner corners, where vertical notches above the nose continue the rising pattern of movement. In both cases, this schema has been applied to physical types quite different from that of Decius: the Terme head (fig. 44) portrays a man with a short, triangular face which tapers from a broad cranium to a small and slightly retreating chin. Like Decius, the man has signs of physical fatigue, such as slack throat tendons, sagging cheeks, and deep

---

[29] Ranuccio Bianchi-Bandinelli, *Rome: the Late Empire*, trans. Peter Green (New York: Braziller, 1971), pp. 1-21; Kitzinger, *Byzantine Art in the Making*, 16-18.

[30] Berlin, Staatliche Museen, Antiken-Sammlung, inv. SK 1764. Marble statue, h. 1.65, right arm missing, head reattached to body. Tip of nose, chin, eyebrows and ears chipped. Entered Berlin museum from Schloss Klein-Glienecke in 1922. Published: Bergmann, *Studien*, pp. 169-173, pl. 50, fig. 2, and pl. 52, fig. 4; Jutta Meischner, "Eine römische Porträtstatue der Antiken-Sammlung," *Forschungen und Berichte der staatlichen Museen zu Berlin*, 18 (1977), 67-80, pls. 15-17.

[31] Rome, Museo Nazionale delle Terme, inv. 8652. Marble head, h. 0.28, set on modern bust. Tip of nose and ears restored. Published: Felletti-Maj, *Ritratti*, No. 296; Helbig⁴, No. 2189; *Museo Nazionale Romano: le sculture*, ed. Giuliano, I¹, pp. 12-13, No. 15 (Silvia Allegra Dayan).

pouches under the eyes which suggest not only sorrow but in this case, perhaps, weakness and indecisiveness. The Berlin statue (figs. 43, 45) on the other hand, which represents a public official presiding at some game or contest,[32] portrays a man of skinny and wiry physique, with a gaunt, angular face. Here too, there are furrows at the inner corners of the eyes which suggest weariness, though the skin is more taut. The hollowness of the cheeks and temples enables the sculptor to give the contours of the head a strong undulation comparable to the effect achieved in the Capitoline portrait of Decius (fig. 10), again culminating in the broad, swelling dome of the cranium, which here is widened further by the man's laurel crown.

The preservation of this head together with its body enables us to observe the sharp upward glance of the face, and its accompanying pattern of line and contour, as part of a complete composition. The body, though standing firmly on the right leg, makes a spiraling turn toward the left which culminates in the twist and lift of the head. The dryly carved, linear creases of his pallium, converging on the left shoulder, help to draw the viewer's attention upward toward the focus of interest in the raised face and upturned gaze. This statue bears comparison with a statue with the attributes of Mars (fig. 46),[33] the portrait face of which clearly represents Trajan Decius,[34] though in a slightly more flattering and less harsh manner than the fine Capitoline head. Here too, however, the facial line, complemented by the swelling curves of cheeks and cranium, form a strong upward sweep which culminates the spiraling movement of the body and lift of the head. Neither the statue of the magistrate (fig. 45), which is based on a conventional statuary type for philosophers,[35] nor the statue of Decius (fig. 46), which undoubtedly adapts a Greek sculptural prototype,[36] are entirely original compositions,

[32] Meischner, *Forschungen und Berichte*, 18 (1977), 68-72.

[33] Rome, Palazzo dei Conservatori, marble statue, h. 2.50. Restored: tip of nose, right eyebrow, parts of lips, most of crest of helmet, right leg (except for foot), right hand, left forearm, part of left foot. Provenance: a late Roman wall on the Esquiline. Principal publications: Bernoulli, *Römische Ikonographie*, II³, 153-154; Stuart-Jones, *Palazzo dei Conservatori*, p. 46, No. 4, pl. 7; Felletti-Maj, *Iconografia*, p. 188, No. 234, pl. 30, figs. 93, 94; Helbig⁴, No. 1494; Niemeyer, *Statuarischen Darstellung*, p. 113, pl. 48, fig. 2; Wegner, Bracker and Real, *Herrscherbild*, III³, 67.

[34] Helga von Heintze, in Helbig⁴, No. 1494, proposes that the statue represents Aemilius Aemilianus (brief claimant to power in 252), and rejects the identification as Decius. Wegner, in *Herrscherbild* III³, 67, agrees in rejecting the identification. I believe, however, that the resemblance of the face to that of the Capitoline Decius is striking, and that the differences can be accounted for in this case by somewhat greater idealization of the subject.

[35] Meischner, *Forschungen und Berichte*, 18 (1977), 68.

[36] Helga von Heintze, Helbig⁴, No. 1494, cites the Ares Borghese as the probable source of the figure. Niemeyer, *Statuarischen Darstellung*, p. 62, notes that this statue, like others which seem to follow the type of the Ares of Alkamenes, freely varies and adapts the stance of the prototype.

but in both cases it is significant that statues with such poses have been chosen for such portrait faces.

The spiraling upward turn of the neck is also shared by a portrait of a rather heavy, older man, in the Capitoline Museum,[37] (fig. 47), which is set on a modern bust of colored marble but which preserves enough of the original neck to show that the head was strongly lifted. The technical execution of this work differs slightly from the others in that the creases of the aging skin are shallower, the hair and beard executed with smaller and more delicate chisel incisions, but these details indicate only a difference of workshop practices; the Capitoline head (fig. 47) is probably the close contemporary of the Terme (fig. 44) and Berlin (figs. 43, 45) portraits.

Here, once again, the creases of the lower face, both alongside the nose and at the corners of the lips, form converging diagonals which complement the tensely unhappy arch of the eyebrows toward the root of the nose. Here, the upward movement of these lines is continued by a single long, vertical crease which runs up the center of the forehead, and from which the horizontal creases branch off in either direction. The two notches at the inner corners of the eyebrows also twist outward into horizontal creases. Thus, just as in the Capitoline portrait of Trajan Decius (fig. 10), the lines of the forehead spread outward, fountain-like, from the center, to create a resolution for the upward movement of the face. Here too, as in the portrait of Decius, the weary-looking pouches under the eyes and ripple of the flabby cheeks create a counter-tension to the upward thrust of the facial lines.

Effects of sudden and dramatic facial movement, then, were quite prevalent in portraiture datable to the 240's and early 250's. Not all such portraits, however, necessarily seek to convey a mood of anxiety or sorrow. A calmer and more meditative expression is achieved in the bust of a man,[38] who wears a Greek pallium and neatly groomed beard, slightly longer than that of most of his contemporaries, which presumably identify him as a philosopher (fig. 48). Once again, the furrows around the nose and mouth and at the inner corners of the eyes, together with the vertical creases which rise from the corners of the eyebrows at the root of

---

[37] Rome, Museo Capitolino, Stanza del Fauno, 2, inv. 356, formerly Sala delle Colombe, 61. Marble head, h. 0.32, set on modern bust of lumachella and alabaster. Restored: rims of both ears. Right cheek, tip of nose and chin chipped. Published: Stuart-Jones, *Museo Capitolino*, p. 162, No. 61, pl. 38; Schweitzer, *Zur Kunst der Antike*, II, 276, pl. 65, fig. 10; Helbig[4], No. 1401.

[38] Rome, Museo Capitolino, Sala delle Colombe, 12, marble bust, h. 0.79. Head, bust, inscription tablet, and foot preserved in one piece. Restored: tip of nose, rim of left ear, tip of scroll-tablet below bust and fingers of hand. Published: Stuart-Jones, *Museo Capitolino*, p. 86, No. 1, pl. 26; Paribeni, *Il Ritratto*, pl. 326; Helbig[4], No. 1258.

the nose, form a pattern of diagonals converging upward along a central axis. Here, however, the soft modeling of the facial furrows creates diffuse shadows, rather than strong lines, while the regular, graceful curves of the facial creases, together with the man's slender physique and delicate features, combine to express thoughtful preoccupation.

In addition to glancing upward, this man turns his head to the left, while the fine chisel strokes which represent the texture of his beard swirl in a series of S-curves toward the right, as though swung by a sudden movement. The twist of neck and torso, however, is graceful and restrained, the pattern of the swirling beard smooth and elegant. The leftward movement of the head is complemented by the gesture of the right arm, which is bent across the chest so that the hand emerges from the pallium, and appears to play absent-mindedly with the folds of the fabric. Hands can often be as expressive of human moods and personality as the face, and the better works of Roman portrait sculpture had exploited the possibilities of gesture since early republican times. This handsome bust is among the few well-preserved portraits of the period under study to demonstrate how good use could be made of both face and hands in the composition of a portrait bust.

Another aristocratic-looking and well-groomed man is represented in one of the finest surviving works from this era in the Palazzo dei Conservatori[39] (fig. 49). This portrait, far from looking sorrowful or anguished has a sly and rather enigmatic smile, though it is perhaps possible to detect a mood of suspicion or apprehension in the sharp glace to one side.[40] Here, all emphasis is on lateral movement: the eyes turn almost as far as it is physically possible for them to turn in their sockets, and the corners of the fleshy lips pull back sharply into the planes of the cheeks. As in the bust of the philosopher, (fig. 48), the short beard seems to have been ruffled by a sudden turn of the head, since the stubbly hair sweeps sharply to the left across the chin. The hair of the head is brushed in the opposite direction, toward the right temple, thus following the turn of the gaze and forming an opposition to the pattern of movement in the beard. The extraordinary care and skill with which the texture of all areas of hair has been executed, the tiny chisel strokes forming little ridges and

---

[39] Rome, Museo Nuovo del Palazzo dei Conservatori, inv. 2302. Head, made for insertion into statue, h. 0.35. Part of neck on left broken, left ear chipped, preservation otherwise good. Provenance: Rome, Via dei Fori Imperiali. Major publications: Mustilli, *Museo Mussolini*, p. 112, No. 27, pl. 69, figs. 272-274; Domenico Mustilli, *BullCom*, 61 (1933), 99-100, pls. 6, 7; Otto Brendel, *AA*, 48 (1933), 610, figs. 16, 17; Bovini, *MonAnt*, 39 (1943), 218, fig. 29; Helbig[4], No. 1753; George M. A. Hanfmann, *Roman Art* (Greenwich, Conn.: W. W. Norton & Co., 1964), p. 98.

[40] See Hanfmann, *Roman Art*, p. 98.

grooves of varying depths which catch the light at multiple angles, make these swirling patterns of movement especially conspicuous.

The sense of vibrant life conveyed by this work owes much also to the vigorous modeling, which gives every surface a restless, surging undulation. The forehead is corrugated by deep furrows, the cheekbones swell out strongly over the concave cheeks, and the middle of the mouth is thrust forward while the tapering corners slant sharply backward to tuck in under the corners of the moustache. This treatment of the cheeks and mouth bears comparison with a slightly earlier work, from the late Severan period (fig. 29), in the Capitoline Museum.[41] Conceivably we are dealing here with an artistic convention for the representation of an ethnic type,[42] but it is more likely that this type of modeling marks another experiment with expressive abstraction. The almost exaggerated projection and recession of features does not produce an organically modeled image of a human face; on the contrary, the modeling undermines the organic unity of the whole. On the other hand, the dramatic play of light and shadow over the surface captures quite successfully the effect of a mobile, living face.

This use of line, highlight, and shadow to suggest that the face has been captured in motion and will change its configuration a moment later, is perhaps the most significant factor which unites the five works just discussed. The portraits of Philip the Arab and Trajan Decius have aptly been described as "impressionistic,"[43] in that they capture a momentary visual impression and do so more through patterns of light than through organic representation of anatomic reality.

One of the latest examples of this "impressionistic" style is a magnificent portrait type which survives in four replicas,[44] (fig. 50), and which

[41] Rome, Museo Capitolino, Sala delle Colombe, 18. For references, see Chapter II, note 51.

[42] Von Heintze in Helbig⁴, No. 1753.

[43] Kaschnitz-Weinberg, *Die Antike*, 2 (1926), 41; H. P. L'Orange, "The Antique Origins of Medieval Portraiture," *Likeness and Icon*, 92-93.

[44] Three of the replicas were found at Ostia; the fourth, in the Vatican, may also have come from Ostia.

A. Ostia Antica, Museo, inv. 68, marble head, h. 0.34. Broken through neck. Lower half of nose, rim of left ear damaged, surface chipped and corroded. Provenance: Villa Aldobrandini, Ostia. Principal publications: Raissa Calza, "Ritratto Ostiense severiano," *Arti Figurative*, 1 (1945), 69-72, pl. 36, and "Sui Ritratti ostiense del supposto Plotino," *BdA*, 38 (1953), 203-210, figs. 1-2; H. P. L'Orange, "The Portrait of Plotinus," *CahArch*, 5 (1951), 15-30, figs. 1-2, and "Plotinus-Paul," *Likeness and Icon*, pp. 32-42, fig. 1; Gisela M. A. Richter, *Three Critical Periods in Greek Sculpture* (Oxford, 1951), p. 61, fig. 136, and *The Portraits of the Greeks* (London, 1965), III, 289, figs. 2056-2058; Helbig⁴, No. 3136.

B. Ostia Antica, inv. 436. Head in white marble, h. 0.30. Neck broken through diagonally, head broken into two halves and reconstructed. Lower half of nose is missing. Upper half of head found in 1940, in the Semita dei Cippi, Ostia, lower half in the Domus

seems to represent some well-known philosopher or man of letters. L'Orange has proposed to identify the subject as Plotinus, the neo-Platonic philosopher and friend of the emperor Gallienus.[45] This hypothesis is perfectly possible, though not definitely proveable, since the identification cannot be verified by coin profiles as in the case of imperial portraits. The discovery of one replica and part of another in a courtyard at Ostia which had been adapted during the third century as a lecture-hall[46] seems to indicate the man's reknown in intellectual circles, though the fact that all four replicas apparently come from Ostia suggests that his fame was limited to that city.

Whether or not the identification as Plotinus can be accepted, there is little doubt that L'Orange's dating to the Gallienic period is correct. The hair is worn in rather long locks combed forward from the back of the skull, a fashion which returned to favor during the reign of Gallienus, though the beard of one of the replicas, Ostia 436 (fig. 50) is still patterned with the isolated chisel strokes typical of the 240's and early 250's. This treatment of the texture of the beard, and the rather dry, angular chiseling of the locks of hair, indicate that the Severan date favored by some scholars[47] cannot be accepted. The dramatic facial expression shows by far the closest affinities to works like the Capitoline Trajan Decius (fig. 10), datable 249-251.

Little can be added to the excellent stylistic analysis of these four portraits by L'Orange. Suffice it to observe that here again the pattern of facial line and undulating contour has been used to create an effect of movement which strives upward. As in the Conservatori head (fig. 49), the gaunt cheeks and hollow temples have been deeply carved out, and the swelling cheekbones thrown into strong relief, giving the surface a

---

del Filsofo in 1951. Major publications: Calza, *BdA*, 38 (1953), 203-210, figs. 5, 6; L'Orange, *CahArch*, 5 (1951), 15-30, figs. 5-6, and "Plotinus-Paul," *Likeness and Icon*, pp. 32-42, figs. 3-4; Richter, *Portraits of the Greeks*, III, 289; Helbig⁴, No. 3137.

C. Ostia Antica, inv. 1386. Marble head, h. 0.28. Neck broken along line of beard. Tip of nose and part of rim of right ear broken away. Major publications: Calza, *BdA*, 38 (1953), 203-210, figs. 7, 8; L'Orange, "Plotinus-Paul," *Likeness and Icon*, pp. 32-42, figs. 5-6; Richter, *Portraits of the Greeks*, III, 289; Helbig⁴, No. 3135.

D. Vatican, Braccio Nuovo, inv. 2203. Marble head, probably from Ostia, h. 0.37. Restored: lower half of nose, both ears, chin and beard, neck, bust. Cracks in forehead and left eye. Surface cleaned in modern times. Principal publications: Amelung, *Die Skulpturen des vaticanischen Museums*, I, 28-29, No. 16, pl. 3; Calza, *Arti Figurative*, 1 (1945), 69-72, pl. 37, left, and *BdA*, 38 (1953), 203-210, figs. 3-4; L'Orange, *CahArch*, 5 (1951), 15-30, figs. 7-8, and "Plotinus-Paul," *Likeness and Icon*, 32-42, fig. 2; Helbig⁴, No. 412.

[45] L'Orange, *CahArch*, 5 (1951), 15-30, and "Plotinus-Paul," *Likeness and Icon*, pp. 32-42.

[46] Calza, *BdA*, 38 (1953), 203.

[47] Calza, *Arti Figurative*, 1 (1945), 70-71. This opinion was later rejected by her in *BdA*, 38 (1953), 203. See also Helbig⁴, Nos. 412 and 3135-3137 (von Heintze).

restless surge which culminates in the swelling dome of the skull. The schema of facial lines bears especially close comparison to the portraits of Decius (fig. 10), in particular the steep diagonals of the naso-labial folds and the fountain-like pattern of creases which spread from the root of the nose across the forehead. Here, the triangular shape of the long, gaunt face and the asymmetrical quiver of the flaring eyebrows make the upward thrust of the movement particularly effective.

This impressionistic treatment of the face, and the emotional intensity of the expressions which it is often used to convey, are somewhat less common in portraits of women than of men. The wife of Philip the Arab, Otacilia Severa, can probably be recognized in a portrait type[48] (fig. 51) which resembles that of her husband in its massive, rectangular shape, and its emphasis on the heavy, fleshy forms and features of the face. The unifying movement and pattern of line which characterized the Vatican bust of Philip (fig. 9) is, however, not present here, despite the fact that the unflattering frankness with which Otacilia's age is represented would make such a pattern of facial furrows eminently possible. Herennia Etruscilla, the wife of Trajan Decius, has yet to be identified with any certainty in surviving sculptural portraits, but the two most likely candidates—a head in the Terme museum[49] and a slightly over-life-sized

----

[48] Three replicas of the type exist:

A. Rome, Palazzo dei Conservatori, Braccio Nuovo, inv. 2765. Marble head, h. 0.26. Most of nose, part of left eyebrow, part of hair below right ear, broken away. Provenance: Via dei Fori Imperiali. Published: Domenico Mustilli, *BullCom*, 61 (1933), 109, No. 15, fig. 14; Meischner, "Frauenporträt," 114-116, No. 99, figs. 77-78; Felletti-Maj, *Iconografia*, p. 182, No. 228; Helbig⁴. No. 1632; Wiggers and Wegner, *Herrscherbild*, III¹, 213; Bergmann, *Studien*, p. 39, pl. 7, figs. 5-6; Wegner, Bracker and Real, *Herrscherbild*, III³, 57, 61, pl. 25.

B. Florence, Uffizi, inv. 1914.271. Head set on a bust to which it may not belong, marble, h. of head and neck 0.29, in toto, 0.61. Restored: nose, chips of drapery. Cleaned with acid. Published: Bernoulli, *Römische Ikonographie*, II³, 233; Mansuelli, *Galleria degli Uffizi*, II, 116, No. 146; Meischner, "Frauenporträt," 114-116, No. 100; Felletti-Maj, *Iconografia*, p. 239, No. 325; Wiggers and Wegner, *Herrscherbild*, III¹, 206-207; Wegner, *Festschrift Kleiner*, p. 124, pl. 26, fig. 2; Bergmann, *Studien*, p. 39; Wegner, Bracker and Real, *Herrscherbild*, III³, 57, 60-61.

C. Petworth, Leconfield Collection, marble head, made for insertion into a statue, h. 0.52. Restored: nose, part of lips, foot of bust. Surface polished and reworked. Major publications: Frederik Poulsen, *Greek and Roman Portraits in English Country Houses* (Oxford: Clarendon Press, 1923), p. 105 and note 5; Meischner, "Frauenporträt," pp. 114-116, No. 98, figs. 75-76; Wiggers and Wegner, *Herrscherbild*, III¹, 211; Bergmann, *Studien*, pp. 39-41; Wegner, Bracker, and Real, *Herrscherbild*, III³, 57, 60-61.

[49] Rome, Museo Nazionale delle Terme, inv. 121016, marble head, h. 0.30. No restorations. Chips missing from diadem and ears; chin battered. Provenance: St. Maria, 2 km. from Via Appia Nuova, found in 1934. Published: G. Annibaldi, *NSc,*, 1935, pp. 88-90, pl. 8; Felletti-Maj, *Ritratti*, p. 144, No. 287, and *Iconografia*, pp. 193-194, No. 245, pl. 31, fig. 100, and pl. 32, fig. 99; Bergmann, *Studien*, pp. 43-44; Wegner, Bracker, and Real, *Herrscherbild*, III³, 78-81, pl. 33.

head in the British Museum[50] (fig. 64)—are both characterized by smooth skin areas and composed, if rather dour, facial expressions. The British Museum head, indeed, belongs more to the abstract style to be discussed in the next chapter, with the immobile expression and wide-eyed, hypnotic stare which frequently characterize such works; it thus differs quite considerably from the style of the Capitoline portrait of Decius.

Some private portraits of women do exist, however, which use formal devices comparable to those of the "impressionistic" male images, and achieve comparable emotional poignancy. An excellent though unfortunately somewhat weathered portrait of an old woman in Berlin[51] (fig. 52), whose coiffure resembles that of Tranquillina, and therefore indicates a date in the 240's, bears close comparison to the portrait of Philip the Arab in its use of a pattern of converging diagonals. Here again, the troubled contraction of the eyebrows, which arch toward their inner corners, is emphasized by the repetition of the rising diagonal in the orbital folds of the deeply hooded eyes. The furrows around the nose and mouth, which are softly modeled but nonetheless deeply carved, again form rising lines the movement of which is continued by the notches above the root of the nose. Here, as in the unflatteringly realistic male portraits of the same period, the artist has been at pains to represent details such as the lumpy, irregular shape of the thick nose and fleshy cheeks. The pouches under the eyes, and the cheeks which obey the law of gravity, once again produce an acute impression of fatigue, since they pull against the upward movement of the raised eyes and accompanying pattern of facial line.

A superb series of small relief portraits of women, either on sarcophagi or on fragments presumably from sarcophagi, employ similar formal devices. Two strigilated bathtub-sarcophagi, decorated at either end with lions and in the center with a bust of the deceased, provide the most complete examples of such monuments. Though one of them was found in Tarragona, Spain[52] (fig. 53), it bears such close resemblance to the one in

---

[50] London, British Museum, cat. no. 1924. Head in marble, h. 0.38. Tip of nose restored. Published: Smith, *Catalogue, British Museum*, III, 69, No. 1924, pl. XVII; Bernoulli, *Römische Ikonographie*, II³, 156; Felletti-Maj, *Iconografia*, p. 194, No. 246, pl. 32, fig. 101; Bergmann, *Studien*, pp. 43-44; Wegner, Bracker, and Real, *Herrscherbild*, III³, p. 80.

[51] Berlin, Staatliche Museen, Antiken-Sammlung, R111, inv. 447. Head in coarse-grained gray marble, h. 0.245. Restored: tip of nose. Surface weathered. Major publications: Blümel, *Römische Bildnisse*, p. 46, No. R111, pl. 72; Bergmann, *Studien*, p. 93, pl. 26, fig. 3.

[52] Tarragona, Spain, Museo de la Necropolis Romanochristiana, strigilated marble sarcophagus, bathtub-shaped, decorated at ends with groups of lions killing fawns and at center with half-body bust of the deceased, set against a curtain. Cover lost. Length 2.05, height 0.65. Published: Frederik Poulsen, *Sculptures antiques des musées de province espagnols*

the Terme museum[53] as to suggest that the two are products of the same workshop, presumably based in Rome, though its products might be exported to Spain. Fragmentary reliefs in Ostia[54] (fig. 54) and Berlin[55] (fig. 55) closely resemble the portraits on the lion sarcophagi, and can conceivably be attributed to the same atelier.

The impression of individuality and sensitive observation of the subject's features which one feels when viewing each of these portraits is belied by their striking physical similarity to each other. Despite the skill with which the formula has been applied in each case, the faces seem to conform to stereotyped conventions for representation of older women. All but one of the portraits have gaunt faces with hollow cheeks; only the Terme sarcophagus differs in representing a plump woman, and even in her case the slackness of the flesh of her cheeks throws the cheekbones into relief. In every case, moreover, the eyes are large, rounded, and strongly three-dimensional, with heavy upper lids. Thus, despite the small scale of the portraits, the play of light and shadow over the strong rise and fall of the surfaces is as vivid as that in many male portraits of the impressionistic style. Here again, there are opposed patterns of upward and downward movement: the upturned eyes and arched brows are complemented by the high arches of the foreheads and, as usual, by the diagonals of the facial furrows, while the pouches under the eyes and rippling cheeks obey the law of gravity. And in these cases, again, the resulting effect of fatigue lends poignancy to the anxious and somewhat sorrowful tension expressed by the direction of the gaze.

As in male portraits, interest in capturing the effect of a fleeting facial movement did not necessarily entail the use of dramatically sad or troubled expressions. A fine portrait in Copenhagen of a middle-aged

(Copenhagen, 1933), p. 64, pl. 68, fig. 107; Giorgio Gullini, "Recenti scoperte di sculture tardo-romane nei dintorni di Roma," *BdA*, 34 (1949), 56; J. Melida, *Arqueologia Espagnol* (Barcelona, 1929).

[53] Rome, Museo Nazionale delle Terme, inv. 124745, marble bathtub-shaped sarcophagus, strigilated, decorated at ends with groups of lions killing fawns and at the center by a half-body bust of the deceased. Lid has form of gabled roof with antefixes. Length 1.70, width 0.60, height 0.63. Height of cover 0.35. Provenance: Via Praenestina, near Rome, between Acqua Bulliante and Tor dei Schiavi, 1946. Published: Gullini, *BdA*, 34 (1949), 56-59; Salvatore Aurigemma, *The Baths of Diocletian and the Museo Nazionale Romano*, 4th ed. (Rome: Istituto Poligrafico dello Stato, 1963), p. 15, No. 2; *EAA*, VII (1966), s.v. "Sarcofago," 28, fig. 41 (Friedrich Matz).

[54] Ostia Antica, Museo, inv. 213-A. Fragment of a sarcophagus: left-hand short end and corner figure of front preserved. Of portrait figure itself, tip of nose chipped, preservation otherwise good. Precise measurements unavailable; to my knowledge, the piece is not published.

[55] Berlin, Staatliche Museen, Antiken-Sammlung, cat. R110. Small head, broken from a relief, in marble, h. 0.13. Nose restored. Published: Blümel, *Römische Bildnisse*, p. 46, No. R110, p. 67; Bergmann, *Studien*, p. 93, pl. 26, fig. 4.

woman[56] (fig. 56) resembles the magnificent male portrait in the Palazzo dei Conservatori (fig. 49) in its quizzical, sidelong glance and wry smile. This female portrait, datable by its coiffure to the 240's, is perhaps not a masterpiece on the level of the Conservatori head, but it shares with that work an emphasis on a strong lateral movement, and a use of emphatically three-dimensional modeling of certain features. Here, it is the prominent eyebrow-ridges, deeply carved eye-sockets, and large, rounded eyeballs which create the most dramatic contrasts of highlight and shadow, while the asymmetrical modeling of the sagging cheeks contributes a more subtle play of light over the rippling surfaces of the flesh. The crimped waves of the coiffure here have the effect of forming a jagged, lively pattern of line around the face and thus increasing the overall impression of animation.

The richness and diversity of the veristic portraits from the fourth and fifth decades of the third century defy simple summation. One common trend can be observed in the examples discussed here, however: the fact that an interest in realistic detail seems to have been inspired not only by a desire to portray the subjects without idealization, but by the possibilities presented by facial line and asymmetry for emotional expression. Furrows which interrupt the skin with dark lines of shadow, strong projections and deep hollows which give complexity to the surfaces of the face, are increasingly used to lend the features an impression of lifelike movement. The trend, already well established in the portraits of Caracalla, of connecting this play of light and shadow into a tightly unified pattern is developed with great sophistication during these years. A variety of patterns and formulae, conveying emotions which range from wry amusement to sadness, and from serious meditation to dramatically tense anxiety, appears in mid-third century portraiture.

The best of these works make a highly convincing impression of a sudden and vivid flash of emotion, revealing of individual personality, yet these effects are achieved through thoroughly calculated means. Another trend was developing in portrait sculpture of the 240's which allowed the pattern behind the facial expression to become more obvious, and which tended to freeze features and lines into a geometric abstraction. These portraits remain to be discussed in the following chapter.

---

[56] Copenhagen, Ny Carlsberg Glyptotek, cat. 752. Marble head, h. 0.44. Nose formerly restored, restoration now removed. Published: Felletti-Maj, *Iconografia*, p. 165, No. 188; Meischner, "Frauenporträt," p. 150, No. 66; Wiggers and Wegner, *Herrscherbild*, III[1], 123; V. Poulsen, *Les Portraits romains*, II, 185, No. 192.

CHAPTER FOUR

# THE EMERGENCE OF AN ABSTRACT STYLE

The impressionistic style of sculpture, particularly as represented in portraits datable to the 240's and 250's, involved an occasional willingness to sacrifice strict anatomic accuracy for the sake of an overall pattern and an emotional effect. The portrait of Trajan Decius, for example, showed deep undercutting of facial furrows and an almost exaggerated emphasis on the concavity of the temples, stylistic features which tended slightly to undermine the organic structure of the head. This same tendency could be observed clearly in the strong projections and recessions of forms in the fine Museo Nuovo head (fig. 49). The more rigidly geometric style which coexists with this impressionism in the fourth and fifth decades of the third century should therefore, perhaps, be regarded as a different manifestation of the same phenomenon: a growing indifference toward faithful representation of a human being's physical appearance, together with increasing interest in conveying emotional or spiritual qualities.

As discussed in the first chapter, the earliest datable portraits which make use of a noticeably abstract style are the relief faces on the sarcophagus of Balbinus (figs. 5, 35), and the portraits of Gordian III (figs. 7, 8) and his wife Tranquillina (fig. 57). The former are particularly significant in that they appear on the same monument with life-sized portraits in a more organic style, thus clearly demonstrating that within a single atelier, artists of high technical competence were working in both manners. The likenesses of Gordian (figs. 7, 8) closely resemble the relief portraits of the sarcophagus of Balbinus (figs. 5, 35), particularly in the shape of the long, narrow eyes, the pattern used to convey a frowning facial expression, and the linear incision of detail, but differ in their more radical simplification of the volumes of the skull. Those of his wife, Furia Sabina Tranquillina,[1] (fig. 57), closely resemble Gordian's portraits in the use of a triangular form for the face, the smooth and simple curvature of forehead and cheeks, and the deeply incised grooves which outline and emphasize a few significant features such as the eyes and mouth. These

---

[1] The portrait type accepted here as Tranquillina has been identified by some scholars as Otacilia Severa, wife of Philip the Arab. For recent and in my opinion conclusive arguments in favor of the identification as the wife of Gordian III, see Bergmann, *Studien*, pp. 39-41; Wegner, Bracker, and Real, *Herrscherbild*, III[3], 51-52 and 57-58.

traits can be clearly observed in the British Museum bust (fig. 57) illustrated here.[2]

The facial expression of Tranquillina's portraits differs from that of her husband: she does not frown, but has a dreamy, downcast gaze emphasized by the heaviness of her eyelids. The orbital folds and the eyebrows above them have a very regular, almost semicircular arch and the small mouth is relaxed. Nonetheless, these female portraits share with those of Gordian the small, dipping point at the center of the upper lip, and the strikingly regular symmetry of the features. A comparison of photographs of the portraits of Gordian (figs. 7, 8) and of Tranquillina (fig. 57) will reveal that the types were probably designed as pendants, since they share so many formal devices, and furthermore that they seem to reflect the personality of the same sculptor. The reappearance of many of these same formal devices in the first portrait type of Gallienus (fig. 12) suggests that it too is the work of the same portraitist.

Though Roman sculpture of all sorts appears to have been a matter of workshop production in which gifted individual artists were not accorded any great status or recognition, it is important to bear in mind that some masters must have existed whose contributions were to some extent influential on the sculptural practices of their times. It is, of course, true that imperial portraits were copied for dissemination around the empire by many artisans of varying styles and abilities, with the result that copies of a single portrait type may vary considerably in details such as the treatment of the hair. Some portraits of Gordian III, for instance, represent the hair in the old-fashioned "*a penna*" technique, with each lock carefully outlined, while others use the sketchier pattern of isolated chisel strokes scattered over the surface of the scalp, and still others use a mixture of techniques.[3] On the other hand, it is reasonable to assume that each official prototype, before it was handed over to be widely copied, had to be created by one artist or, at most, by a small group of portraitists.

Whenever it is possible to trace common elements in imperial portraits which suggest an artist's idiom, as is the case with the portraits of Gordian III, Tranquillina, and the young Gallienus, the contributions of that individual should not be altogether overlooked. Such artists were not the single-handed creators of artistic trends: their work was the product of tradition, training, and major political pressures which dictated many of

---

[2] London, British Museum, cat. 1923, marble head set on modern bust, h. 0.415. Published: Smith, *Catalogue*, III, 169, No. 1923; Bernoulli, *Römische Ikonographie*, II³, 138-139, 145, pl. 43a, b; Bovini, *MonAnt*, 39 (1943), 240, fig. 46; Felletti-Maj, *Iconografia*, p. 179, No. 217; Bergmann, *Studien*, p. 39, pl. 7, figs. 3-4; Wegner, Bracker and Real, *Herrscherbild*, III³, 52, 54.

[3] See Bracker, "Bestimmung der Bildnisse Gordians III," pp. 52-55.

their choices. However, the artistic movements in which they participated were not purely impersonal and mechanical occurrences, but the results of the acts of individual men using, adapting, and altering the sculptural traditions which they had learned from other men.[4]

With these considerations in mind, then, let us examine the significance of the style of the portraits of Gordian, Tranquillina, and Gallienus. In the portraits of all three of these imperial figures (see figs. 7, 8, 12, 57), skin surfaces tend to be smooth and regular—a fact not necessarily due to the youth of the subjects, since Gallienus was old enough to wear a mature beard. These surfaces are interrupted by only a few significant features, which tend to be treated as isolated patterns, and to be strongly outlined or emphasized by linear means. The eyes, in all three, for example, are surrounded above and below by deeply cut creases, the eyebrows form sharp and angular ridges where the surfaces of forehead and eyesocket intersect, and the shapes of the mouths are emphasized by a deeply cut groove between the lips. The male portraits, which share a slight contraction of the forehead and pursing of the lips, display a strikingly similar pattern in the eye area: the eyebrows of both Gordian (figs. 7, 8) and the young Gallienus (fig. 12) flare toward their outer corners and slope downward toward the nose, where vertical notches rise at abrupt angles above their inner corners, and the long, almond-shaped eyes have almost the same form in the portraits of both men. The portraits of all three individuals also share a tendency to reduce the head to simple geometric forms: the terms "triangular" and "prismatic" are not mere conveniences to help us describe the shape of a human face, but striking formal aspects of these portraits as works of art.

Linearity, symmetry, a tendency toward geometric patterning both of the overall form and of individual features—all these elements were to become increasingly prominent in the sculptural style of the later third century. To what extent the "Gordian master" was an innovator of these techniques, to what extent merely one member of a widespread artistic movement, is difficult to assess, but the prominent visibility and broad distribution of his work may well have played some role in the gradual acceptance of the more abstract style. The later portrait type of Gallienus, datable after the death of his father in 260, of which perhaps the best copy is the head in the Terme museum[5] (fig. 13) differs considerably from his

---

[4] See Otto Brendel, *Prolegomena to the Study of Roman Art* (New Haven and London: Yale University Press, 1979), pp. 37, 112, 125. Originally published as "Prolegomena to a Book on Roman Art," *MAAR*, 1953.

[5] Rome, Museo Nazionale delle Terme, inv. 644. Marble head, h. 0.38, made for insertion into a statue. Tip of nose and part of hair over forehead broken off. Provenance: Roman forum, house of the Vestals. Principal publications: Alföldi, *25 Jahre römisch-germanische Kommision*, p. 40, pl. 2, fig. 2; L'Orange, *Studien*, p. 5, fig. 11; Bovini,

earlier portraits, and is almost certainly the work of a different portraitist. The face is much broader and flatter, the hair a longer and fuller mane which tumbles outward from a central part in a manner reminiscent of the images of Alexander the Great.[6] Yet many of the formal devices are continuations of those of his earlier portrait: the sharp ridge of the jawline, again, has a half-hexagonal shape, within which the line of the beard forms a neat, regular trefoil around the cheekbones and mouth. The features tend to be strongly outlined and isolated from one another in the broad, neutral surfaces of the face, and the frowning facial expression reduced to a stiff, symmetrical pattern of line.

The earlier and later portraits of Gallienus also share a very hard and dry treatment of the hair and beard, in which locks are represented as angular ridges rather than softly rounded volumes. The later Terme head (fig. 13) demonstrates a more complete commitment to the use of the hair as a decorative pattern in the stiff, mannered arrangement of the hook-shaped curls around the face. The hair, and the other features of the later type, thus show a more radical use of abstraction, but one developing logically from the formal devices of the earlier portrait.

Unfortunately, aside from Gallienus, few other imperial figures from the 250's and 260's can be recognized with any certainty in extant portrait sculpture, though a few tentatively identified works can profitably be discussed here. The iconography of Trebonianus Gallus (A.D. 251-253), as mentioned in the first chapter, has yet to be satisfactorily solved, but a colossal bronze statue in New York (fig. 11), because of its dimensions, has perhaps the best claim of the various candidates. This work follows the tradition of Caracalla's portraits in its use of a scowling expression which causes the facial musculature to knot and bulge, but resembles the portraits of Gordian III in its reduction of that scowl to a stiffly symmetrical pattern of line. The compact ovoid of the skull and firmly closed oval contour of the face also demonstrate the trend toward geometric simplification of forms seen in Gordian's and Gallienus's portraits.

Clearly identifiable portrait types are also lacking for the women of the family of Gallienus. However, a recently discovered statue of a seated woman with the attributes of Venus[7] (figs. 58, 59) might well represent

---

MemLinc, 7th ser., 2 (1941), 136-137, No. 1, fig. 7, pl. 1, and MonAnt., 39 (1943), 226, figs. 33, 34; Felletti-Maj, Ritratti, pp. 152-153, No. 304, and Iconografia, p. 225, No. 293, pl. 42, fig. 138; Helbig[4], No 2315; Fittschen, JdI, 84 (1969), 217, fig. 32, and RömMitt, 77 (1970), pl. 65, fig. 2; Bergmann, Studien, pp. 51-54; Wegner, Bracker and Real, Herrscherbild, III[3], 108-110, 117-118, pl. 45; Museo Nazionale Romano: le sculture, ed. Giuliano, pp. 296-297, No. 181 (Silvia Allegra Dayan).

[6] Breckenridge, Likeness, p. 214, and Aufstieg und Niedergang, II.12.2, 507-508.

[7] Rome, Museo Nazionale della Villa Giulia, provisional deposit, formerly in Civitavecchia, Museo Nazionale. Statue of a woman accompanied by a small figure of

Salonina, the wife of Gallienus, though until more replicas of this portrait type are discovered, this proposed identification can be no more than tentative. Evidence in favor of the identification includes the coiffure, a variant of the *Scheitelzopf* in which the hair is not braided but drawn up in soft, twisted coils to form a broad coronet at the top of the cranium. The empress whose coins most closely approximate this arrangement is Salonina,[8] though it should be noted that in these coins, the coil of hair seems to be drawn more vertically up the back of the skull, rather than wrapped in an oval around the cranium, as in the statue. Salonina's numismatic portraits also share with this sculpture the large, strongly arched eyes, fleshy lower face, and square jaw line.

The explicit identification of the subject with a goddess does not necessarily indicate imperial rank, since private funerary portraits are frequently endowed with divine attributes. The statue, however, has some other regalia associated with imperial status, such as the cutting of the coiffure for an attachment in metal which was probably a crescent-shaped diadem.[9] This attribute routinely appears on coin-profiles of third-century *Augustae*, though again it is not the exclusive prerogative of empresses.[10] The balance of evidence, then, though far from conclusive, suggests that this woman was of imperial rank, and perhaps that she can be identified as Salonina or some woman of the family of Gallienus.

The statue represents a woman seated on a backless chair, her left foot advanced and her right drawn back under the stool. Her right forearm lies in her lap, but her left arm is raised slightly and bent upward at the elbow, in a gesture now difficult to interpret, since the hand does not seem to have touched the cithara which is offered to her by the Eros at her side.[11] The torso spirals slightly in the direction of the raised arm, and the

---

Eros. Marble, height of statue 1.25, of head, 0.25, of face (chin to hairline), 0.16. Length at base: 0.76. Missing: both hands and wrists of the woman, the arms and legs of the putto, part of the cithara. The head is broken off and reset, but clearly belongs to the statue; likewise, the figure of the putto and the right half of the cithara. Tip of nose broken, mouth area battered. Coiffure at top of head shows cutting for an attachment, probably a crescent diadem. Found accidentally in 1962, in Cazzonella, near Tarquinia, amid remains of what appears to be a villa. Published: *Nuove Scoperte e acquisizioni nell'Etruria Meridionale*, exh. cat. ed. Mario Moretti (Rome, 1975), pp. 254-258, No. 7, pls. 76-77.

[8] Richard Delbrueck, *Die Münzbildnisse von Maximinus bis Carinus*, Vol. III, part 2 of *Das römische Herrscherbild*, ed. Max Wegner (Berlin: Mann, 1940), 99, pl. 12, fig. 12; pl. 13, figs. 18, 25; pl. 14, figs. 30, 33, 35, 38; pl. 15, fig. 52; pl. 16, figs. 58, 63; pl. 18, fig. 88. See also Wessel, *AA*, 61 (1946-47), 65-70. I am indebted to a seminar paper given by Margaret Rhea, and to Professor Richard Brilliant, for pointing out the evidence in favor of a late Gallienic date for this statue. Brilliant believes that the subject may be Mariniana, the mother of Gallienus.

[9] *Nuove Scoperte*, ed. Moretti, p. 256.

[10] Bergmann, *Studien*, p. 43.

[11] *Nuove Scoperte*, ed. Moretti, p. 255.

head is turned more strongly upward toward the left. The body thus forms a classic contraposto, even though the figure is seated: the right shoulder is relaxed and the left hip lowered, the right arm and left leg extending forward in a relaxed position while the right leg and left arm and shoulder are drawn backward and flexed. Both in its pose and in the skillful rendering of the *chiton* which the woman wears, the statue is strongly reminiscent of fifth-century Greek prototypes, particularly those of the Pheidian school.[12] The statue does not reproduce any known classical type exactly, but does share with the reclining female figures of the Parthenon pediments both the relaxed yet dignified pose and the detail of a strap slipping provocatively (but not immodestly) off one shoulder.

This skillful imitation of fifth-century models is typical of the philhellenism and nostalgia for the classical past which dominated the tastes of the emperor Gallienus, and which have given rise to the term "Gallienic renaissance."[13] The portrait head (fig. 58), on the contrary, is strongly abstract, sharing with the later portrait of Gallienus a tendency to broaden and flatten the face, to arrange all the features in a single plane, and to treat them more as decorative than as organic elements. The lower face, particularly the fleshy cheeks and small mouth, are modeled with great sensitivity, but the large, lunette-shaped eyes and the high, regular arches of the eyebrows show a very stiffly patterned treatment. As with the later portraits of Gallienus, the origins of this portrait's style can be traced in the more subtly abstract works of the 240's and 250's. The portraits of Tranquillina (fig. 57), for example, bear striking resemblances to the face of the Tarquinia statue,[14] particularly in the regular, semicircular arches of the eyebrows and orbital folds, and the use of deeply incised grooves to outline the upper curves of the eyeballs. The Gallienic statue has thick, puffy eyelids, like the portraits of Tranquillina, but they lack the dreamy, sensuous droop of the eyelids in the earlier work. Instead, the eyes are widely opened in an almost hypnotic stare which suggests other-worldliness.

To what extent, and how rapidly, was the abstract style of Gordian's and Gallienus's portraits accepted in non-imperial art? Private portraits datable to the time of Gordian III which seem to reflect the influence of his portraits and those of Tranquillina are comparatively scarce, though they do exist. As is frequently the case, it would seem that private patrons

---

[12] Ibid., pp. 255-256.

[13] For a fuller discussion of this phenomenon, see Alföldi, *25 Jahre römisch-germanische Kommission*, pp. 21-23, 44-45; Mathew, *JRS*, 33 (1943), 65-70; Schweitzer, *Zur Kunst der Antike*, II, 272.

[14] I am indebted for this observation to Prof. Richard Brilliant.

were slightly more conservative, and the artists employed by them more cautious than artists in the service of imperial patrons in adopting stylistic innovations. By the time of Gallienus, an elegant and inorganically decorative approach to the human face is as widely represented in private as in imperial portraiture.

One work, a slightly under-life-sized bust in the Ny Carlsberg Glyptotek, seems to show a very direct imitation of the portraits of Gordian (fig. 60).[15] This portrait is comparatively well-preserved, since the head survives in one piece with a bust which includes the upper chest and shoulder-caps, and is represented nude. The slim neck and sloping shoulders suggest a light physique. The strong emphasis on the triangular shape of the face, the flaring eyebrows which plunge sharply toward the nose, and the almond form of the narrow, puffy-lidded eyes all resemble the formal elements of Gordian's portraits very strongly, despite the fact that the subject is a more mature man. The scowling X-pattern of Caracalla's portraits can readily be recognized here in the tensed forehead and deep naso-labial folds, but this portrait, like those of Gordian, demonstrates a tendency to freeze that pattern into strict symmetry, allowing its geometric structure to become more obvious. There is a tendency to regularize and repeat patterns: the V-shaped hairline and the diagonal furrows which traverse the forehead (but, significantly, do *not* set off the swelling form of the forehead muscle), form parallel chevrons, while the more curvilinear crease across the skin of the forehead neatly parallels the flare and dip of the tensed eyebrows. Likewise, the hard, angularly cut crease under the lower lip forms a regular arc as it outlines and nearly isolates the knobby chin.

A detail which confirms the dating of this very patterned and abstract work to Gordian III's time is the treatment of hair and beard as purely linear designs, without volume, engraved in isolated chisel strokes, which are scattered on the scalp and cheeks. The bust can thus be dated in the 240's, prior to the return to fashion of longer hair and beards which accompanied the general trends toward abstraction at the time of Gallienus. Two other works, both in the Capitoline museum, which make use of the same technique for representation of the hair (figs. 61[16]

---

[15] Copenhagen, Ny Carlsberg Glyptotek, cat. 761, inv. 827. Bust in marble, showing chest and shoulders, h. 0.38. Tip of nose chipped and forehead battered, front cleaned but back still covered with calcareous accretions. No restorations. Published: F. Poulsen, *Catalogue*, No. 761, and *English Country Houses*, p. 111; Vagn Poulsen, *Les Portraits romains*, II, 178, No. 181, pls. 293-294, with full literature.

[16] Rome, Capitoline Museum, Stanza Terrena a Destra I, No. 21, formerly in Sala delle Colombe, No. 4. Marble head and neck, h. 0.54, of head alone 0.28. Restored: tip of nose, ears, bust and foot. Published: Stuart-Jones, *Museo Capitolino*, pp. 139-140, No. 4, pl. 36, No. 4.

and 62[17]) demonstrate a similar use of some of the devices of Gordian III's portraits, though because these heads are not so slavishly dependent on imperial models, they both achieve greater immediacy and convey a more vivid sense of the personality of their subjects.

These two Capitoline portraits share with the portraits of Gordian a tendency to reduce the volumes of the head to simple and severely geometric forms: the cheeks, for example, form almost flat planes which converge toward the front of the face and intersect the area under the chin in hard angles. The bulge of the cheekbones is almost completely suppressed. The foreheads too are planar: they cant outward, but the brow muscle has no rounded bulge in relief. The spareness of detail, and the use of dark, deeply cut grooves to call attention to a few significant features—eyes, lips, and creases of the forehead—demonstrate close technical relationships with the portraits of Gordian (figs. 7, 8) and Tranquillina (fig. 57). It is in the facial expressions, wry sidelong smiles rather than energetic frowns, that the sculptures display their independence of contemporary public portraiture.

Several details of execution suggest that these two works can perhaps be attributed to the same artist, or at least to the same atelier. The beards in both cases are sketched as a purely linear design on the "skin," but the beards, unlike the hair, are not represented by small, isolated chisel strokes. Instead, the engraved design outlines small, pointed locks with graceful curves. This pattern, which is far less common than the more perfunctorily executed stubble of the hair, seems to suggest a personal idiom, as do the characteristic almond forms of the eyes, and certain aspects of overall structure—most notably the prominent brow ridge and retreating, almost nonexistent cheekbones. All these similarities could conceivably be coincidental results of physical similarities between the subjects of the portraits, but since both works clearly make use of some abstraction and simplification of natural forms, it is perhaps safe to interpret the treatment of eyes, eyebrows and cheeks as stylistic features.

Many of these stylistic elements can also be observed in two earlier works discussed previously: a late-Severan bust in Munich (fig. 19)[18] and a head in the Fogg Art Museum (fig. 20),[19] which can therefore be more tentatively attributed to the same master. Within this series of four

---

[17] Rome, Museo Capitolino, Stanza degli Imperatori, No. 49, marble head on modern bust of lumachella and white alabaster. H. 0.79, of ancient part 0.30. Restored: nose, rims of ears, connecting piece between neck and bust. Weathered. Published: Stuart-Jones, *Museo Capitolino*, p. 209, No. 65, pl. 50; Bernoulli, *Römische Ikonographie*, II[3], 123; Paribeni, *Il Ritratto*, p. 319; Felletti-Maj, *Iconografia*, pp. 133-134, No. 155; Helbig[4], No. 1317.

[18] See Chapter II, note 23.

[19] See Chapter II, note 24.

works, changes can be traced which provide an intriguing example of the development of an artist's style in response to the trends of his time. The Munich bust (fig. 19) showed the influence of the portraits of Caracalla in its bombastic, scowling facial expression. Emotion was conveyed through a complex pattern of line, furrow, and undulation of surfaces. The Fogg head (fig. 20) was quieter both in mood and in style. The hair had lower relief and was arranged in a more regular pattern of locks, which swirled inward toward the center; the forehead, though still heavy, and prominent, was not contracted or corrugated with creases, and the mouth, with its ironic twist to one side, suggested a less intense mood. Yet with the wry smile of this portrait, the artist came closer than he had before to capturing a lifelike moment of emotion.[20]

The head in the Stanza Terrena a Destra (fig. 61) of the Capitoline Museum is very close in style, format and execution to the Fogg head, (fig. 20), differing primarily in the reduction of the hair on the scalp to a pattern of single chisel strokes. The full lips, with the quirk to one side, accompanied by a sharp turn of the eyes, reveal an almost identical pattern applied to both faces, though the Capitoline head simplifies the formula, eliminating all but the most essential details. Finally, in the head in the Stanza degli Imperatori (fig. 62), the sidelong glance and asymmetrical smile are reduced almost to a linear pattern superimposed onto a geometric solid. Yet paradoxically, the features, as they stand out vividly from this austerely executed face, capture more successfully than any of the other three a revealing moment of emotion. The contraction of the brows, now reduced to a pattern of a few lines, the sharp gaze and enigmatic twitch of the mouth, express a mood which could be interpreted as humorous, or as troubled, or as both. However one interprets the expression, it conveys well a sense of individuality.

If the attribution of these four works to the same sculptor, or at least the same workshop, is correct, the development which they reveal casts an interesting light on the increasing taste for abstraction in the 230's and 240's. The Munich bust (fig. 19) shows a great wealth of anatomically accurate detail; clearly, this artist understood the structure of the human head. His work, however, shows a progressive abandonment of all details superfluous to the portrayal of an emotion. The artist seems to give priority to vividness of facial expression, an effect which, he has discovered, can be more effectively achieved when the pattern of features is simplified to a few telling lines.

Many of the same trends can be observed in female portraiture datable to about the time of Gordian III. Here, as with male portraits, two

---

[20] Hanfmann, *Latomus*, 11 (1952), 207-208.

stylistic currents seem to have coexisted, the one more naturalistic, the other gradually beginning to exploit the possibilities of abstraction. The female portraits discussed in the previous chapter which shared the fluid, subtle modeling of the life-sized portrait of the wife of Balbinus, and those which reflected the dramatically anxious or sad facial expressions of their male contemporaries, represent the former trend. But other female portraits which wear coiffures datable prior to the Gallienic period already show a stiffening of the feature into hard, symmetrical patterns, and a use of line to emphasize detail.

A bust in the Biblioteca Marciana in Venice[21] (fig. 63) and a head in the British Museum[22] (fig. 64) illustrate these trends. Both these portraits show the hair worn in a flat, oval chignon at the base of the skull, a fashion most popular at the time of Julia Mammaea, but still in evidence in the coin portraits of Herennia Etruscilla[23] as late as 251. After Etruscilla, however, the coiffure does not appear again on the coins of empresses, and seems to have definitely passed from fashion, a fact which indicates that these two portraits should be dated not later than the 240's. The waves of hair around the foreheads of both women form stiffly symmetrical arabesques, their eyebrows have broad, regular arches, and the large eyes in both cases seem to be given a deliberately inorganic form. Those of the Venice bust (fig. 63) bear close comparison with the portraits of Gordian III in their simple almond shapes, outlined above and below by deeply cut creases. The eyes of the London head (fig. 64) have a lunette-shape, with almost horizontal lower lids, which seems to foreshadow the more obviously patterned and abstract eyes of works like the Tarquinia statue (fig. 58).

The London head also displays striking affinities with the portrait of a little boy in Munich[24] (fig. 65): the pattern of eyes and eyebrows are vir-

---

[21] Venice, Biblioteca Marciana, inv. 203, marble head set on modern bust, h. of ancient part 0.23. Restored: nose, neck. Published: Bernoulli, *Römische Ikonographie*, II³, 92; Buchholz, *Kaiserinnen*, p. 156; Traversari, *Ritratti*, p. 91, No. 72; Wiggers and Wegner, *Herrscherbild*, III¹, 176.

[22] London, British Museum, inv. 1924, marble head, h. 0.38. Tip of nose restored. Published: Smith, *Catalogue*, III, 69, No. 1924, pl. XVII. Bernoulli, *Römische Ikonographie*, II³, 156; Felletti-Maj, *Iconografia*, p. 194, No. 246, pl. 32, fig. 101; Bergmann, *Studien*, pp. 43-44; Wegner, Bracker, and Real, *Herrscherbild*, III³, pp. 78-80. The head has been identified as Herennia Etruscilla, wife of Trajan Decius, an identification which is possible though not, in my opinion, definitely provable. A date of 249 would be compatible with the style of the work.

[23] For the coins of Etruscilla, see *RIC*, Vol. IV³, 127-129, Nos. 55-76, and 137-138, Nos. 132-137; pl. II, figs. 2-8.

[24] Munich Glyptotek, cat. 360, inv. KH150. Head and neck in marble, measurements not available. Restorations now removed: bust. Well preserved except for chips from ears. Published: Bernoulli, *Römische Ikonographie*, II³, 149, No. 12, and p. 151; Felletti-Maj, *Iconografia*, p. 85, No. 1, pl. I, fig. 4; Furtwängler, *Beschreibung*, p. 340, No. 360. I am indebted to Sheldon Nodelman for the suggestion that this head may represent Philip II, an identification consistent with the date proposed here.

tually identical in the two works, while the hard, squarish jawlines and smooth, flat skin surfaces give the overall form of both heads an austere and geometric appearance. The broad, thin-lipped mouths, which curl slightly upward at the corners are also very similar, suggesting that once again we can trace the style of a particular sculptor in two different works. In this case, the identification of a common hand is of interest in that these two works display similar formal devices applied to very different subjects: a mature woman and a young child. The Munich portrait, like the London head, should not be dated later than the time of Gordian III, since the hair is still treated in the "*a penna*" technique, but it too shows a definite and clearly thought-out, if still rather subtle, use of abstraction and a taste for stiff angularity of contour.

One more female portrait datable probably to the time of Gordian is a head, set on a modern bust, in the Palazzo dei Conservatori (fig. 66).[25] This artistically mediocre sculpture follows imperial portraiture so unimaginatively that it could represent Gordian III in a female wig. It is of interest primarily because it, like the Venice and London portraits, demonstrates how the coiffure popular since Severan times has been frozen into a stiffly decorative and non-naturalistic pattern of waves. Little clusters of curls which resemble grapes can be seen escaping from the coiffure under each ear, but they too are treated in a hard, dry manner which does not suggest the texture or resilience of real hair.

Inferior works like the Conservatori portrait (fig. 66) might contribute to the impression that the abstract style was the result of a decline in artistic ability during the third century. It is important therefore to place this work in context through comparison with a genuine masterpiece of about the same date, a head formerly in the Lateran collection and now in the Vatican (fig. 67).[26] The coiffure of the young woman represented in this work most closely resembles that of Tranquillina (fig. 57), allowing the portrait to be dated with reasonable certainty in the 240's. Here, however, the hair is not parted in the middle and crimped into tight ridges but swept back from the hairline in soft, full waves, on which the strands of hair are engraved in richly decorative, undulating lines. A short fringe of hair escapes from the coiffure to frame the forehead, while

---

[25] Rome, Palazzo dei Conservatori, Scala, inv. 428. Head and neck set on modern bust of colored marble. H. of ancient part 0.34. Restored: tip of nose. Published: Bernoulli, *Römische Ikonographie*, II³, 92, 107; Stuart-Jones, *Museo Capitolino*, pp. 205-206, No. 58, pl. 48; Buchholz, *Kaiserinnen*, pp. 53, 155; Helbig⁴, No. 1801; Wiggers and Wegner, *Herrscherbild*, III¹, 172.

[26] Vatican, former Lateran collection, inv. 10206. Head and neck in white marble, h. of ancient part 0.31. Restorations now removed: lower part of bib-bust, tip of nose. Published: Giuliano, *Catalogo*, p. 78, No. 96, pl. 57; Bovini, *MonAnt*, 39 (1943), 311, fig. 104, pl. 2, fig. 2; Helbig⁴, No. 1099.

at the neck a row of thick corkscrew-curls contribute to the decorative treatment of the hair. In the care lavished on these details, the Vatican head (fig. 67) bears comparison with the lovely bust in Copenhagen discussed in the previous chapter (fig. 42).

The face, in contrast, is depicted without prettification or flattery. Standards of beauty have of course changed constantly during history, rendering modern judgments on the beauty of a subject somewhat invalid. Still, it seems unlikely that the small, close-set eyes, hard, thin-lipped mouth, and heavy square jaw of this woman would have been considered attractive by Roman standards any more than by modern. Yet the portrait itself is beautiful, even if its subject is not. The squarish lower face, level eyebrows, narrow eyes and horizontal mouth have been exploited to form an austerely harmonious structure of rectilinears. Emotion is suggested only by the slight contraction of the eyebrows over the nose; the symmetry, simplicity of detail, and emphasis on geometric form which typify Gordian III's portraits are all clearly in evidence here. The combination of subtle abstraction in the face with restrained elegance in the design of the coiffure is immensely successful.

Several observers[27] have noted that this portrait (fig. 67) is almost certain to be the work of the same sculptor as another work in the Vatican collection,[28] which portrays an older woman. The artist's "handwriting" is most obvious in the handling of the coiffures, in particular the undulating pattern of engraved strands. The shapes of the eyes and hard, angular chiseling of the mouths also bear close comparison. The Galleria dei Busti head, however, is the more technically clumsy of the two works, and therefore probably the earlier one. The portraits also have some striking stylistic differences, in that the Galleria dei Busti sculpture makes a more complex use of detail in the wrinkles and sagging flesh of its subject, and has more noticeable asymmetries. The sculptor of these two works appears, therefore, to have abandoned the older tradition of rich, three-dimensional modeling and expressive irregularity, which are more evident in the earlier head, in favor of the current of geometric abstraction. The change, in the case of this sculptor's work, seems definitely to have been for the better.

---

[27] Giuliano, *Catalogo*, p. 78, No. 96; Helga von Heintze in Helbig⁴, No. 177, and No. 1099.

[28] Vatican, Sala dei Busti, No. 333. Head and neck in marble, set on modern bust. H. in toto 0.68; measurements of ancient part not available. Head life-sized. Restored: bust, except for small piece of drapery to left of neck; foot, lower half of nose, parts of coiffure alongside ears. Neck and rear of head broken in several places, right eye and lower lip battered, surface cleaned in modern times. Published: Amelung, *Skulpturen des vaticanischen Museums*, II, 525, No. 333, pl. 72; Giuliano, *Catalogo*, p. 78, under No. 96; Helbig⁴, No. 177.

Most of the more abstract portraits from prior to the middle of the third century tend to be harshly austere and almost anti-decorative in the treatment of detail. The Berlin bust of Gordian III (fig. 7) typifies this severity, which makes so many of these works unattractive and inaccessible to modern viewers. Works like the lovely head in the former Lateran collection (fig. 67), however, demonstrate a rediscovery of the possibilities of line and texture, particularly in the hair, for the creation of a pattern which is pleasing in itself as pure design. Both male and female portraits of the Gallienic period demonstrate a delight in such decorative elegance, which now definitely begins not only to dominate but to supplant anatomic realism in portrait sculpture.

# CHAPTER FIVE

# THE VICTORY OF ABSTRACTION

The reign of Gallienus formed a significant turning-point in the development of sculptural style of the third century. The taste for decorative elegance and emotional calm which dominated portraiture during the late 250's and 260's fostered the abstract style which had been emerging in the preceding decade. The period roughly coinciding with the rule of Gallienus also produced some of the more aesthetically pleasing works to survive from the third century and has, not altogether without justification, been described as a "renaissance".

Self-conscious revivals and references to earlier works of art undoubtedly played a significant role in portrait sculpture at this time. The earlier portraits (fig. 12) of Gallienus made an obvious reference to those of Augustus in the bifurcation of the hair slightly to the left of the middle of the forehead, while the later ones, with the full aureole of hair around the face, recall both the Antonine emperors[1] and Alexander the Great.[2] It has also been suggested that the popularity at this time of longer hair for men was inspired in part by literary descriptions of the long-haired warriors of the heroic age and of historic Sparta.[3] The revival of the fashion would thus reflect a romantic nostalgia for the Greek past. Another layer of reference may also be suggested by the similarities of the later portraits of Gallienus (fig. 13) to those of Hadrian,[4] with their full hair, short-clipped beards and broad faces. Gallienus shared many attitudes and policies with Hadrian, most notably a respect for the traditions of Greek culture.

Such a complex use of visual references would not be at all surprising in the portraiture of an intellectual philhellene like Gallienus, or in the private portraits of aristocrats who emulated him. On the other hand, these revivals were far from reactionary in effect, since they were applied with freshness and imagination, and integrated harmoniously with the new taste for geometric abstraction. Until fairly recently, our understanding of the Gallienic period has been distorted by a tendency to date to those years any male portrait with long, full hair tumbling outward from a central part. Fittschen has demonstrated that many such works

---

[1] Mathew, *JRS*, 33 (1943), 68.
[2] Breckenridge, *Likeness*, p. 214.
[3] Alföldi, *25 Jahre römisch-germanische Kommission*, pp. 44-45.
[4] Breckenridge, *Aufstieg und Niedergang der römischen Welt*, II.12.2, 507.

actually show closest affinities with the childhood portraits of Caracalla and Geta, and that they therefore belong in the early Severan period.[5] The works which remain securely datable to the Gallienic period yield an overall picture of an era far more progressive than previously supposed. In addition to the hardness of modeling and general abstraction in these works, they incorporate—perhaps unconsciously and unintentionally—new elements of spirituality, new expressions of mystic transcendancy which were to have a long life in Medieval art.[6]

In a few cases, replicas of a single portrait type can provide intriguing evidence of the emergence of Gallienic taste. Bergmann has pointed out[7] that the portraits of the young Gallienus himself vary considerably, though recognizably following a common type, and that a head in the Capitoline Museum[8] is far more asymmetrical and less decorative than the Berlin head (fig. 12). Bergmann would, therefore, date the Capitoline head earlier, nearer in time to the veristic portraits of emperors like Decius (fig. 10), and place the Berlin head later during the coregency of Valerian and Gallienus, after a taste for elegant pattern had become better established. It should however be noted that the Capitoline head is a work of inferior quality, and that the clumsily lopsided treatment of the cranium and eyes may well be unintentional.

A clearer example of the same phenomenon can be observed in the replicas of the portrait of a philosopher whom L'Orange has identified as Plotinus[9] (fig. 50). By far the best and most evocative example of the type, Ostia 436 (fig. 50) demonstrates that the prototype was a work of the dramatically impressionistic style which exploited effects of movement to the fullest. Two other replicas, Ostia 68 and the head in the Vatican unmistakably follow the same prototype, since not only the features but the arrangement of the locks of hair follow an identical pattern. But the Gallienic taste for harder and drier chisel work, more angular outlines and stiffer contours have vitiated the sense of movement conveyed in Ostia 436 through curving surfaces and lines. These two

---

[5] Fittschen, *RömMitt.*, 77 (1970), 132-143, and *JdI*, 84 (1969), 197-236.

[6] See Mathew, *JRS*, 33 (1943), 68, for a discussion of this phenomenon not only in art but in other aspects of life and thought of Gallienus's time.

[7] Bergmann, *Studien*, pp. 57-58.

[8] Rome, Museo Capitolino, Stanza degli Imperatori, marble head, h. 0.21. Restored: part of nose, fragments of ears, bib-bust. Published: Stuart-Jones, *Museo Capitolino*, p. 149, No. 27, pl. 37; Bernoulli, *Römische Ikonographie*, II³, 167, No. 2; Alföldi, *25 Jahre römisch-germanische Kommission*, p. 32, fig. 4; L'Orange, *Studien*, p. 5; Bovini, *MemLinc*, 2 (1941), 146, fig. 10; Felletti-Maj, *Iconografia*, p. 223, No. 290; Helga von Heintze, "Drei antike Porträtstatuen," *Antike Plastik*, I (1962), 15-16; Helbig⁴, No. 1324; McCoull, *Berytus*, 17 (1967-68), 71, No. 1, pl. 22, fig. 1; Bergmann, *Studien*, p. 51, No. 2, pp. 57-58, pl. 12, figs. 1-2; Wegner, Bracker and Real, *Herrscherbild*, III³, 107-108, 116-117, pl. 43.

[9] For references, see Chapter III, note 44.

replicas seem to express not so much a sudden thrill of mystic inspiration[10] as a calmly meditative mood.

The fourth replica of the series, Ostia 1386, has so thoroughly eliminated all movement and emotion from the face as to reduce the expression to vapidity. Even the slight touseling of the hair on the sides of the head has been regularized; the hair is now combed forward alongside the bald spot in regular undulations. In frontal view, the gaunt face and pointed beard form a stiff, regular triangle, without the surging undulations of contour seen in Ostia 436. In this case, the use of an abstract style would seem to mark a definite change for the worse in the interpretations of the "Plotinus" type, though here again the quality of the replicas must be borne in mind, and Ostia 1386 perhaps regarded as a clumsy reproduction by a copyist who failed to understand the original.

The tradition of philosopher portraits to which the "Plotinus" type belongs was far from dead; on the contrary, it was to produce some compelling works in the abstract style of the later third century. A portrait in the Liebighaus Museum at Frankfurt[11], (fig. 68), datable probably between 260 and 280,[12] can be profitably compared with the "Plotinus." Again, the subject is a gaunt-faced older man with a pointed beard and broad, domed cranium which give the face roughly the form of a long triangle. Again, too, the eyes gaze upward, the eyebrows are raised, and the skin of the forehead corrugated with the tension of concentration. This time, however, the semicircular arches of the eyebrows have been regularized and their symmetry emphasized. The eyebrows are strongly canted outward, the eyesockets deeply carved and the eyeballs very rounded, but it is the linear pattern—the concentric semicircles of eyebrows and orbital folds—which first capture the viewer's attention. A look of momentary emotion has been replaced by a trance-like, immobile stare. The subsequent mutations of the tradition of philosopher portraits, and its eventual adaptation in Christian art to the images of prophets and saints, has been thoroughly analyzed by L'Orange, and requires no further elaboration here.[13]

---

[10] See L'Orange, "Plotinus-Paul," *Likeness and Icon*, for an extraordinarily sensitive analysis of Ostia 436.

[11] Frankfurt, Liebighaus Museum No. 87. Marble head, h. 0.315. Part of right ear restored, left ear chipped. Surface cleaned in modern times, but polish of marble appears to be ancient. Published: *Bildwerke aus dem Liebighaus* (Frankfurt am Main, 1962), pl. 13, No. 13; Helga von Heintze, *Römische Porträtplastik* (Stuttgart: H. E. Gunter, 1961), p. 15, pl. 37, and *Jahrbuch für Antike und Christentum*, 6 (1963), 42, pl. 7a; F. Eckstein and H. Beck, *Antike Plastik im Liebighaus* (Frankfurt am Main, 1973), pl. 96, No. 96.

[12] On the date, see von Heintze, *Römische Porträt-Plastik*, p. 15, and Eckstein and Beck, *Liebighaus*, No. 96.

[13] L'Orange, "Plotinus-Paul," *Likeness and Icon*, pp. 41-42, and "The Antique Origins of Medieval Portraiture," *Likeness and Icon*, pp. 96-102.

To return to the early years of the coregency of Gallienus and Valerian, however, a number of male portraits which resemble those of the young Gallienus in their treatment of the hair and beard document how the dramatic facial expressions of the preceding decades were frozen into decorative patterns. A head in the Museo Nuovo of the Palazzo dei Conservatori[14] (fig. 69), for example, shows the hair and beard still worn short, but in slightly longer locks than were fashionable in the era of the soldier emperors. The relief of the hair is still very shallow but allows for a decorative elaboration of line and texture over the scalp, cheeks and throat. The face also resembles that of the young Gallienus in its emphasis on the angularity of the jawline and the rigidly regular diagonals of the plunging eyebrows. Many more private portraits of the 250's resemble this one in their continuation of the trends of Gordian III's portraits, the reduction of the frowning expression to a starkly geometric formula.

Other works of this period are strongly reminiscent of late Severan portraiture in their return to a more subdued and melancholy, rather than intensely anguished facial expression. A head in the Munich Glyptotek,[15] (fig. 70), in which the stubbly beard is still represented by the "picked" pattern but the slightly longer hair of the scalp indicates Gallienic fashions, a veristic pattern of facial furrows has been applied in a remarkable manner. Creases still spread across the forehead and around the eyes, but they are separated from one another, isolated in neutral surfaces, and rather shallowly engraved. The effect of movement conveyed by earlier works like the Capitoline Decius (fig. 10) seems here to have been deliberately nullified by the breaking up of the pattern of line. This work also shows a renewed emphasis on aristocratic delicacy in the features: though the face is lined, its fine-boned features and regular rectangular structure are quite attractive.

These qualities are even more striking in a particularly fine work in the former Lateran Collection[16] (fig. 71). Here again, the subject is a man of

---

[14] Rome, Museo Nuovo del Palazzo dei Conservatori, marble head, inv. 184, h. 0.355, set on a small modern bust. Restored: nose, chin, right ear, part of cranium. Published: Mustilli, *Museo Mussolini*, p. 149, pl. 91, No. 339; Antonio Giuliano, *BullCom*, 80 (1965-67), 119-120, fig. 5; Bovini, *MonAnt*, 39 (1943), 216, fig. 28; Bergmann, *Studien*, pp. 61, 67, pl. 15, fig. 3.

[15] Munich Glyptotek, inv. 362, head in marble. Present measurements (without modern bust to which it was formerly attached) not available. Life-sized. Restorations now removed: tip of nose, left ear, bust. Published: Furtwängler, *Beschreibung*, p. 36, No. 362; Hekler, *Bildniskunst*, pl. 295b; Hans Diepolder, "Römische Bildnisse in München," *RömMitt*, 54 (1939), 278; Bergmann, *Studien*, p. 17, pl. 11, fig. 1.

[16] Vatican, formerly in the Lateran collection, inv. 10205. Head and neck in marble, h. 0.29, of head alone 0.25. Restorations now removed: bust, nose, part of chin. Surface scratched. Published: Giuliano, *Catalogo*, p. 76, No. 93, pl. 54; Helga von Heintze, *Gnomon*, 32 (1960), 159; Jocelyn M. C. Toynbee, *JRS*, 48 (1958), 200 (review of Giuliano, *Catalogo*); Helbig⁴, No. 1100.

aristocratic handsomeness, ravaged by signs of fatigue and anxiety such as the furrows of the forehead and gauntness of the cheeks. Here, too, the contour of the head is a severely simple rectangle, unbroken by the volume of the hair which still lies smoothly along the scalp in a shallow cap. The beard is still represented by chisel incisions on the cheeks and throat, though the units are no longer short pick-marks but slightly longer curving lines which suggest a curly texture. The locks of hair over the forehead are longer and fuller, forming an elegant row of hook-shaped locks, which along with the little curls on the temples make a decorative frame for the face.

This portrait bears striking resemblances both in facial type and in its gently sorrowful expression to a work of the late Severan period, a type represented by copies in the Terme Museum (fig. 21), Vienna, and Smith College.[17] Were it not for the considerable technical differences between those three works and this head, it would be tempting to regard the Vatican head as a fourth replica of the same type, but the dry, angular chiseling of the hair clearly indicates that it must be a work of some thirty years later. Conceivably, this portrait could represent the same man, if he was of sufficient importance to his family or community to merit the duplication of his portrait a generation after the prototype was made. But in the absence of evidence concerning the subject's identity, it is safer to interpret the Vatican head (fig. 71) as a vivid demonstration of the return to favor of some of the formal devices popular in the late Severan age: deep-set, brooding eyes, subtle muscular tensions, and a suggestion of sadness in the way the corners of the mouth are pulled slightly down.

The differences between the style of the Severan and Gallienic periods, on the other hand, can be readily observed by comparing the treatment of hair in the earlier and later works (figs. 21, 71). The quality of the surfaces also present interesting differences: a glossy, polished finish in the Severan works which emphasizes the unity of the subtly modeled skin areas; a matt-like finish in the later work, interrupted by harshly angular chiseling.

A work very similar in style to the Vatican head is an under-life-sized head in the Terme museum (fig. 72).[18] Here again, the brooding, heavy brow ridge, deep-set eyes and gaunt cheeks are strongly reminiscent of

---

[17] For references see chapter II, notes 25-27.

[18] Rome, Museo Nazionale delle Terme, cat. 301, inv. 108607. Marble head, about half life-sized, h. 0.245. Half of neck preserved, tip of nose and left nostril broken off, rim of right ear chipped, surface root-marked. Provenance: Ostia. Published: Felletti-Maj, *Ritratti*, p. 151, No. 301; Moretti, *NSc*, 1920, p. 53, fig. 8; Paribeni, *Il Ritratto*, pl. 305; Bergmann, *Studien*, p. 67, pl. 20, figs. 3-4.

late-Severan portraits, with their relatively subtle suggestion of emotional tensions. On the other hand, the long locks of hair on the scalp and chin are carved in a flat, dry manner, while the fuller and shorter curls of the sideburns form angular, abstract ridges which indicate Gallienic date. The Terme and Vatican heads both still show considerable three-dimensionality in the treatment of the features. Profile views of the works demonstrate that the foreheads cant forward, the forehead muscles swell in relief, and the gaunt cheeks are deeply carved out. As the abstract style of the Gallienic period became better established, however, the faces of portraits tended to become flatter and broader, the features more two-dimensional.

A handsome and exceptionally well-preserved bust in the Metropolitan Museum in New York[19] (fig. 73) provides an intriguing contrast with the small portrait from Ostia (fig. 72). The subject's facial type is similar: long, thin and triangular, tapering to a pointed chin and short, pointed beard. The hair, too, seems to belong to the same phase of third-century fashion: it is worn comparatively long, but combed forward smoothly along the scalp and represented with almost no volume. The beard is, if anything, more conservative in treatment than that of the Ostia head (fig. 72), being engraved as an almost volumeless pattern of line on the cheeks. But the features are simpler, more symmetrical, and more crowded into a single, frontal plane. A frontal view of the head (fig. 73) indicates that the curvature of cheeks and cheekbones is minimal: the contours of the face form almost flat sides of an isoceles triangle. In profile, the forehead and chin form segments of a single, almost perfectly straight line. The abstraction in this work is still rather subtle, and the sense of individual likeness fairly strong, but the artist has emphasized the geometric regularity of the face. A pattern of simple horizontal accents in the features enhances a mood of calm meditation: the eyebrows, for example, are not only very level but meet over the nose to form a single line, while the thin-lipped mouth, though not apparently tense, is severely straight and simply drawn.

Another portrait with comparable treatment of the hair and beard, and therefore presumably a roughly contemporary date, shows a more extreme tendency to flatten the face into a mask-like design. This head, in the Capitoline Museum,[20] (fig. 74) had been identified by von Heintze as

[19] New York, Metropolitan Museum of Art, inv. 08.258.46. Marble bust, h. 0.658. Tip of nose and a few chips of drapery lost, surface root-marked. Published: Gisela M. A. Richter, *Handbook of the Classical Collection* (New York, 1927), p. 305, fig. 214; 1930 ed., p. 305; Richter, *Roman Portraits*, fig. 96; *BMMA*, 5 (1909), 64-65, fig. 5; Frederik Poulsen, *From the Collections of the Ny Carlsberg Glyptotek*, 3 (1942), 113-114, fig. 26.
[20] Rome, Museo Capitolino, Sala delle Colombe, inv. 340. Marble head, H. 0.31. Restored: tip of nose, ears, bust and foot. Major publications: Stuart-Jones, *Museo*

Hostilianus, the younger son of Decius, though her theory is not widely accepted.[21] The identity of the portrait is not of primary importance here, though it should be noted in passing that the profile does indeed bear striking resemblances to the coin profiles of Hostilianus.[22] Those coins, of course, invariably represent a beardless boy, while the Capitoline head portrays a youth with a light beard. However, the sculptural portrait still has very soft, immature features which indicate an age not necessarily too much later than the age of Hostilianus as represented on his coins. The marble portrait could conceivably have been made at the very end of his life, after the numismatic images. On the other hand, the patterned treatment of the hair, in parallel S-curves which flow forward and downward from the rear of the skull, suggest a date somewhat later than 251. Furthermore, the portrait face on the great Ludovisi battle sarcophagus, which definitely seems to portray the same person,[23] displays not only a more mature beard but a more advanced stage of Gallienic style. This replica of the Capitoline portrait is difficult to reconcile either with the ages of the sons of Decius as represented on their coins or with a date as early as 252.

The face of the Capitoline head (fig. 74), in frontal view, forms a broad, regular triangle across which the features are spread in a basically flat design. The wide-set eyes, horizontal eyebrows, and full-lipped mouth have some three-dimensionality in their execution, but are arranged basically parallel to the frontal plane of the face. The skin areas are not only smooth but devoid of any signs of muscular tension. Only the graceful drawing of the large eyes and the mouth saves the face from inexpressiveness. The calligraphic elegance of these details, however,

---

*Capitolino*, p. 178, No. 92, pl. 39; Gerhard Rodenwaldt, "Der Große Schlachtsarkophag Ludovisi," *Antike Denkmäler*, IV (1929), 26, figs. 12, 13, and *AA*, 43 (1928), pp. 266-267; Bovini, *MonAnt*, 39 (1943), 186-187, fig. 4; Felletti-Maj, *Iconografia*, p. 166, No. 189; Helga von Heintze, "Studien zu den Porträts des 3. Jahrhunderts n.Chr. IV: Der Feldherr des grossen Ludovisichen Schlachtsarkophags," *RömMitt*, 64 (1957), 74; Cornelius Vermeule, "A Graeco-Roman Head of the Third Century A.D.," *DOPapers*, 15 (1961), 6, fig. 10; Fittschen, *JdI*, 84 (1969), 219, fig. 38; Wegner, Bracker and Real, *Herrscherbild*, III³, pp. 75-76.

[21] Von Heintze, *RömMitt*, 64 (1957), 69-91. For dissenting opinions on the iconography of Hostilianus, see Wegner, Bracker and Real, *Herrscherbild*, III³, pp. 75-76, and Klaus Fittschen, "Sarkophage römischer Kaiser oder vom Nutzen der Porträtforschung," *JdI*, 94 (1979), 581-584; Bergmann, *Studien*, p. 44.

[22] *RIC* IV³, pp. 143-150, pl. 11, figs. 19, 20, and pl. 12, figs. 1-4.

[23] For major publications of the problem, see Rodenwaldt, *Antike Denkmäler*, IV (1929), 61-68; von Heintze, *RömMitt*, 64 (1957), 69-91; Pelikàn, *Vom antiken Realismus zur spätantiken Expressivität*, pp. 116-127, 143; Fittschen, *JdI*, 94 (1979), 581-584. I personally believe that the Capitoline head and the general of the Ludovisi sarcophagus probably do represent the same man, but that a head now in the Munich Glyptotek, inv. DV46, which is sometimes also identified as a member of this type, differs considerably from the other two, sharing with them little besides the cross-shaped scar on the forehead.

and of the hair, makes the portrait a very aesthetically pleasing work. Here too, as is often the case in portraits of roughly Gallienic date, there may be a conscious allusion to the styles of an earlier period, since the hair bears close comparison with that of Trajanic portraits.[24]

The portrait figure of this young man on the Ludovisi sarcophagus, where he appears as a triumphant general on horseback, displays many of the same stylistic traits as the Capitoline head (fig. 74). The face has the same geometric simplicity of contours, the same full and graceful curves outlining the eyes and lips, and the same mood of transcendant calm, which here forms a striking contrast with the tumult of the battle scene around him. The execution is stiffer and drier, however, the features set off more sharply by hard, angular ridges, and the hair and beard are both fuller. The tendency of artists at the time of Gallienus to convert hair and beard to decorative textures is very evident here, as is the dry and angular chisel work in the carving of the locks.

Another portrait type which presents vexing problems of identification, but which can be dated with some security to the 250's, is a group of three male statues[25] which were apparently found together, in the ruins of the same building,[26] and are now in the Villa Doria Pamfili (figs. 75, 76, 77). The three works represent, respectively, a man dressed in a toga and two nude men, the latter apparently portrayed as hunters, since one carries a

---

[24] For a particularly attractive example of this calligraphic treatment of the hair from the Trajanic period, compare the bust of a child in Berlin, Staatliche Museen, Antiken-Sammlung, cat. R48, Blümel, *Römische Bildnisse*, pp. 20-21, No. R48, pl. 31.

[25] A) Rome, Villa Doria Pamfili, statue of a man wearing a toga. H. without plinth 1.80, of head 0.25. Lower half of nose and left nostril restored, also chip by right nostril and piece of rear of head. On rest of body: scroll restored along with part of left little finger, chips of drapery.

B) Rome, Villa Doria Pamfili, statue of a hunter, nude except for chlamys, marble, h. without plinth 1.97, of head 0.275, length of foot 0.32, h. of support 0.90. Head broken off and reset, but belongs to statue. Hair, tip of nose, rims of ears chipped. Drapery around hips restored. Body broken in several places, pieced together with plaster. Two outer folds of mantle as it falls from the left shoulder, drapery below left hand, parts of fingers of hand restored. Attribute originally held in left hand now lost.

C) Rome, Villa Doria Pamfili, statue of a hunter, nude except for a chlamys. Marble, h. without plinth 2.0, of head 0.28, length of foot 0.32, h. of support 0.88 (without restorations, 0.79). Restored: part of forehead and hair on left, piece of rim of right ear. Tip of nose, nostrils, left cheek chipped. Head broken off and reset, but belongs to body. Drapery across groin is modern. Arms and legs broken in several places, pieced together. Restorations to right calf, left foot and knee, right forearm, hand and end of treetrunk, boar's head, part of sword hilt and left hand.

Publications of the three statues: von Heintze, *Antike Plastik*, I (1962), 7-31, pls. 1-18; Niemeyer, *Statuarischen Darstellung*, pp. 47, 62, 86, 109, 114, Nos. 20, 102 130; *Antichità della Villa Doria Pamfili*, ed. Raissa Calza (Rome: Liberia dello Stato, 1977), Nos. 372-374, pp. 299-301 (Calza); Bergmann, *Studien*, p. 65.

[26] Calza, in *Villa Doria Pamfili*, pp. 299, 303.

sword while the other originally carried a spear, and is accompanied by a dog.

The two nude statues typify the admiration of the Gallienic period for the high-classic art of the fifth century, since both are strongly reminiscent in proportion and stance of the works of Polykleitos, and since one is unmistakably a copy of his *doryphoros*.[27] Even here, a slight alteration to the type has been made by the addition of a chlamys, in accordance with the Roman taste for adapting rather than literally copying classical prototypes.[28] The togate statue, however, which conforms to more recent and more strictly Roman traditions, is by far the most successful composition of the three, demonstrating a remarkably graceful exploitation of the stiff, cumbersome folds of the contabulate toga. The broad horizontal folds across the chest and the long, vertical column of pleats which gradually tapers to soft folds as it curves around under the left knee achieve, in terms wholly belonging to the third century, the poise and stability which the other two statues attempt to borrow from older Greek artistic traditions. In the togate statue the thorough understanding of plastic form evident in the execution of the folds of cloth is subordinated to a taste for linear design, achieved through rather sharp and dry cutting of the furrows which produce the lines of shadow. Style and technique are entirely consistent with the subtly abstract and linear rendering of the features of the face.

The faces of the Doria Pamfili statues are so strikingly similar that it is hard to escape the conclusion that they represent the same man in three different guises. It is rather surprising, however, that three statues of the same man, even a man of imperial rank, should have been displayed in the same building. Calza has suggested that all three statues depict the young Gallienus in his various capacities as a statesman and heroic hunter.[29] But if the identification of the young Gallienus is to be accepted for the type represented by the Berlin head (fig. 12), as I believe it must be, then it must be rejected for these statues. Despite certain general resemblances to that type, these faces differ too much from those of Gallienus, in the shape of the hairline, eyebrows and mouths, to allow them to portray the same man.

Von Heintze's suggestion that these statues represent three different men, a father and his two sons,[30] is one that should therefore not be rejected too hastily. The presence in the same building of a statue of a

---

[27] Niemeyer, *Statuarischen Darstellung*, pp. 62, 109, No. 102, and von Heintze, *Antike Plastik*, I, pp. 24-27.

[28] Niemeyer, *Statuarischen Darstellung*, pp. 62, 109.

[29] Calza in *Villa Doria Pamfili*, pp. 299-300.

[30] Von Heintze, *Antike Plastik*, I (1962), 31.

dignified patriarch in senatorial dress and of heroically nude statues of his two young sons or heirs has good precedents in Roman imperial sculpture, most notably a group of statues from Corinth of Augustus and of his grandsons Gaius and Lucius.[31] The Corinth statues illustrate further how a family resemblance can be emphasized so strongly that the distinction of the individual features requires close scrutiny. Given the tendencies toward idealization and abstraction in Gallienic sculpture, it is entirely possible that a similar phenomenon accounts for the resemblances between the three Doria Pamfili statues.

The question of the identity of these statues must, for the moment, be relegated to the exasperatingly large group of unsolved problems of third century iconography. Of more significance for the present study is the hard-edged, dry carving of the features in all three faces and the tendency to regularize them into symmetrical patterns. The hair and beards are still represented primarily through the picked pattern of isolated chisel strokes, though the hair is now long enough to lie in smooth strands along the scalp. The faces also show some slight reminiscences of the impressionistic works of a few years earlier: the eyebrows, for example, twist upward at their inner corners into vertical furrows above the nose.

This pattern was common in the portraits which sought a dramatic effect of facial movement, but the Villa Doria Pamfili statues (figs. 75, 76, 77) could not differ more drastically in their effect from works like, for example, the bust of Philip the Arab (fig. 9). Here, the naso-labial furrows, far from creating an upward surge of movement, build neat and regular triangles around the mouths which are repeated by the narrow lines of the moustaches. The creases of the foreheads are too shallowly engraved to suggest much tension, instead contributing to the general effect of stability in the faces by creating additional nearly-horizontal accents. The planes of cheeks and foreheads are smooth and flat, the contours of the faces stiff, and here again, as in the portraits of Gallienus (figs. 12, 13) the narrow chin-strap beards have been used to emphasize the angularity of the jawlines. These statues resemble the portraits of the young Gallienus (fig. 12) in their comparatively short hair and beards, a fact which argues for a date in the 250's. Their sculptural style, on the other hand, approaches that of his later type (fig. 13) not only in the breadth and flatness of the faces but in the sharp ridges of the eyebrows, and the crisp angles used to set off the borders of the lips from the skin.

---

[31] Cornelius Vermeule, *Roman Imperial Sculpture in Greece and Asia Minor* (Cambridge, Mass.: Harvard University Press, 1968), pp. 179-180, figs. 106, 110, 111; E. H. Swift, "A Group of Roman Imperial Portraits at Corinth," *AJA*, 25 (1921), 337-362; Franklin P. Johnson, *Corinth*, IX (Cambridge, Mass.: Harvard University Press, 1931), 72-76, and "Gaius and Lucius Caesar?" *AJA*, 45 (1941), 607-609.

Most of the male portraits discussed so far can probably be dated prior to 260, before the death of Valerian and the introduction of the more heroic portrait type of Gallienus (fig. 13) which represent him as sole ruler. The essential elements of Gallienic style had, however, already been firmly established in these portraits; works datable to the 260's merely demonstrate more extreme use of the same devices. Decorative detail becomes more extravagant: the use of the drill, for example, is revived for carving masses of curls. This technique can be seen in a bust at Ostia (fig. 78)[32] and a statue of a young man represented as a hunter (figs. 79-80) in the Capitoline museum.[33] The breadth and flatness of the faces in both those works indicates a simplification of anatomic forms commensurate with the elaboration of decorative detail.

A particularly abstract device, typical of the 260's, which is noticable to some degree is these two works, is the treatment of the eyes as large lunette shapes, surrounded by the concentric semicircles of orbital folds and eyebrows. This pattern, already noted in the statue of an empress (fig. 58) and the portrait of a philosopher in Frankfurt (fig. 68) can also be observed in a bust in the Palazzo dei Conservatori of a young man who still wears the short hair and beard of the earlier Gallienic period[34] (fig. 81). The Conservatori head is probably not earlier than about 260, but it illustrates one of the steps by which the subtle abstractions in portraits of the 240's and 250's advanced toward the blatantly anti-naturalistic style of the later third century.

---

[32] Ostia Antica, Museo, inv. 62. Bust in marble, h. 0.64, of head 0.26. Head broken off at base of neck and reset, but belongs to bust. Lower half of nose battered, rims of ears broken off. Foot of bust missing. Provenance: Domus della Fortuna Annonaria. Published: Giovanni Becatti, "Nuovo contributo ostiense di ritratti romani," *Le Arti*, 2 (1939-1940), 9, 10, pl. 4, figs. 15-16; Bovini, *MonAnt*, 39 (1943), 259, figs. 61, 62; Nikolaus Himmelmann-Wildschutz, "Sarkophag eines gallienischen Konsuls," *Festschrift für Friedrich Matz* (Mainz: von Zabern, 1962), p. 119, pl. 35; Helbig[4], No. 3133; Bergmann, *Studien*, p. 70, pl. 21, figs. 3-4.

[33] Rome, Museo Capitolino, Salone, No. 27, inv. 645. Statue of a hunter, adapted from an early-classical prototype of Perseus with the head of Medusa. H. of figure 1.98, of tree 2.52. Restored: tip of nose, large part of left arm and spear, parts of right hand, hare (except for parts of forepaws and hind feet), upper branch of tree, part of plinth. Major publications: Stuart-Jones, *Museo Capitolino*, p. 292, No. 27, pl. 71; Ernst Langlotz, *Der triumphierende Perseus* (Cologne: Westdeutscher Verlag, 1960), pp. 17-18, and "Eine neue Replik des triumphierenden Perseus," *RömMitt*, 70 (1963), 20-21; Konrad Schauenburg, *Perseus in der Kunst des Altertums* (Bonn: R. Habelt, 1960), p. 108; Helbig[4] No. 1388; Werner Fuchs, "Zum Antinous Hope und 'Cacciatore' im Kapitolinischen Museum," *AA*, 81 (1966), pp. 76-86; Bergmann, *Studien*, pp. 68-70, pl. 20, figs. 5-6.

[34] Rome, Palazzo dei Conservatori, Museo Nuovo, inv. 1794. Marble bust of a man in toga and tunic, h. 0.78. Nose, earlobes and rims of ears missing. Polish is ancient. Head broken off and reset, but belongs to bust. Published: L. Mariani, *BullCom*, 29 (1901), 176-177, fig. 7; Mustilli, *Museo Mussolini*, p. 111, No. 23, pl. 68, fig. 270; von Heintze, *Antike Plastik*, I (1962), 16, pl. 19b; Helbig[4], No. 1745.

The Gallienic tendency to reduce the face to a mask-like pattern is illustrated even more dramatically by female portraits. Here, the taste for cold and elegant abstraction was fostered by long traditions of treating female faces in a slightly more flattering, and consequently less individualized, manner than their male counterparts. Furthermore, women's faces tend in the nature of things to have less prominent bone and muscle structures, and to lend themselves to a more regularized treatment in art. It was possible, however, for magnificent likenesses of older women to be produced in the veristic style (e.g., figs. 40, and 52-56), and these works can profitably be compared with Gallienic sculptures which also portray ageing subjects.

A portrait head in Copenhagen (fig. 82)[35] and a very similar work in Vienna (fig. 83)[36] both represent rather stout, middle-aged women who wear a coiffure well attested on the coins of Salonina.[37] The hair is drawn up the back of the cranium, not in braids but in a thick, soft coil which forms a rounded topknot in frontal view. It has in fact been suggested that both these works portray Salonina;[38] however, despite their formal resemblances, it is unlikely that these two heads can represent the same woman. The Vienna portrait shows a much heavier person, with a thicker neck and more pronounced double chin. Her eyes are also longer, narrower and deeper-set than those of the Copenhagen head.[39] It is probably more accurate, therefore, to regard these works as two private portraits, from Salonina's time, which happen to resemble one another because they use the same formal devices to achieve a sober and dignified presentation of the subject. They may well be attributable to a common atelier.

Simple, symmetrical shapes dominate both these faces. The straight hair is drawn smoothly down on either side of the part to outline the forehead as a broad triangle, while the contours of the cheeks and of the

---

[35] Copenhagen, Ny Carlsberg Glyptotek, 757, inv. 1493. Marble head, h. 0.36. Nose, part of upper lip broken away. Surface corroded by modern cleaning. Published: F. Poulsen, *Catalogue*, No. 757; Felletti-Maj, *Ritratti*, p. 154, and *Iconografia*, p. 194, No, 247; Weber, *JdI*, 68 (1953), 128; von Heintze, *RömMitt*, 64 (1957), 79; V. Poulsen, *Les Portraits romains*, II, 173-174, No. 178, pls. 287-288.

[36] Vienna, Kunsthistorisches Museum, inv. 257. Head in marble on modern bust. Restored: nose, piece on left of rear of head. H. of ancient part 0.34, of head 0.26. Published: Bernoulli, *Römische Ikonographie*, II³, 155, pl. 47; Frederik Poulsen, *Porträtstudien in Norditalischen Provinzmuseen* (Copenhagen, 1928), p. 41; F. Poulsen, *Catalogue*, under No. 757; Felletti-Maj, *Iconografia*, p. 195, No. 248; V. Poulsen, *Les Portraits romains*, II, 173-174, under No. 178.

[37] Wessel, *AA*, 61 (1946-47), p. 67; Bergmann, *Studien*, p. 90.

[38] V. Poulsen, *Les Portraits romains*, II, 173-174, under No. 178. The two portraits had earlier been identified as Etruscilla: see Bernoulli, *Römische Ikonographie*, II³, p. 155; F. Poulsen, *Catalogue*, p. 525, No. 757; Felletti-Maj, *Iconografia*, pp. 194-195, Nos. 247-248.

[39] Felletti-Maj, *Iconografia*, p. 195, No. 248.

fleshy areas under the chins form regular half-ovals. The eyebrows of both faces are almost perfectly straight horizontals, though in the Vienna head this feature is more noticeable because of the parallel line of the long and narrow eyes. Despite the obvious maturity of the subjects, the skin areas are very smooth, regular, and simply modeled, while the facial expressions betray almost no trace of muscular tension. The relaxed and graceful curves of the lips, as well as the smooth skin surfaces, illustrate this point.

A work of somewhat greater individuality and livelier character is a portrait in the Getty Museum,[40] (fig. 84), again of a plump older woman. She wears the same type of coiffure as the Vienna and Copenhagen heads, except that her hair, instead of being parted, is swept smoothly back from the hairline. Here, the sagging flesh of the cheeks is modeled in more detail, and the rather determined set of the small mouth clearly indicated by the slight ripple of the muscles around the lips. The taste for simplicity and clarity of form is evident here too, however, in the broad, symmetrical arch of the hairline and the regular contour of the jowly lower face. The trefoil shape formed by the cheeks and chin[41] is reminiscent of the pattern outlined in many Gallienic male portraits by the beards. Furthermore, linear rather than plastic devices predominate in the rendering of the features: it is the dark grooves of the orbital folds, eyelids, and line between the lips which first strike the attention. A profile view reveals how flat the face is: all the features are crowded into a shallow space and aligned parallel to a frontal plane.

The flattening of the face in the Getty portrait is still rather subtle, and is not readily noticeable from a frontal view. Two portraits of younger women, probably roughly contemporary with it, show a much more obviously broad and mask-like treatment of the features. One of these is a somewhat crude head in the Terme museum,[42] which however shares many technical devices with an artistically better work in Copenhagen[43]

---

[40] Malibu, J. Paul Getty Museum, 73.AA.47. Marble head, h. 0.37. Surface somewhat damaged by modern cleaning. Nose and left eyebrow battered. Published: Bergmann, *Studien*, p. 92, pl. 26, figs. 5-6; Jiři Frel, *Roman Portraits in the Getty Museum*, exh. cat. (Philbrook Art Center and the J. Paul Getty Museum, 1981), pp. 106-107, No. 88, and p. 132.

[41] See Bergmann, *Studien*, p. 92.

[42] Rome, Museo Nazionale delle Terme, inv. 72251, cat. 284. Marble head and neck, h. 0.45. Nose missing, lips battered, face chipped. Provenance: Poggio Sommavilla. Published: *NSc*, 1916, pp. 281-282; Felletti-Maj, *Ritratti*, p. 143, No. 284, and *Iconografia*, p. 164, No. 185, pl. 22, figs. 70, 71. Bergmann, *Studien*, p. 92, pl. 26, figs. 1-2.

[43] Copenhagen, Ny Carlsberg Glyptotek, inv. 824, cat. 751. Marble head, h. 0.34. Nose, left eyebrow and chin battered. Red patina. Published: *NSc*, 1916, p. 283; F. Poulsen, *Catalogue*, No. 751; Hekler, *Bildniskunst*, pl. 304; Bovini, *MonAnt*, 39 (1943), 224; Felletti-Maj, *Iconografia*, p. 165, No. 187; Weber, *JdI*, 68 (1953), 130, fig. 7; V. Poulsen, *Les Portraits romains*, II, 186, No. 193, pl. 314; Bergmann, *Studien*, p. 96, pl. 31, figs. 1-2.

(fig. 85). The shallow, dry chiseling of the eyes and lips, the alignment of the features in a frontal plane, and the emphasis on a hard, rectilinear bone structure under the smooth cheeks are all evident at a glance. These works also share with their male counterparts a taste for more extravagant decoration in the treatment of the hair, and a reappearance of the use of the drill for chiaroscuro effects.

The faces of female portraits from slightly later in the Gallienic period have a blocky structure which foreshadows the stereometric heads in sculpture from the Tetrarchy. The tendency can be observed in the bust of a woman in the Palazzo dei Conservatori,[44] (fig. 86), whose face is given a very prismatic form by the projection of the fine cheekbones and jaw under the taut skin of the cheeks. This lady, too, wears her hair drawn up from the nape in a soft coil, but this time the hair forms a broad loop across the top of the squarish head, thus contributing one more broad, horizontal emphasis to the composition. The features, like those of the Copenhagen head (fig. 85) are drily and shallowly carved, yet still convey considerable character because of the subtle sensitivity of their execution. A sense of life is also achieved through the animated turn of the head to the right, and through the opposite movement of the right lower arm, which is bent across the body toward the left, and can be seen through the drapery. The body, however, is tightly swathed in a heavy and opaque palla which is both physically and visually confining.

Another bust of a woman, which bears a funerary inscription to one Aurelia Monina,[45] (fig. 87), and a closely related head in the Terme museum,[46] are thoroughly drained of movement, individuality , and almost of any trace of human life. These unimaginative funerary portraits were probably commissioned from artisans who made no more than a minimal effort to achieve likenesses, but it is revealing of the taste of the period that so little effort should have been required. The blocky, prismatic structure of the heads in these two works is more arbitrary and less anatomically justified than in the Conservatori bust (fig. 86), and the

---

[44] Rome, Palazzo dei Conservatori, inv. 2767. Bust, marble, h. 0.65, of head 0.23. Nose broken away, but head and bust preserved in one piece. Surface slightly corroded. Major publications: Helbig⁴, No. 1638; Bergmann, *Studien*, pp. 94-95, 97-98, 189, pl. 28, figs. 5-6 and pl. 31, fig. 5.

[45] Berlin, Staatliche Museen, Antiken-Sammlung, cat. R118. Bust in marble, bearing a funerary inscription to Aurelia Monina. H. 0.84. Head broken off and reset, but belongs to bust. Nose, part of neck, chips of drapery restored. Part of back of head lost. Face reworked from the eyes down, but the stylistic nature of the upper face has not been altered. Published: *CIL*, VI 13360 (inscription); Blümel, *Römische Bildnisse*, p. 49, No. 118, pl. 75; Bovini, *MonAnt*, 39 (1943), 312-313, fig. 105; Bergmann, *Studien*, pp. 96-97.

[46] Rome, Museo Nazionale delle Terme, inv. 136, cat. 309. Head in marble, h. 0.29. Restored: nose, fragment of forehead. Chips of ears missing. Published: Felletti-Maj, *Ritratti*, No. 309.

posture of the heads stiffly frontal. In the bust of Aurelia Monina, (fig. 87), which is preserved almost intact, the arms are pinned to her sides by the heavy drapery—a striking contrast with the Conservatori bust (fig. 86) which allowed the right arm some movement. But it is the eye areas of these portraits which makes the most strikingly abstract impression: the eyes are large and lunette-shaped, their upper arches repeated by the concentric circles of orbital folds and eyebrows. This scheme was noted in some contemporary male portraits (e.g. figs. 78, 81), but the artificial symmetry and regularity of the pattern used to express a hypnotic stare is perhaps most obvious here.

Second-rate works like these can, if taken in isolation, create the impression of a decline in artistic ability and imagination. It must be emphasized, therefore, that these dreary workshop products have been discussed here since they illustrate certain schemata which were being developed at this time, but that such works must be viewed in the context of an artistic movement which also produced some masterpieces. The later portraits of Gallienus, in particular the Terme replica (fig. 13) succeed magnificently, both as aesthetically pleasing abstractions and as portraiture. The face, it is true, may bear little resemblance to the physical appearance of Gallienus or any other man, but the patterned and linear features clearly convey their message of strength, energy and coolly disciplined intellectual control.

This portrait is an intelligently conceived and highly sophisticated ideogram of the face of an ideal ruler, a "philosopher king." Similar devices could be used in private portraiture to equally successful effect, when applied by sensitive artists: the female bust in the Palazzo dei Conservatori (fig. 86), with its air of quiet but intense thoughtfulness, illustrates the point. The abstract style of the Gallienic period, furthermore, was one with a long future. Some of its decorative elegance may have been again rejected in the 270's and 280's, but the portraits of the Tetrarchs and of Constantine, with their compelling, mask-like stares, can be seen as its lineal descendants.

# CONCLUSIONS

The preceding chapters have attempted to demonstrate that an un-broken process of development can, indeed, be traced in the portrait sculpture of the third century, despite the rapidity of innovation during these years. It is true that the period from 217 until 260 saw bold and radical experimentation in sculpture which led, eventually, to a com-pletely different approach to the human form, and to very different aesthetic principles from those of the sculpture of preceding centuries. It is also true that many revivals of earlier styles which can be recognized in these works are the result of self-conscious visual allusions, rather than reflections of living artistic traditions. On the other hand, at no point during these years can one observe a genuine break with traditions of the past; many apparent schisms in art vanish when they are examined more closely.

The portraits of Maximinus Thrax are frequently cited as works which break completely with the style of the imperial portraiture of the preceding dynasty.[1] Yet the intense expression, the vigorous modeling and coarse realism of Maximinus's portraits have good precedents in the portraits of Caracalla. Futhermore, the anonymous male portraits datable to Alexander Severus's time seem to prove that the format of Caracalla's portraits was used continuously through the 220's, though in subdued form. The portraitist who created the official type for Max-iminus broke with the style of the immediately preceding years only in that he used the scowling expression and bulging facial musculature with a renewed vigor. These choices by the artist were in part governed by the political needs of his client; the choice, however, concerned only how the artist was to use the traditions of earlier portrait sculpture, not whether he was to use them.

Another seeming schism occurs at the time of Gordian III, in whose portraits we can trace the work of a very innovative artist who ex-perimented freely with new forms of abstraction. In the portraits of both Gordian and Tranquillina (see figs. 7, 8, 57), we can observe an austere simplification of detail, a strong linear emphasis upon the most ex-pressive facial features—the eyes and mouth—and a subordination of anatomic forms to severely geometric outlines. In the portraits of Gor-dian, however, the portraitist is not creating an original design for the features. Instead, he is again working variations on the theme of

---

[1] E.g., Zinserling, *Klio*, 41 (1963), 200-203.

Caracalla's later portraits. The tension of the forehead muscle, the V-shaped pattern produced by the contraction of the eyebrows, and the tension of the mouth are, again, traditional elements. The innovation of the Gordian master consists primarily in the freezing of this configuration of features into a hard, symmetrical, and immobile pattern.

These innovations, in turn, form the basis for the style of the portraits of Gallienus (fig. 12, 13), another emperor whose artistic program is often described as a deliberate break with that of his predecessors.[2] It is true that Gallienus, for political reasons, had a need to present himself in a calm and aristocratic guise, according to the traditions of portraiture of designated heirs to imperial power. This propaganda goal was quite different from that of Philip, Decius, and Gallus, who were "soldier emperors," and who needed therefore to emphasize their soldierly qualities. For the purposes of conveying transcendant calm, the stylized immobility of the portraits of Gordian III would have provided Gallienus's portraitist with an appropriate model to follow; indeed, there is good reason to believe that the same artist created the types of Gordian and of the young Gallienus. Once again, the "schism" in imperial portraiture between the reigns of Philip, Decius and Gallus and that of Gallienus consisted only in the manner in which traditions were used, not in a complete break with the developments of the immediately preceding years.

Space has not allowed in the present study for a systematic tracing of the traditions of third-century portraiture further back than the time of Caracalla. Schweitzer[3] was undoubtedly correct, however, in observing that the "verism" of the soldier-emperor period has very deep roots in Roman art, and that relationships can be observed between these works and the realistic portraits of republican and Flavian times. Schweitzer is probably also correct in arguing that this tradition never entirely died out in Roman art at any time, but existed as a stylistic substratum, even at times when a more classicizing manner was preferred in official art.[4] The portraits of Maximinus, Philip, and Decius belong to the "plebeian" trend of Roman art, as it was defined by Bianchi-Bandinelli, though the fact that this style did not always enjoy favor in official monuments does not in any way imply that it is a primitive or folk-art style. A coarse, unflattering presentation of the subject is not at all the same thing as coarseness of technique; the portraits of Caracalla, Maximinus, Philip and Decius are in fact highly sophisticated works of art.

---

[2] Alföldi, 25 Jahre römisch-germanische Kommission, pp. 33-49; L'Orange, Studien, pp. 5-14.

[3] Schweitzer, Zur Kunst der Antike, II, 266-268.

[4] Ibid., p. 277.

No small knowledge of the musculature and bone structure of the human face is required to produce a portrait such as that of Maximinus Thrax (fig. 3). More important is the skill with which the artists of such portraits have employed light and shadow for optical effect, and have manipulated the movement of surfaces and lines so as to capture very lifelike moments of emotion. The portraits of the soldier-emperors display a continuous process of experimentation with such devices, as was discussed in the first chapter. The development of impressionistic devices and patterns of movement traceable in imperial portraits is amply attested in many fine private portraits as well. A portrait statue in Berlin, for example (figs. 43, 45) displays basically the same principles of composition as the portraits of Decius (fig. 10). We are dealing, therefore, not merely with a style dictated by necessities of political propaganda, by the ethnic backgrounds or the taste for "plebeian" style of certain emperors, but with a thriving artistic movement.

From the time of Gordian onward, this movement coexisted with the rather different stylistic current of geometric abstraction. Two schools of sculpture seem to have flourished, conceivably inspired by the examples set by different master portraitists. The "impressionistic" style was favored by the artists of Philip's and Decius's portraits, the more abstract manner by the Gordian master. These schools should not, however, be regarded as rigidly divided from one another. Sculptors who favored one style could learn from practitioners of the other: Philip's portraitist, for example, treats detail in a linear manner reminiscent of the Gordian master. Private portraits, furthermore, show combinations of elements of the two trends. Two portraits in the Capitoline museum, for example (figs. 61, 62) are datable contemporaneously with the portraits of Gordian III, works with which they share a hard, geometric form, a simplification of detail, and a few strong linear accents on certain features. Yet neither of these works show the stiff immobility or mannered symmetry of the facial expression of Gordian's portraits (see figs. 7, 8). Both, instead, seem to seek for an effect of movement, a transient moment of life. This is an aesthetic goal more typical of the "impressionistic" style.

The harder, more geometric style typical of Gordian's and Gallienus's portraits seems to have had a longer life in Roman art, and ultimately, a more profound impact upon late-Roman and Byzantine art than the other, "impressionistic" trend. In a larger sense, however, both these schools of sculpture can be regarded as two aspects of the same trend toward abstraction in the treatment of the human form. Works of the "impressionistic" style show an increasing distortion of anatomic form for the purpose of creating an expressive pattern of movement. The depth of facial furrows, for instance, and the curvature of the surfaces of the face, often seem to be exaggerated to the point where the organic structure of the face is undermined.[5] This subordination of organic accuracy to expressive pattern is shared by both the "impressionistic" and the "abstract" style; they differ primarily in that one type of composition involves movement while the other does not.

Some overall observations must be added concerning the relationships of private and imperial portraits if the question of stylistic schools, and the influence of the court masters, is to be properly understood. The artists who created imperial portrait types would have enjoyed the most influence and yet, in many ways, the least freedom, of the portraitists working at any given time. The court portraitists would have borne the heavy responsibility of presenting the ruler to the public, in whatever manner was required by that emperor's program of propaganda. For this reason, the choices and options available to these artists would have been limited by external circumstances. In order to convey certain messages to the public, artists often seem to have relied upon visual associations, and references to the portraits of earlier emperors. As discussed above, there was a tradition of portraying "crown princes" in a calm, aristocratic manner, a tradition which can be traced from the portraits of Gallienus, Gordian, Maximus, and Alexander Severus back to Antonine times. The arrangement of the locks of hair in Gallienus's earlier portrait, and its seeming reference to Augustus, is another example of such a visual association. This necessity for reliance on tradition could have had the effect of discouraging innovation. On the other hand, the art of visual persuasion involves the necessity of capturing and holding the attention of the viewer, and for this purpose, fresh and new means of presentation are desirable. In this sense, therefore, imperial portraitists would have had an incentive for constant experimentation with new uses of existing styles.

During the politically turbulent third century, the incentive for experimentation would have been especially strong. The frequent military uprisings would suddenly thrust into power men who had little legitimate claim to imperial status, and who therefore had an urgent need to impress their personalities upon the consciousness of the public as quickly and as strongly as possible. Zinserling has cited this motivation as the probable cause of a preference for an intensely veristic style which emphasized the individuality of the subject.[6] A flattering style like that of Gallienus's portraits can, however, serve as well as a veristic style for the

---

[5] See L'Orange, *Studien*, p. 4.
[6] Zinserling, *Klio*, 41 (1963), 200-201.

purposes of making a strong impression on the public, so long as the style is sufficiently original to attract attention.

The artistic freedom of portraitists who fulfilled private commissions was also in some ways restricted, but by different concerns than that of the imperial masters. Given the high visibility of imperial portraits, the tastes of clients who commissioned private portraits could hardly avoid being affected by the styles of public works. The tastes of the artists themselves would presumably also be affected by exposure to the publicly displayed work of the portraitists in the service of the imperial family. Private portraiture, therefore, would tend to follow the trends set by public portrait sculpture. On the other hand, the artists who filled these commissions did not need to consider the impression which their works were likely to make on a large audience, and the ways in which those impressions might affect public opinion. The artist would need to satisfy his clients by presenting the subject in an appropriately dignified manner, but the audience for whom such a work was intended would be smaller, and the consequences of their impressions less momentous, than in the case of public portraits.

Private portraitists, in short, would have been governed to some extent by the stylistic trends established by imperial portrait types. They would, however, have enjoyed somewhat greater freedom in the ways in which they could use these stylistic innovations than did the imperial portraitists themselves. The consequences of this relative lack of restriction can be seen in the variety of private portraits discussed in this study which use devices and schemata closely similar to those of the contemporary imperial types, but use them for considerably different effects. Some examples which can be cited include a male and female portrait (figs. 39, 40), both of which show configurations of facial line very similar to that of Maximinus Thrax (fig. 3). Neither of the two works, however, show the strong contraction of facial muscles, nor the expression of anger, seen in Maximinus's portraits. The male bust in Venice (fig. 39), like the portraits of Maximinus, seeks to impress the viewer with the subject's physical strength, but does not seem to try to intimidate through the portrayal of an intensely aggressive mood. The woman's portrait (fig. 40), merely through a slight raising of the eyebrows and a softening and curvilinearity of contours, manages to convey a mood of gentleness and meditation.

Another example is a bust of a philosopher in the Capitoline museum (fig. 48), datable in the 240's. This bust shares with the portraits of Philip the Arab a pattern of facial lines which sweep inward and upward, complementing the movement of the body as a whole, since the head turns to one side and gazes upward. The subject of the Capitoline bust, however, unlike Philip, is a slender man with a delicate bone structure. His portrait therefore lacks the sense of physical energy conveyed by Philip's. The movement of the body and of the facial lines suggest instead a more spiritual, otherworldly concentration.

We can, then, describe an artistic movement in such a cultural milieu as a stylistic trend likely to be pioneered by the imperial portraitists, but then to be enlarged and enriched by the variety of ways in which the style was employed by private portraitists. It has been my contention throughout this analysis of third-century style that despite the political pressures which affected the aesthetic aims of official portraitists, the stylistic developments of these years were "inner directed" as well as "other directed," and that as is often the case, art had a life of its own not wholly dependent on the demands and wishes of its patrons. The portraitists at work during the third century were still members of a living tradition, which they could use, and upon which they could build, in order to convey the various messages which were required by imperial propaganda. The fact that the innovations of the imperial artists were often enthusiastically accepted and elaborated by artists fulfilling private commissions seems to indicate that the formal solutions which were developed for the problems of imperial propaganda succeeded in touching a responsive chord in the minds of the public, and of other artists. These stylistic innovations were accepted because third-century society was ready to accept them; because the new ways of portraying the human face and body somehow reflected the ways in which people of this time perceived themselves.

The social history of the Roman empire during the third century does not lend itself to facile generalizations. Even the material discussed in the present monograph, a small and specialized part of the life of the society which produced it, has revealed a great wealth of complex developments. During these years, sculptural style evolved with a rapidity which was to lead to a radical change in the nature of art and in the aesthetic concepts of late antiquity. We can, however, draw one conclusion from the present survey: that the ages of the late Severans and the soldier emperors produced many intelligent and imaginative artists, men who were able to use and build upon the traditions of the past even as they developed new ways in which to respond to the tastes and needs of their rapidly changing society.

# APPENDIX

# ICONOGRAPHY

It is not my intention to add to the many fine studies of imperial iconography of the third century which are already in print. This monograph has dealt with the stylistic development of portraiture in the early and middle third century, using as the chronological basis for the study those imperial portraits already securely identified by other scholars. In many cases, however, it has been necessary to choose which identifications to accept and which to reject. Therefore, the following list will briefly outline which portraits I believe to have been correctly identified.

A few general principals must be explained here. First, no identification can be accepted unless it finds reasonable justification in the comparison of the sculptured types in question with inscribed likenesses which, for the third century, appear almost exclusively on coins. For imperial figures such as Herennia Etruscilla, whose coin profiles vary so much as to be virtually useless for iconographic study, or Timesitheus, the father-in-law of Gordian III, who was not represented on coins, any identification must remain pure hypothesis. Second, for emperors who reigned for a period of three years or less, it is highly unlikely that more than one official type could have been made and duplicated, or indeed that it would have been desirable to replace an official image so quickly. In a very few cases, such as that of Macrinus, the coin profiles clearly attest the existence of different official images, some with a shorter beard and some with a long, Antonine-style beard, but when portraits of a very short-lived emperor like Balbinus display stylistic variations, these can usually be attributed to the interpretations of copyists rather than to the existence of differing prototypes. Boy-emperors like Elagabalus, Alexander Severus and Gordian III, may have wished to change their official portrait types rather more often than adult emperors in order to demonstrate their increasing maturity. In the cases of Alexander Severus and Gordian III, it is undeniable that some portraits represent them as beardless boys while others show them as young men with facial hair. On the other hand, it is not credible that Gordian III should have had five official types during a reign of only six years, as Bracker has suggested[1].

---

[1] Wegner, Bracker, and Real, *Herrscherbild*, III[3], 13-20. For a refutation of Bracker's theory, see Fittschen, *JdI*, 84 (1969), 204.

Ockham's razor has therefore been applied with ruthless liberality to many proposed distinctions between imperial types.

In the interests of space, only the most recent or crucial bibliography can be cited here for each work. The books and articles cited, however, should give the interested reader fuller literature on each object.

## Macrinus, 217-218

Type I, with shorter beard:

1. Cambridge, Fogg Art Museum, Harvard University, inv. 1949.47.138. Mutilated marble head, h. 0.28. Major publications: Hanfmann, *Latomus*, 11 (1952), pp. 209-215, figs. 5-6; Salzmann, *JdI*, 98 (1983), 361-371, figs. 11, 15, 19.

2. Rome, Palazzo dei Conservatori, inv. 1757. Mutilated marble head and neck, h. 0.25. Major recent publications: Helbig[4], No. 1755; Wiggers and Wegner, *Herrscherbild*, III[1], 134-136, 139, pl. 32; Salzmann, *JdI*, 98 (1983), 361-371, figs. 12, 16, 20.

Variant on Type I, with longer beard:

3. Rome, Museo Capitolino, Stanza degli Imperatori, No. 48, inv. 460. Over life sized, heavily restored head on modern bust. H. of head 0.37. Recent publications: Helbig[4], No. 1307; Wiggers and Wegner, *Herrscherbild*, III[1], 134-136, 138-139, pl. 33; Salzmann, *JdI*, 98 (1983), 361-371, figs. 14, 18, 22.

Type II, with Marcus-Aurelius beard:

4. Belgrade, City Museum, inv. 2636. Bronze head, h. 0.41, of head 0.33. Published: Kondić, *JRS*, 63 (1973), 47-48, plates V, VI, VII. Salzmann, *JdI*, 98 (1983), 362; 371-379, figs. 13, 17, 21, 28, 29, 30.

## Elagabalus, 218-222

Securely accepted:

1. Rome, Capitoline Museum, Stanza degli Imperatori 55, inv. 470. Marble head, h. 0.46. Recent publications: Wiggers and Wegner, *Herrscherbild*, III[1], 151; Bergmann, *Studien*, p. 22, pl. 1, figs. 3-4.

Tentatively accepted:

2. Oslo, Nasjonalgalleriet, head and neck in marble. H. 0.33, of head alone 0.22. Published: L'Orange, *Symbolae Osloenses*, 20 (1940), 152-159; Bergmann, *Studien*, 22. This work is an exact replica of the Capitoline head, though the modeling is somewhat more sensitive. Bergmann raises questions as to its authenticity, but the fact that the surface is root-marked is strong, if not conclusive, evidence in favor of its acceptance.

It is possible that, as L'Orange[2] and Vermeule[3] suggest, a second type was created for Elagabalus. L'Orange has identified such a type in a bust in the Museo Torlonia,[4] while Vermeule proposes that an exceptionally fine bust in Boston[5] represents Elagabalus at a slightly younger age than the Capitoline/Oslo type. In both cases, however, the physical similarities are not strong enough to allow certainty in the identification.

## Alexander Severus, 222-235

Type 1, Boyhood portrait, c. 222

1. Rome, Museo Nuovo del Palazzo dei Conservatori, inv. 2457. Marble head, h. 0.255. Published: Felletti-Maj, *Iconografia*, p. 96, No. 24; Helbig[4], No. 1633; Wiggers and Wegner, *Herrscherbild*, III[1], 192-193, pl. 46.

2. Rome, Museo Capitolino, Stanza degli Imperatori, 69, inv. 480, bust in marble, h. 0.76. Recent publications: Helbig[4], No. 1319; Wiggers and Wegner, *Herrscherbild*, III[1], 191-192; Bergmann, *Studien*, pp. 26-27, pl. 2, fig. 2; Wegner, Bracker and Real, *Herrscherbild*, III[3], 43, 46-47, pl. 17a and 18a, with literature.

3. Copenhagen, Ny Carlsberg Glyptotek, cat. 756, inv. 1283. Head and neck unit, marble, h. 0.34. Recent publications: V. Poulsen, *Les Portraits romains*, II, 142, No. 140, pl. 224; Wiggers and Wegner, *Herrscherbild*, III[1], 188; Wegner, Bracker and Real, *Herrscherbild*, III[3], 43, 45, pl. 20.

4. Oslo, Nasjonalgalleriet, marble, h. 0.32. Recent publications: Wiggers and Wegner, *Herrscherbild*, III[1], 189, pl. 49; Bergmann, *Studien*, p. 26, No. 8, and p. 29.

5. Berlin, Staatliche Museen, Antikenabteilung R100. Marble, h. 0.26. Recent publications: Wiggers and Wegner, *Herrscherbild*, III[1], 184, pl. 48b; Bergmann, *Studien*, p. 26, no. 6.

6. Leningrad, Hermitage Museum, inv. A281, h. of head 0.285, marble. Published: Aleksandra Vostchinina, *Le Portrait romain*, French trans. T. Gourevich (Leningrad: Aurore, 1974), No. 64, plates 86-87, and p. 182 with complete Russian bibliography.

7. Rome, Museo Torlonia, Cat. 589. Marble bust, h. 0.62. Recent publications: Wiggers and Wegner, *Herrscherbild*, III[1], 195, pl. 48a; Bergmann, *Studien*, p. 26.

---

[2] L'Orange, *SymbOslo*, 20 (1940), 158-159.

[3] Cornelius Vermeule, *Iconographic Studies* (Boston: Museum of Fine Arts, 1980), 36-38.

[4] Rome, Museo Torlonia, 574. Published: L'Orange, *SymbOslo*, 20 (1940), 156-159; Vermeule, *Iconographic Studies*, 55-57.

[5] Boston Museum of Fine Arts, inv. 77.337, marble bust, h. 0.71, of face 0.23. Published: Vermeule, *Iconographic Studies*, 35-39, photos pp. 49-51.

8. Vatican, Museo Chiaramonti, 674, inv. 1481. Marble, h. 0.28. Recent publications: Wiggers and Wegner, *Herrscherbild*, III[1], 197; Bergmann, *Studien*, p. 26; Wegner, Bracker, and Real, *Herrscherbild*, III[3], 48.

9. (Provincial replica) Corinth, Museum, inv. 42. Life-sized; precise measurements not available. Published: Wiggers and Wegner, *Herrscherbild*, III[1], 188, pl. 47.

Type 2, Adolescent type, c. A.D. 226

1. Florence, Uffizi Gallery, inv. 1914.245, bust wearing trabeated toga. Marble, h. 0.68. Recent publications: Wiggers and Wegner, *Herrscherbild*, III[1], 186, pl. 53, 65a; Bergmann, *Studien*, pp. 26-27.

2. Paris, Musée du Louvre, MA 1051. Marble, h. 0.39. Recent publications: Wiggers and Wegner, *Herrscherbild*, III[1], pp. 182, 190, pl. 52; Bergmann, *Studien*, pp. 26-27.

Type 3, Young-Adult Type, c. A.D. 230

1. Vatican, Sala dei Busti, 361, inv. 632, head set on modern bust. H. 0.28, marble. Recent publications: Wiggers and Wegner, *Herrscherbild*, III[1], 197, pl. 54; Bergmann, *Studien*, pp. 26-27, pl. 2, fig. 3.; Helbig[4], no. 186.

2. Naples, Museo Nazionale, 5993, colossal nude statue, h. 3.79, marble. Recent publications: Klaus Fittschen and Paul Zanker, "Die Kolossalstatue in Neapel—eine wiederverwendete Statue des Elagabal," *AA*, 85 (1970), 248-253; Wiggers and Wegner, *Herrscherbild*, III[1], 189, pls. 50, 56a; Bergmann, *Studien*, pp. 26-27.

3. Rome, Museo Torlonia, 365, nude statue, marble, h. 2.25. Recent publications: Wiggers and Wegner, *Herrscherbild*, III[1], 194; Bergmann, *Studien*, pp. 26-27.

4. (Provincial replica) Cairo Museum, inv. 27480. Head, in marble, h. 0.24. Recent publication: Wiggers and Wegner, *Herrscherbild*, III[1], 187, pl. 51, with full literature.

## Julia Mammaea, Mother of Alexander Severus

Type 1, probably datable c. 222-230.

1. Vienna, Kunsthistorisches Museum, inv. 18, head set on modern bust, marble, h. 0.255. Recent publications: Meischner, "Frauenporträt," p. 105, No. 82; Wiggers and Wegner, *Herrscherbild*, III[1], 217.

2. Rome, Museo Torlonia, 563. Marble, h. 0.56, of head 0.23. Recent publications: Meischner, "Frauenporträt," p. 105, No. 83; Wiggers and Wegner, *Herrscherbild*, III[1], 213.

3. Rome, Museo Torlonia, 578, head on modern bust. Marble, h. 0.88. Recent publications: Meischner, "Frauenporträt," p. 106, No. 85; Wiggers and Wegner, *Herrscherbild*, III[1], 213, pls. 58b, 62.
4. Rome, Museo Torlonia 590, head on bust to which it does not belong. Marble, h. 0.20, with bust 0.56. Recent publications: Meischner, "Frauenporträt," p. 106, No. 84; Wiggers and Wegner, *Herrscherbild*, III[1], 214.
5. Rome, Museo Torlonia, 595, head set on damaged bust, marble, h. 0.53. Recent publications: Meischner, "Frauenporträt," p. 106, No. 86; Wiggers and Wegner, *Herrscherbild*, III[1], 214.
6. London, British Museum, bust, cat. 1920, marble, h. 0.60. Recent publications: Meischner, "Frauenporträt," p. 105, No. 81, fig. 71; Wiggers and Wegner, *Herrscherbild*, III[1]. 208.
7. Vatican, Sala dei Busti, h. 0.64, marble. Recent publications: Meischner, "Frauenporträt," pp. 105, 107, No. 79, figs. 68-69; Helbig[4], No. 172; Wiggers and Wegner, *Herrscherbild*, III[1], 214-215.

Type 2, possibly datable c. 230
1. Paris, Louvre, MA 3552, diademed head with fragment of bust, marble, life-sized. Recent publications: Meischner, "Frauenporträt," pp. 112-113, No. 97; Wiggers and Wegners, *Herrscherbild*, III[1], 211, pl. 60.
2. London, British Museum, 1922, head in marble, h. 0.38. Recent publications: Meischner, "Frauenporträt," pp. 109-112, No. 96, fig. 74; Wiggers and Wegner, *Herrscherbild*, III[1], 208; Bergmann, *Studien*, p. 30.
3. Rome, Museo Capitolino, Stanza degli Imperatori, 47, inv. 457, marble bust, h. 0.43. Recent publications: Meischner, "Frauenporträt," p. 105, No. 80, Fig. 70; Helbig[4], No. 1305; Wiggers and Wegner, *Herrscherbild*, III[1], 212, pls. 59, 64a; Bergmann, *Studien*, p. 30.
4. Rome, Museo Torlonia, 134. Head on modern bust, marble, h. 0.23. Recent publications: Meischner, "Frauenporträt," p. 107, No. 93, p. 109. Wiggers and Wegner, *Herrscherbild*, III[1], 213.
5. Ostia Antica inv. 26. Over-life-sized head in marble, made for insertion into statue, h. 0.42. Recent publications: Meischner, "Frauenporträt," pp. 109-112, No. 95, figs. 72-73; Wiggers and Wegner, *Herrscherbild*, III[1], 209, pl. 61.

## Maximinus Thrax, 235-238

1. Copenhagen, Ny Carlsberg Glyptotek, cat. 744, marble head, h. 0.43. Recent publications: Bergmann, *Studien*, pp. 30-31; V.

Poulsen, *Les Portraits romains*, II, 161-162, No. 164; Wiggers and Wegner, *Herrscherbild*, III[1], 226-227, pl. 69a.

2. Rome, Museo Capitolino, Stanza degli Imperatori 62. Marble, h. of head 0.30. Recent publications: Helbig[4], No. 1314; Wiggers and Wegner, *Herrscherbild*, III[1], 227-228, with complete recent references. Bergmann, *Studien*, pp. 30-31.

3. Paris, Louvre, MA 1044. Marble bust, h. 0.58, of head 0.265. Recent publications: Wiggers and Wegner, *Herrscherbild*, III[1], 227, pl. 64b, with complete literature; Bergmann, *Studien*, pp. 30-31.

4. Rome, Museo Nazionale delle Terme, cat. 278, inv. 52681. Marble fragment of the upper part of a head, h. 0.21. Recent publications: Wiggers and Wegner, *Herrscherbild*, III[1], 228, pl. 68 and 70b; Bergmann, *Studien*, pp. 30-31.

5. Rome, Casino Aurora, formerly in Villa Ludovisi. Head, made for insertion, now set into togate statue to which it may not belong. Over-life-sized; precise measurements not available. Recent publication: Klaus Fittschen, "Siebenmals Maximinus Thrax," *AA*, 92 (1977), 324, figs. 3, 4.

6. Rome, Casino Aurora, formerly in Villa Ludovisi. Marble, over-life-sized; precise measurements not available. Recent publication: Fittschen, *AA*, 92 (1977), 324, figs. 5-6.

## Maximus, Son of Maximinus Thrax

1. Copenhagen, Ny Carlsberg Glyptotek, cat. 745, inv. 819. Head in marble, h. 0.42. Recent publications: Wiggers and Wegner, *Herrscherbild*, III[1], 232 and 234, pl. 71; V. Poulsen, *Les Portraits romains*, II, No. 166, pp. 162-163; Bergmann, *Studien*, pp. 32-33.

2. Copenhagen, Ny Carlsberg Glyptotek, cat. 746, inv. 823, marble head, h. 0.42. Recent publications: Wiggers and Wegner, *Herrscherbild*, III[1], 234, pl. 70a; V. Poulsen, *Les Portraits romains*, pp. 162-163, No. 165.

3. Copenhagen, Ny Carlsberg Glyptotek No. 759, inv. 826. Head made for insertion into a draped statue. Marble, h. 0.34. Recent publications: Wiggers and Wegner, *Herrscherbild*, III[1], 232, 234; Bergmann, *Studien*, pp. 32-34.

## Pupienus, April-July, A.D. 238.

1. Paris, Louvre, MA 1020. Italian marble head with small bib-bust, made for insertion into statue. H. 0.35. Recent publication: Wiggers and Wegner, *Herrscherbild*, III[1], 244, pl. 76a.

2. Rome, Vatican, Braccio Nuovo, No. 54. Marble bust, h. in toto 0.69. Recent publications: Wegner, *Festschrift Kleiner*, p. 106; Wiggers and Wegner, *Herrscherbild*, III[1], 245, pls, 65b and 77.
3. Rome, Museo Capitolino, Stanza degli Imperatori, No. 66. Marble, h. 0.34. Recent publications: Helbig[4], No. 1318; Wiggers and Wegner, *Herrscherbild*, III[1], 255, pl. 76b.
4. Rome, Museo Torlonia, 588. Marble, h. 0.34. Recent publication: Wiggers and Wegner, *Herrscherbild*, III[1], 245.

Of suspect authenticity:
5. Copenhagen, Ny Carlsberg Glyptotek, cat. 467, inv. 788. Head in marble, h. 0.29. Recent publications: V. Poulsen, *Les Portraits romains*, II, 183, pl. 306-307; Britt Haarløv, *New Identifications of Third Century Roman Portraits* (Odense: Odense University Press), 1975, pp. 13-14. The identification of this head as a replica of the portraits of Pupienus, suggested by Haarløv, is undoubtedly correct. However, some deviations from the type in the form of the hairline, as well as the very unusual treatment of the hair, arouse suspicions that the copy may not be ancient.

## Balbinus, April-July, A.D. 238

1. Rome, Museum of the Catacomb of the Praetextatus, marble sarcophagus, with reclining portrait figures of Balbinus and his wife on the cover, portraits of them in relief on the box. Height 1.17, length 2.32, depth 1.31. Cover: height 0.83, length 2.32, depth 1.17. Principal publications: Gütschow, *MemPontAcc*, 4 (1934-38), 77-106, pls. X-XII; Jucker, *AA*, 81 (1966), pp. 501-514, figs. 7-13; Jucker, *Bulletin of the Cleveland Museum of Art*, 1967, pp. 15-16; Wiggers and Wegner, *Herrscherbild*, III[1], 248, pl. 79.
1a. Cleveland Museum of Art, inv. 25.945, head from relief, identified beyond doubt as belonging to sarcophagus in the museum of the Catacomb of the Praetextatus. Published: Jucker, *AA*, 81 (1966), 501-514, and *Bulletin of the Cleveland Museum of Art*, 1967, pp. 11-16, figs. 1-3; Wiggers and Wegner, *Herrscherbild*, III[1], 247.
2. Vatican library, bronze head, h. 0.38. Recent publications: Wiggers and Wegner, *Herrscherbild*, III[1], 248, pl. 78a; J. and J. Ch. Balty, *Bulletin de l'Institut Historique Belge de Rome*, 44 (1974), 31, 35; Helbig[4], No. 472.
3. Brussels, Musée du Parc du Cinquantenaire, A 3753. Marble, h. 0.245. Published: J. and J. Ch. Balty, *Bulletin de l'Institut Historique Belge de Rome*, 44 (1974), 24-45.

4.  (Provincial portrait) Piraeus Museum, marble statue. H. 2.02. Principal publications: Gräfin von Schlieffen (R. West), *ÖJh*, 29 (1935), 97-108. For recent publications with full references, see Wiggers and Wegner, *Herrscherbild*, III[1], 248, and J. and J. Ch. Balty, *Bulletin de l'Institut Historique Belge de Rome*, 44 (1974), 40-42, pls. 4-5.

## Gordian III, 238-244

Type 1, Childhood portrait, probably datable 238 through 241

1.  Rome, Palazzo dei Conservatori, Sala degli Orti Meceneziane, inv. 995. Marble, h. 0.28. The root marks on the surface indicate that the ancient surface has not been reworked. Recent publications: Fittschen, *JdI*, 84 (1969), 200-201, No. 14; pp. 209-210, figs. 13-16; Wegner, Bracker, and Real, *Herrscherbild* III[3], 16, 26.
2.  Rome, Villa Albani, Galleria 1023. Marble head set on a bust to which it does not belong, h. 0.24. Recent publications: Fittschen, *JdI*, 84 (1969), 200-201, No. 23, pp. 206, 209, figs. 17-20; Wegner, Bracker and Real, *Herrscherbild*, III[3], 28.
3.  Berlin, Staatliche Museen, R102, bust with trabeated toga, marble, h. 0.56. Recent publications: Fittschen, *JdI*, 84 (1969), 200-201, No. 1, and p. 206; Wegner, Bracker and Real, *Herrscherbild*, III[3], 16-17, 21, pl. 7.
4.  Rome, Vatican, Museo Chiaramonti 699, inv. 1232. Marble bust, h. 0.30. Recent publications: Fittschen, *JdI*, 84 (1969), 200-201, No. 21, and p. 206; Wegner, Bracker, and Real, *Herrscherbild*, III[3], 28, pl. 2.
5.  Rome, Museo Nazionale delle Terme, 4178. Marble head, h. 0.21. Recent publications: Fittschen, *JdI*, 84 (1969), 200-201, No. 17, pp. 206, 207, figs. 9-12; Wegner, Bracker and Real, *Herrscherbild*, III[3], p. 27.
6.  Rome, Villa Albani, Tempietto di Giove. Marble, h. of head 0.18. Recent publications: Fittschen, *JdI*, 84 (1969), 200-201, No. 22, p. 206, and figs. 3-4; Wegner, Bracker, and Real, *Herrscherbild*, III[3], 28.
7.  Rome, Museo Torlonia, 606, marble, h. 0.22. Recent publications: Fittschen, *JdI*, 84 (1969), 200-201, No. 19, and p. 206; Wegner, Bracker and Real, *Herrscherbild*, III[2], 27.
8.  Rome, Museo Torlonia, 620. Marble, h. 0.24. Recent publications: Fittschen, *JdI*, 84 (1969), 200-201, No. 18, and p. 206; Wegner, Bracker, and Real, *Herrscherbild*, III[3], 27.
9.  Palermo, Museo Archeologico. Head on modern bust, in marble, slightly under-life-sized; precise measurements not available. Recent publications: Fittschen, *JdI*, 84 (1969), 200-201, No. 8, and p. 206; Wegner, Bracker, and Real, *Herrscherbild*, III[3], p. 25.

10. Paris, Bibliothèque Nationale, marble head on modern bust, h. 0.165. Recent publications: Fittschen, *JdI*, 84 (1969), 200-201, No. 9, and p. 206; Wegner, Bracker and Real, *Herrscherbild*, III³, 25.

11. Paris, Louvre, 2331. Head on modern bust, h. of ancient part 0.26. Recent publications: Fittschen, *JdI*, 84 (1969), 200-201, No. 11, and p. 206; Wegner, Bracker and Real, *Herrscherbild*, III³, 26.

12. Rome, Museo Nuovo del Palazzo dei Conservatori, inv. 479, head on bust to which it does not belong, h. 0.70, of head 0.245. Recent publications: Fittschen, *JdI* 84 (1969), 200-201, No. 13, and p. 206; Wegner, Bracker and Real, *Herrscherbild*, III³, 26.

13. Rome, Latini collection, marble head, h. 0.21. Recent publications: Fittschen, *JdI*, 84 (1969), 200-201, No. 15, and p. 206; Wegner, Bracker and Real, *Herrscherbild*, III³, 28.

14. Rome, Museo Capitolino, Stanza degli Imperatori, 78. Life-sized head set on bust to which it does not belong, h. 0.455. Recent publications: Fittschen, *JdI*, 84 (1969), 200, No. 12; Wegner, Bracker, and Real, *Herrscherbild*, III³, 26, pl. 7a; Helbig⁴, No. 1321.

15. Turin, Museo di Antichità. Recent publications: Fittschen, *JdI*, 84 (1969), 200-201, No. 25; p. 206, figs. 5-8; Wegner, Bracker and Real, *Herrscherbild* III³, 29.

16. Vienna, Kunsthistorisches Museum, miniature bronze bust, h. 0.095. Recent publication: Wegner, Bracker and Real, *Herrscherbild*, III³, 29.

Type 2, adolescent type, datable probably 242-244

1. Florence, Palazzo Medici-Riccardi, head with laurel wreath, in marble, set on modern bust. Over-life-sized; precise measurements not available. Recent publications: Fittschen, *JdI*, 84 (1969), 200-201, No. 3, p. 206, figs. 21a-b, p. 210; Wegner, Bracker and Real, *Herrscherbild*, III³, 22.

2. Vatican, Sala dei Busti, inv. 618, head in marble, h. 0.75. Measurements without restorations not available. Recent publications: Helbig⁴, No. 189; Fittschen, *JdI*, 84 (1969), 200-201, No. 20 and p. 206; Wegner, Bracker and Real, *Herrscherbild*, III³, 28, pl. 5.

3. Rome, Museo Nazionale delle Terme, inv. 326. Colossal head in marble, h. 0.63. Recent publications: Fittschen, *JdI*, 84 (1969), 200-201, No. 16, and pp. 206, 211, figs. 1-2; Wegner, Bracker and Real, *Herrscherbild*, III³, 19, 27, pl. 9.

4. Paris, Louvre, MA 1063, half-body bust in marble, h. 0.75. Recent publications: Fittschen, *JdI*, 84 (1969), 200-201, No. 10 and p. 206; Wegner, *Festschrift Kleiner*, p. 122; Wegner, Bracker, and Real, *Herrscherbild*, III³, 19, 26, pl. 8, with full literature.

Tranquillina, married to Gordian III in 241

1. London, British Museum, cat. 1923, head set on modern bust, marble, h. 0.415. Recent publications: Bergmann, *Studien*, p. 39, pl. 7, figs. 3-4; Wegner, Bracker and Real, *Herrscherbild*, III³, 52, 54.

2. Liverpool Museum, formerly in Rossie Priory, head in marble, h. 0.23. Recent publications: Bergmann, *Studien*, p. 39, No. 2; Wegner, Bracker, and Real, *Herrscherbild*, III³, 52, 54 pl. 23.

3. Copenhagen, Ny Carlsberg Glyptotek 754, inv. 1572. Head in marble, h. 0.23. Recent publications: V. Poulsen, *Les Portraits romains*, II, 165-166, No. 169, pl. 271; Wegner, Bracker and Real, *Herrscherbild*, III³, 52, 54.

4. Toulouse, Musée St. Raymond, marble bust, h. 0.50. Published: Felletti-Maj, *Iconografia*, p. 179, No. 220; Wegner, Bracker and Real, *Herrscherbild*, III³, 52, 56.

5. Dresden, Albertinum. Staatliche Skulpturensammlung, No. 380, marble. Recent publication: Wegner, Bracker, and Real, *Herrscherbild*, III³, 52, 53.

6. Florence, Uffizi Gallery, 1914.265. Head in marble set on modern bust, h. of ancient part 0.26. Recent publication: Wegner, Bracker, and Real, *Herrscherbild*, III³, 52, 53.

7. Rome, Vatican, Museo Chiaramonti, head in marble, set on ancient bust to which it does not belong. H. 0.655, of ancient parts 0.59. Recent publication: Wegner, Bracker and Real, *Herrscherbild*, III³, 52, 56, pl. 22.

8. Rome, Museo Torlonia 592, marble bust, h. in toto 0.53, of head 0.24. Recent publication: Wegner, Bracker and Real, *Herrscherbild*, III³, 52, 55.

9. Rome, Vatican, former Lateran collection, head in marble, h. 0.25. Recent publications: Wegner, Bracker and Real, *Herrscherbild*, III³, 52, 56, pl. 22.

10. Basel, art trade. Head in marble, h. 0.23. Published: *Antike Kunst*, sale catalogue (Basel: Palladini gallery, 1976), p. 106, No. 123, with photographs. Wegner, Bracker, and Real, *Herrscherbild*, III³, 53.

Though this type has been identified by some scholars as Otacilia Severa,[6] wife of Philip the Arab, the form of the coiffure and the stylistic similarities to the portraits of Gordian III argue in favor of its identification as Tranquillina.[7]

---

[6] E.g. F. Poulsen, *Catalogue*, p. 108, No. 108, and Felletti-Maj, *Iconografia*, pp. 177-180.

[7] See Bergmann, *Studien*, p. 40; Wegner, Bracker, and Real, *Herrscherbild*, III³, 51-52 and 57-58.

## Philip the Arab, 244-249

1. Rome, Vatican, Braccio Nuovo, inv. 2216, bust wearing trabeated toga, marble, h. 0.71. Recent publications: Helbig[4], No. 456; Wegner, Bracker, and Real, *Herrscherbild*, III[3], 32-33, 40, pls. 11a, 12a; Kiang, *Acta ad Archaeologiam et Artium Historiam Pertinentia*, 8 (1978), 75-84, pls. III, IV.

2. Leningrad, Hermitage Museum, togate bust in marble, h. 0.70, of head 0.27. Recent publications: Bergmann, *Studien*, p. 34, No. 2; Vostchinina, *Le Portrait romain*, No. 66, pls. 90-91, p. 184, with complete Russian bibliography; Wegner, Bracker and Real, *Herrscherbild*, III[3], 32-33, 36, pl. 13; Kiang, *Acta ad Archaeologiam et Artium Historiam Pertinentia*, 8 (1978), pl. V-a.

## Otacilia Severa, Wife of Philip the Arab

1. Rome, Palazzo dei Conservatori, inv. 2765. Marble head, h. 0.26. Recent publications: Helbig[4], No. 1632; Wegner, *Herrscherbild*, III[1], 213; Bergmann, *Studien*, p. 39, pl. 7, figs. 5, 6; Wegner, Bracker, and Real, *Herrscherbild*, III[3], 57, 61, pl. 25.

2. Petworth, Leconfield collection, head made for insertion into statue, h. 0.52. Recent publications: Wegner, *Herrscherbild*, III[1], 211; Bergmann, *Studien*, p. 39; Wegner, Bracker and Real, *Herrscherbild*, III[3], 57, 60-61.

3. Florence, Uffizi Gallery, 1914.271, head set on bust to which it may not belong. H. 0.61, of head and neck 0.29. Recent publications: Bergmann, *Studien*, p. 39; Wiggers and Wegner, *Herrscherbild*, III[1], 206-207; Wegner, Bracker and Real, *Herrscherbild*, III[3], 57, 60-61.

## Philip II, Son of Philip the Arab

1. Toulouse, Musée Saint Raymond, 30.128. Marble head, life sized. Recent publications: Fittschen, *JdI*, 84 (1969), 211, fig. 24; Wiggers and Wegner, *Herrscherbild*, III[1], 199; Bergmann, *Studien*, pp. 36-38, pl. 5, figs. 1-3; Wegner, Bracker, and Real, *Herrscherbild*, III[3], 44, 49, pl. 15.

2. Ostia, Museum inv. 1129. Marble head, h. 0.18 m. Recent publications: Helbig[4], No. 3070; Wiggers and Wegner, *Herrscherbild*, III[1], 189-190; Bergmann, *Studien*, pp. 35-38, pl. 4, figs. 1-2; Wegner, Bracker, and Real, *Herrscherbild*, III[3], 25, 46.

3. Malibu, J. Paul Getty Museum, inv. 79.AB.120. Bronze head, h. 0.22 m. Published: Jiří Frel, *Roman Portraits*, catalogue for the exhibition "Citizens and Caesars," Philbrook Art Center, Tulsa, Oklahoma, April 26—July 12, 1981, pp. 104 and 131, No. 86.

4. Munich Glyptothek, cat. 360. Formerly set on bust to which it did not belong. Recent publications: Wiggers and Wegner, *Herrscherbild*, III¹, 189; Wegner, Bracker, and Real, *Herrscherbild*, III³, 46.

## Trajan Decius, 249-251

1. Rome, Museo Capitolino, Stanza degli Imperatori, head in marble, h. 0.24. Recent publications: Helbig⁴, No. 1320; J. and J. Ch. Balty, *Bulletin de l'Institut Historique Belge de Rome*, 44 (1974), 45-54, pl. 6, fig. 1, and pl. 8, fig 1; J. and J. Ch. Balty, *RömMitt*, 83 (1976), 177-178, pl. 43, fig. 1, pl. 44, fig. 2; Bergmann, *Studien*, pp. 42-43, pl. 6, figs. 3-4; Wegner, Bracker and Real, *Herrscherbild*, III³, 64, 66, pl. 26.

2. Rome, Palazzo dei Conservatori, statue of Mars with portrait head, marble, h. 2.17. Recent publications: Niemeyer, *Statuarische Darstellung*, p. 113, pl. 48, fig. 2; Helbig⁴, No. 1494; Wegner, Bracker and Real, *Herrscherbild* III³, 67.

3. Florence, Museo Archeologico, inv. 14013, bronze head, h. 0.27. Recent publications: J. and J. Ch. Balty, *Bulletin de l'Institut Historique Belge de Rome*, 44 (1974), 47-48, pl. 7; Wegner, Bracker and Real, *Herrscherbild*, III³, 65, 84-86, 87-88.

4. Würzburg, University museum, marble head and neck, h. 0.32, of head alone 0.24. Recent publications: Th. Lorenz, *Führer durch die Antikenabteilung des Martin von Wagner Museum der Universität Würzburg*, ed. E. Simon (Mainz, 1975), p. 254, No. H2406, pl. 64; J. and J. Ch. Balty, *RömMitt*, 83 (1976), 177-178, pl. 45, fig. 1, and pl. 47, figs. 1-2.

5. (Provincial replica) Deva, regional museum, bronze head, h. 0.25, broken at chin. Provenance: Ulpia Traiana (Sarmizegetusa), 1964. Published: J. and J. Ch. Balty, *Bulletin de l'Institut Historique Belge de Rome*, 44 (1974), 48, pl. 9, fig. 2, with full earlier literature. Wegner, Bracker, and Real, *Herrscherbild*, III³, 64-65.

No portraits of Herennia Etruscilla, the wife of Decius, nor of his two sons Herennius Etruscus and Hostilianus have yet been identified with any certainty.

## Trebonianus Gallus, 251-252

No type has yet been identified with certainty. The bronze statue in New York (discussed in Chapter I, note 44), has perhaps the strongest claim of the various candidates, by virtue of its colossal size, which strongly suggests that it is an imperial portrait. The evidence of the coins, however, is not decisive.

## Valerian, 253-260

1. (Provincial portrait) Copenhagen, Ny Carlsberg Glyptotek, 766c. Marble head, h. 0.425. Recent publications: V. Poulsen, *Les Portraits romains*, II, 169-170, No. 174, pls. 279-280, with full earlier literature; Bergmann, *Studien*, pp. 51, 59-60, 93, pl. 15, fig. 1; Wegner, Bracker and Real, *Herrscherbild*, III³, 101, 102-103.

A number of Sassanian rock-cut reliefs in Iran represent Roman emperors in various positions of defeat and submission before Persian monarchs, and Valerian is probably represented on most if not all of these.[8] However, these reliefs are obviously not based on Roman prototypes, and were produced by artists of a culture which lacked a tradition of realistic portraiture. They are, therefore, of little value for either iconographic or stylistic study of Valerian's Roman portraits.

## Gallienus, 253-268

Type 1, Gallienus as Caesar, c. 253-260
1. Rome, Museo Capitolino, Stanza degli Imperatori, marble head, h. 0.21. Recent publications: Helbig⁴, No. 1324; Bergmann, *Studien*, p. 51, No. 2, pp. 57-58, pl. 12, figs. 1-2; Wegner, Bracker and Real, *Herrscherbild*, III³, 107, 116-117, pl. 43.
2. Rome, Palazzo Braschi (formerly Museo Capitolino, Stanza degli Imperatori). Marble bust, h. in toto 0.66. Recent publications: Fittschen, *RömMitt*, 77 (1970), pl. 68, fig. 2; Bergmann, *Studien*, p. 51, No. 3, pp. 57-58, pl. 12; Wegner, Bracker and Real, *Herrscherbild*, III³, 107-108, 119, pl. 41.
3. Berlin, Staatliche Museen, Antiken-Sammlung, R114, marble head, h. 0.37. Recent publications: Bergmann, *Studien*, p. 51, No. 4, pp. 57-58, pl. 12, figs. 5-6; Wegner, Bracker and Real, *Herrscherbild*, III³, 108, 111, pl. 42.
4. Copenhagen, Ny Carlsberg Glyptotek, inv. 3388. Marble head, h. 0.445. Recent publications: Fittschen, *RömMitt*, 77 (1970), 175, pls. 281-282; Wegner, Bracker and Real, *Herrscherbild*, III³, 112-113.

Type 2, Gallienus as Augustus, c. 260
1. Brussels, Musée du Parc du Cinquantenaire, A 3558. Marble head, life-sized, measurements not available. Recent publications: Bergmann, *Studien*, p. 51, No. 5, p. 53, pl. 13, figs. 1-2; Wegner, Bracker and Real, *Herrscherbild*, III³, 109-110, 111, with full literature.

---

[8] B. C. Mac Dermot, "Roman Emperors in the Sassanian Reliefs," *JRS*, 44 (1954), 76-80; Felletti-Maj, *Iconografia*, pp. 216-217, No. 284.

2. Lagos, Portugal, Museo Regional, inv. 1418. Marble head, somewhat battered, no restorations, h. 0.29. Recent publications: Bergmann, *Studien*, p. 51, No. 6, p. 53, pl. 13, figs. 3-4; Wegner, Bracker and Real, *Herrscherbild*, III³, 110, 113-114, pl. 47.

3. Paris, Louvre, MR 511, over-life-sized head, precise measurements not available. Recent publications with earlier literature: Wegner, Bracker and Real, *Herrscherbild*, III³, 115; Bergmann, *Studien*, p. 52, No. 8.

4. Paris, Louvre, MA 1223. Head with strophion, marble. Measurements not available. Published: Bergmann, *Studien*, p. 52, No. 11, p. 53.

5. Rome, Museo Nazionale delle Terme, inv. 644. Marble head, h. 0.38, made for insertion into a statue. Recent publications: Helbig⁴, No. 2315; Bergmann, *Studien*, pp. 51-54; Wegner, Bracker and Real, *Herrscherbild*, III³, 108-110, 117-118, pl. 45; *Museo Nazionale Romano: le sculture*, ed. Guiliano, pp. 296-297, No. 181 (Silvia Allegra Dayan), with literature.

6. Rome, Museo Torlonia, 604. Marble bust, h. 0.67. Recent publications: Bergmann, *Studien*, p. 52, No. 12; Wegner, Bracker and Real, *Herrscherbild*, III³, 109, 118-119.

Type 3, late in reign of Gallienus
1. Copenhagen, Ny Carlsberg Glyptotek, cat. 768, inv. 832. Colossal head in marble, h. 0.52. Recent publications: V. Poulsen, *Les Portraits romains*, II, 172-173, No. 177, pls. 285-286; Bergmann, *Studien*, p. 52, No. 14, p. 54, pl. 14, figs. 1-2; Wegner, Bracker and Real, *Herrscherbild*, III³, 113, with full earlier literature.

# SELECT BIBLIOGRAPHY

## A) *Catalogues*

*Aquileia*:
Scrinari, Valnea Santa Maria. *Museo Archeologico di Aquileia: Catalogo delle Sculture Romane.* Rome: Istituto Poligrafico dello Stato, 1972.

*Berlin*:
Blümel, Carl. *Römische Bildnisse.* Bd. suppl., *Katalog der Sammlung antiker Skulpturen.* Berlin: Schoetz, 1933.

*Boston*:
Comstock, Mary, and Cornelius C. Vermeule. *Sculpture in Stone.* Boston: Museum of Fine Arts, 1976.

*Copenhagen*:
Poulsen, Frederik. *Catalogue of Ancient Sculpture, Ny Carlsberg Glyptotek.* 2nd ed., trans. W. E. Calvert. Copenhagen: Ny Carlsberg Glyptotek, 1951.
Poulsen, Vagn. *Les Portraits romains.* Printed for the Ny Carlsberg Glyptotek. Copenhagen: Munksgaard,1974. Vol. II.

*Florence*:
Mansuelli, Guido A. *Galleria degli Uffizi: le sculture.* Rome: Istituto poligrafico dello stato, 1961.

*Frankfurt*:
*Bildwerke aus dem Liebighaus.* Frankfurt am Main, 1962.
Eckstein, F., and H. Beck. *Antike Plastik im Liebighaus.* Frankfurt am Main: Liebighaus, 1973.

*Fulda*:
Heintze, Helga von. *Die antiken Porträts in Schloss Fasanerie bei Fulda.* Mainz an Rhein: P. von Zabern. 1968.

*Leningrad*:
Vostchinina, Aleksandra. *Le Portrait romain.* In Russian and French, French trans. T. Gourevich. Leningrad: Aurore, for the Hermitage Museum, 1974.

*London*:
Smith, A. H. *A Catalogue of Sculpture in the Department of Greek and Roman Antiquities, British Museum.* London: British Museum, 1904, Vol. III.

*Madrid*:
Blanco, A. *Museo del Prado, Catalogo de la escultura.* Madrid, 1957.

*Malibu*:
Frel, Jiří. *Roman Portraits in the J. Paul Getty Museum,* exh. cat. Philbrook Art Center, Tulsa, Oklahoma, and the J. Paul Getty Museum, Malibu, California, 1981.

*Munich*:
Furtwängler, Adolf. *Beschreibung der Glyptothek König Ludwig I zu München.* Munich: A. Buchholz, 1910.

*Naples*:
*Guida illustrata del museo nazionale di Napoli.* Ed. Arnold Ruesch. Naples: Richter, 1925.

*New York:*
Richter, Gisela M. A. *Greek, Etruscan and Roman Bronzes.* New York: Metropolitan Museum of Art, 1915.
———.*Handbook of the Classical Collection.* New York: Metropolitian Museum of Art, 1930.

*Paris:*
*Catalogue sommaire des marbres antiques.* Paris: Musée du Louvre, 1896.
Charbonneaux, Jean. *La Sculpture grecque et romaine au Musée du Louvre.* Paris: Ministère d'état, affaires culturelles, 1963.

*Rome:*
British School at Rome. *The Sculptures of the Museo Capitolino.* Ed. H. Stuart-Jones. Oxford: Clarendon Press, 1912.
———.*The Sculptures of the Palazzo dei Conservatori.* Ed. H. Stuart-Jones. Oxford: Clarendon Press, 1926.
Calza, Raissa, M. Bonanno, G. Messineo, B. Palma, P. Pensabene. *Antichità della villa Doria Pamfili.* Ed. Raissa Calza. Rome: Libreria dello stato, 1977.
Felletti-Maj, Bianca-Maria. *Museo nazionale romano: i ritatti.* Rome: Libreria dello stato, 1953.
*Museo Nazionale Romano: le sculture.* Ed. Antonio Giuliano. Rome: De Luca, 1979.
Gütschow, Margarete. *Das Museum der Praetextatkatakombe.* Vol. IV of *MemPontAcc,* 3rd ser. 1938.
Heintze, Helga von. Entries in Helbig⁴.
de Luca, Gioia. *I monumenti antichi di Palazzo Corsini in Roma.* Rome: Accademia Nazionale dei Lincei, 1976.
Mustilli, Domenico. *Il Museo Mussolini.* Rome: Libreria dello stato, 1939.
Visconti, Charles Ludovico. *Les Monuments de sculpture antique du musée Torlonia.* Rome, 1884.

*Vatican:*
Amelung, Walther, *Die Skulpturen des vaticanischen Museums.* Vol. I, Berlin: Georg Reimer, 1903. Vol. II, Berlin: Georg Reimer, 1908.
Lippold, Georg. *Die Skulpturen des vaticanischen Museums.* Vol. III, Berlin: De Gruyter, 1956.
Giuliano, Antonio. *Catalogo dei ritratti romani del museo profano Lateranense.* Vatican: Tipografia poliglotta Vaticana, 1957.

*Venice:*
Anti, Carlo. *Il regio museo archeologico nel palazzo reale di Venezia.* Rome: Libreria dello stato, 1930.
Traversari, Gustavo. *Museo archeologico di Venezia: i ritratti.* Rome: Istituto poligrafico dello stato, 1968.

*Miscellaneous Catalogues:*
Brunn, Heinrich, and Paul Arndt: *Griechische und römische Porträts.* Text. Munich: Friedrich Bruckmann, 1891. Plates. Munich: Friedrich Bruckmann, 1891.
Dütschke, Hans. *Antike Bildwerke in Oberitalien.* Leipzig: Engelmann, 1874-1882.
Espérandieu, Emile, et. al. *Recueil général des bas-reliefs, statues, et bustes de la Gaule Romaine.* Paris: Imprimerie nationale, 1907-1966. 14 vols., including supplements.
*Nuove Scoperte e acquisizioni nell'Etruria Meridionale.* Exh. cat., ed. Mario Moretti. Rome: Museo Nazionale della Villa Giulia, 1975.
Poulsen, Frederik. *Greek and Roman Portraits in English Country Houses.* Oxford: Clarendon Press, 1923.
———.*Porträtstudien in norditalischen Provinzmuseum.* Copenhagen: Høst, 1928.
———.*Sculptures antiques des musées de province espagnols.* Copenhagen, 1933.

B) *Iconographic Studies*

Balty, Janine and Jean-Charles. "Notes d'iconographie romain," *Bulletin de l'Institut Historique Belge de Rome*, 44 (1974), 24-45.

——."Notes d'iconographie romain II," *RömMitt*, 83 (1976), 175-193, plates 43-56.

Bernoulli, Johann Jakob. *Römische Ikonographie*. Stuttgart: W. Spemann, 1882-1894, Vol. II, part, 3.

Bracker, Jörgen. "Bestimmung der Bildnisse Gordians III nach einer neuen ikonographischen Methode." Diss. Westfälische Wilhelms Universität zu Münster,1966.

Buchholz, Käte. *Die Bildnisse der Kaiserinnen der Severerzeit nach ihren Frisuren, 193-235 n. Chr.* Frankfurt am Main, 1963.

Delbrueck, Richard. *Die Münzbildnisse von Maximinus bis Carinus*. Vol. III, part 2, of *Das römische Herrscherbild*. Ed. Max Wegner. Berlin: Mann, 1940.

Felletti-Maj, Bianca-Maria. *Iconografia romana imperiale*. Rome: L'Erma di Bretschneider, 1958.

Fittschen, Klaus, "Sarkophage römischer Kaiser oder vom Nutzen der Porträtforschung," *JdI*, 94 (1979), 578-593.

Giuliano, Antonio. "Due ritratti di Alessandro Severo nel museo Lateranense," *ArchCl*, 3 (1951), 181-185, plates XLV-XLVIII.

Gräfin von Schlieffen, Anna (Robert West), "Eine römische Kaiserstatue im Piraeus Museum" *ÖJh*, 29 (1935), 97-108.

Haarløv, Britt. *New Identifications of Third-Century Roman Portraits*. Odense: Odense University Press, 1975.

Heintze, Helga von. "Studien zu den Porträts des 3. Jahrhunderts n.Chr. I, Gordian III," *RömMitt*, 62 (1955), 174-184.

——"Studien zu den Porträts des 3. Jahrhunderts n. Chr. II, Trebonianus Gallus—Trajan Decius; III, Gordians I-II," *RömMitt*, 63 (1956), 56-65.

——.Studien zu den Porträts des 3. Jahrhunderts n. Chr. IV, Der Feldherr des grossen Ludovisischen Schlachtsarkophags," *RömMitt*, 64 (1957), 69-91.

——."Studien zu den Porträts des 3. Jahrhunderts n. Chr. V, Der Knabe des Acilia Sarkophags," *RömMitt*, 66 (1959), 175-191.

——."Studien zu den Porträts des 3. Jahrhunderts n. Chr. VI, Eine Porträtbüste des Severus Alexander aus Veji," *RömMitt*, 69 (1962), 164-171.

——."Studien zu den Porträts des 3. Jahrhunderts n. Chr. VII, Caracalla, Geta, Elagabal und Severus Alexander," *RömMitt*, 73-74 (1966-67), 190-231.

——."Studien zu den Porträts des 3. Jahrhunderts n. Chr. VIII, Die vier Kaiser der Krisenjahre 193-197 n. Chr.," *RömMitt*, 84 (1977), 159-180.

Leeb, Martha. "A New Portrait of Gallienus," *Smith College Museum of Art Bulletin*, 29-31 (1951), 8-10.

Meischner, Jutta. "Ein Porträt des Kaisers Volusianus," *AA* 82 (1967), 220-228.

Weber, Hans. "Zu einem Bildnis der Kaiserin Julia Paula," *JdI*, 68 (1953), 124-138.

Wegner, Max, Jörgen Bracker and Willi Real, *Gordianus III bis Carinus*, Vol. III, part 3 of *Das römische Herrscherbild*. Berlin: Mann, 1979.

Wegner, Max, *Die Herrscherbildnisse in Antoninischer Zeit*, Vol. II, part 4 of *Das römische Herrscherbild*, ed. Max Wegner. Berlin: Mann, 1939.

Wiggers, Heinz, and Max Wegner. *Caracalla bis Balbinus*. Vol. III, part 1 of *Das römische Herrscherbild*. Ed. Max Wegner. Berlin: Mann, 1971.


C. *Other Works Consulted*

Alföldi, Andreas. "Die Vorherrschaft der Pannonier und die Reaktion des Hellenentums unter Gallienus," *25 Jahre römisch-germanische Kommission*. Berlin-Leipzig, 1930.

Anton, John P. "Plotinus's Conception of the Functions of the Artist," *Journal of Aesthetics and Art Criticism*, 26 (1967), 91-101.

Becatti, Giovanni. "Nuovo contributo  ostiense dei ritratti romani," *Le Arti*, 2 (1939-1940), 3-11.

Bergmann, Marianne. *Studien zum römischen Porträt des 3. Jahrhunderts n. Chr.*, Vol. 18 of *Antiquitas*, 3rd ser. Bonn, 1977.

Bianchi-Bandinelli, Ranuccio. *Rome: the Center of Power.* Trans. Peter Green. New York: Braziller, 1970.

——.*Rome, the Late Empire.* Trans. Peter Green. New York: Braziller, 1971.

Bovini, Giuseppe. "Gallieno, la sua iconografia e i riflessi in essa delle vicende storiche e culturali del tempo," *MemLinc*, 7th ser., 2 (1941), 115-162.

——."Osservazione sulla ritrattistica romana da Treboniano Gallo a Probo," *MonAnt.*, 39 (1943), 179-366.

Breckenridge, James D. *Likeness: A Conceptual History of Portraiture.* Evanston: Northwestern University Press, 1968.

——."Imperial Portraiture: Augustus to Gallienus," *Aufstieg und Niedergang der römischen Welt*, II. 12, part 2 (Berlin and New York: De Gruyter, 1981), 477-514.

Brendel, Otto. *Prolegomena to the Study of Roman Art.* New Haven: Yale University Press, 1979. Originally published as "Prolegomena to a Book on Roman Art," *MAAR*, 1953.

Budde, Ludwig. *Jugendbildnisse des Caracalla und Geta.* Münster Westf.: Aschendorffsche Verlagsbuchhandlung, 1951.

Byvanck, Alexander Wilhelm. "Les Origines de l'art du bas-empire," *BABesch*, 39 (1964), 1-47.

Calza, Raissa. "Ritratto ostiense severiano," *Arti Figurative*, 1 (1945), 69-72.

——."Sui ritratti ostiense del supposto Plotino," *BdA*, 38 (1953), 203-210.

Dio Cassius, *Dio's Roman History.* Trans. and ed. E. Capps, T. E. Page and W. H. D. Rouse, Loeb Classical Library, London and New York, 1927.

Ferri, Silvio. "Plotino e l'arte del III secolo," *Critica d'Arte*, 1, fasc. 4 (1935-36), 166-171.

Fittschen, Klaus. "Antik oder nicht Antik? Zum Problem der Echtheit römischer Bildnisse," *Festschrift für Frank Brommer.* Mainz: von Zabern, 1977, pp. 93-99, plates 28-31.

——."Bemerkungen zu den Porträts des 3. Jahrhunderts nach Christus," *JdI*, 84 (1969), 197-236.

——."Zwei römische Bildnisse in Kassel," *RömMitt*, 77 (1970), 132-143.

——."Zum angeblichen Bildnis des Lucius Verus im Thermenmuseum," *JdI*, 86 (1971), 214-252.

Goldscheider, Ludwig. *Roman Portraits.* Oxford and London, 1945.

Gombrich, Ernst H. *Art and Illusion: A Study in the Psychology of Pictorial Representation.* Bollingen Series, 35. Princeton: Princeton University Press, 1956.

Grabar, André. "Plotin et les origines de l'esthétique médievale," *CahArch*, 1 (1945), 15-31.

Gullini, Giorgio. *Maestri e botteghe in Roma da Gallieno alla Tetrarchia.* Turin: Università di Torino, 1960.

——."Recenti scoperte di sculture tardo-romane nei dintorni di Roma," *BdA*, 34 (1949), 50-59.

Hanfmann, George M. A. "Observations on Roman Portraiture," *Latomus*, 11 (1952), 203-215, and 337-347.

——."Personality and Portraiture in Ancient Art," *ProcPhilSoc*, 117, part 4 (1973), 259-270.

Harrison, Evelyn Byrd. *Portrait Sculpture.* Vol. I of *The Athenian Agora.* Princeton: American School of Classical Studies at Athens, 1953.

Hausmann, Ulrich, "Zur Typologie und Ideologie des Augustusporträts," *Aufstieg und Niedergang der römischen Welt*, II. 12, part 2. Berlin and New York: De Gruyter, 1981. 513-598.

Heintze, Helga von. "Aspekte römischer Porträtkunst," *Gymnasium Beiheft*, 4 (1964), 149-162.

——."Drei antike Porträtstatuen," *Antike Plastik*, I (1962), 7-31, plates 1-21.

——.*Römische Porträt-Plastik.* Stuttgart: H. E. Gunter, 1961.

Hekler, Anton. *Die Bildniskunst der Griechen und Römer.* Stuttgart: W. Heinemann, 1912.

——."Studien zur römischen Porträtkunst," *ÖJh.*, 21-22 (1922-1924), 172-202.

Himmelmann-Wildschutz, Nikolaus, "Sarkophag eines gallienischen Konsuls," *Festschrift für Friedrich Matz*. Mainz: von Zabern, 1962, pp. 110-124, plates 31-39.

Hinks, R. P.*Greek and Roman Portrait Sculpture*. London: British Museum, 1935.

Inan, Jale, and Elizabeth Rosenbaum. *Roman and Early Byzantine Portrait Sculpture in Asia Minor*. London: Oxford University Press, for the British Academy, 1966.

Ippel, Albert. *Römische Porträts*. Vol. I, Bilderhefte zur Kunst- und Kulturgeschichte des Altertums. Leipzig: Hans Schaal, 1930.

Jucker, Hans. "Die Behauptung des Balbinus," *AA*, 81 (1966), 501-514.

———."Drei ergänzte Sarkophage," *AA*, 70 (1955), 26-31.

———."A Portrait Head of the Emperor Balbinus," *Cleveland Museum of Art Bulletin*, 54 (1967), 11-16.

Kallipolitis, Basileios. "Portrait grec en bronze de l'epoque de Gallien," *MonPiot*, 54 (1965), 117-130.

Kaschnitz-Weinberg, Guido. "Spätrömische Porträts," *Die Antike*, 2 (1926), 36-60.

Kiang, Dawson, "The Metropolitan Antiochus and the Vatican Philip," *Acta ad Archaeologiam et Artium Historiam Pertinentia*, 8 (1978), 75-84.

Kitzinger, Ernst. *Byzantine Art in the Making*. London: Faber and Faber, 1977.

Kluge, Kurt, and Karl Lehmann-Hartleben. *Grossbronzen der römischen Kaiserzeit*. 2 vols. Berlin-Leipzig: De Gruyter, 1927.

Kondić, Vladimir. "Two Recent Acquisitions in Belgrade Museums," *JRS*, 63 (1973), 47-49.

Lattanzi, Elena. *I Ritratti dei cosmeti nel museo nazionale di Atene*. Rome: L' Erma di Bretschneider, 1968.

L'Orange, H. P. *Apotheosis in Ancient Portraiture*, Institutet for Sammenlignende Kulturforskning, Ser. B., Vol. XLIV. Oslo, 1947.

———."The Antique Origins of Medieval Portraiture," *Likeness and Icon*. Odense: Odense University Press, 1973, pp. 91-102. Originally published in *Acta Congressus Madvigiani*, Proceedings of the Second International Congress of Classical Studies, Vol. III, Copenhagen, 1954, pp. 53-70.

———.*Art Forms and Civic Life in the Late Roman Empire*. Princeton: Princeton University Press, 1965.

———."Plotinus-Paul," *Likeness and Icon*. Odense: Odense University Press, 1973, pp. 32-42. Originally published in *Byzantion*, 25-27 (1955-57), 473-485, reprinted in Italian in *Atti 7 congresso internazionale di archeologia classica*. Rome, 1961. Vol. II, 475-482.

———."The Portrait of Plotinus," *CahArch*, 5 (1951), 15-30.

———.*Studien zur Geschichte des spätantiken Porträts*. Oslo: H. Aschebourg, 1933.

———."Zur Ikonographie des Kaisers Elagabals," *SymbOslo*, 20 (1940), 152-159.

McCann, Anna Marguerite, "Beyond the Classical in Third Century Portraiture," *Aufstieg und Niedergang der römischen Welt*, II. 12, part 2. Berlin and New York: De Gruyter, 1981. 623-645.

McCoull, Leslie. "Two New Third-Century Imperial Portraits in the Ny Carlsberg Glyptotek," *Berytus*, 17 (1967-1968), 66-71.

Mathew, Gervase. "The Character of the Gallienic Renaissance," *JRS*, 33 (1943), 65-70.

Mattingly, Harold, Edward A. Sydenham, and C. V. H. Sutherland. *The Roman Imperial Coinage*. Vol. IV, part 2. London: Spink and Son, Ltd., 1938. Vol. IV, part 3. London: Spink and Son, Ltd., 1949.

Meischner, Jutta. "Das Frauenpörtat der Severerzeit,"Diss., Freie Universität, Berlin, 1964.

———."Eine römische Porträtstatue der Antiken-Sammlung," *Forschungen und Berichte der staatlichen Museen zu Berlin*, 18 (1977), 67-80, pls. 15-17.

———."Zwei Stilrichtungen in der Porträtkunst des mittleren 3. Jahrhunderts nach Christus,"*AA*, 82 (1967), 34-46.

Minto, Antonio. "Nuovo ritratto in bronzo di Filippo l'Arabo," *Rivista d'Arte*, 29 (1954), 5-16.

Niemeyer, Hans Georg, *Studien zur statuarischen Darstellung der römischen Kaiser*. Berlin: Mann, 1968.

Nodelman, Sheldon. "Severan Imperial Portraits, A. D. 193-217." Diss., Yale University, 1965.
——."How to Read a Roman Portrait," *Art in America*, 63 (1977), 27-33.
——."Structural Analysis in Art and Anthropology," *Structuralism*, ed. Jacques Ehrmann. New York: Doubleday Anchor, 1970, pp. 79-93.
Paribeni, Roberto. *Il Ritratto nell'arte antica*. Milan: Fratelli Treves, 1934.
Pelikàn, Oldrich. "A Propos a l'évolution de l'art romain: le rôle du maniérisme dans la sculpture," *Hommages a Marcel Renard*. Vol. 60, *Collection Latomus*. Brussels, 1969, pp. 453-460.
——.*Vom antiken Realismus zur spätantiken Expressivität*. Prague, Státni Pedag, 1965.
Plotinus. *Enneads*. Trans. Stephen MacKenna. 3rd ed., rev. B. S. Page. London: Faber, 1962.
Richter, Gisela M. A. "Four Notable Acquisitions of the Metropolitan Museum," *AJA*, 44 (1940), 428-442.
——."A Portrait of Caracalla," *BMMA*, 35 (1940), 139-142.
Riegl, Alois. *Die spätrömische Kunstindustrie nach den Funden in Österreich-Ungarn*. Vienna: Druck und Verlag der kaiserlich-königlichen Hof- und Staatsdruckerei, 1901. Vol. I.
Rodenwaldt, Gerhard. "Der grosse Schlachtsarkophag Ludovisi," *Antike Denkmäler*, 4 (1929). 61-68.
——."Über den Stilwandel in der Antoninischen Kunst," *AbhBerl*, 1935, pp. 1-25.
Saletti, Cesare. *Ritratti Severiani*. Vol. X of *Studia Archeologica*. Rome: L'Erma di Bretschneider, 1967.
Schefold, Karl. *Die Bildnisse der antiken Dichter, Redner und Denker*. Basel: B. Schwabe, 1943.
Schweitzer, Bernhard. "Altrömische Traditionselemente in der Bildniskunst des 3. nach-Christlichen Jahrhunderts," *Zur Kunst der Antike, Ausgewählte Schriften*. Tübingen: Ulrich Hausmann, 1963. Vol. II, 265-279. Originally published in *Nederlands Kunsthistorisch Jaarboeck*, 5 (1954), 173-190.
——."Spätantike Grundlagen der Mittelalterlichen Kunst," *Zur Kunst der Antike: Ausgewählte Schriften*. Tübingen: Ulrich Hausmann, 1963. Vol. II, 280-303. Originally published in *Leipziger Universitätsreden*, 16 (1949).
*Scriptores Historiae Augustae*. Trans. and ed. David Magie, Loeb Classical Library. Cambridge, Mass.: Harvard University Press. Vol. I, 1921. II, 1924. III, 1932.
Soechting, Dirk. *Die Porträts des Septimius Severus*. Bonn: R. Habelt, 1972.
Strong, Donald. *Roman Art*. Ed. Jocelyn M. C. Toynbee. *Pelican History of Art*. Harmondsworth and Baltimore: Penguin, 1976. 2nd ed., in integrated format, 1980.
Strong, Eugenie. *Art in Ancient Rome*. New York: C. Scribner's Sons, 1929.
——.*Roman Sculpture from Augustus to Constantine*. London: Duckworth and Co.; New York: C. Scribner's Sons, 1907.
Stuart, Merriweather. "How Were Imperial Portraits Distributed Throughout the Roman Empire?" *AJA*, 43 (1939), 601-617.
Swift, E. H. "Imagines in Imperial Portraiture," *AJA*, 27 (1923), 286-301.
Vermeule, Cornelius. "A Graeco-Roman Portrait Head of the Third Century A.D.," *DOPapers*, 15 (1961), 3-22.
——.*Roman Imperial Art in Greece and Asia Minor*. Cambridge: Harvard University Press, 1968.
Wegner, Max. "Bildnisbüste im 3. Jahrhundert n. Chr.," *Festschrift für Gerhard Kleiner*. Tübingen: Wasmuth, 1973. Pp. 105-132.
Wessel, Klaus. "Römische Frauenfrisuren von der severischen bis zur konstantinischen Zeit," *AA*, 61 (1946-47),62-76.
Wilson, Lillian. *The Clothing of the Ancient Romans*. Baltimore: Johns Hopkins Press, 1938.
——.*The Roman Toga*. Baltimore: Johns Hopkins Press, 1924.
Zadoks-Josephus Jitta, Annie N. *Ancestral Portraiture in Rome*. Amsterdam: Allard Pierson, 1932.
Zinserling, Gerhard. "Altrömische Traditionselemente in Porträtkunst und Historienmalerei der ersten Hälfte des 3. Jahrhunderts u.z.," *Klio*, 41 (1963), 196-220.

# INDEX OF PROPER NAMES

## PERSONS

## PLACES AND MUSEUMS

# GENERAL INDEX

Abstraction: x, 22, 23-24, 32, 35, 68, 77, 92-115, 118-119
Antonine style: 13, 15, 18, 28, 30
Anxiety, portrayal of: 78-79
Asymmetry: 23, 34, 62, 87
Attribution: see personality, artistic
Augustan style: 13, 15, 16, 17, 20, 22

Baroque style: 13
Biography, in Latin literature: 2
Busts, typology of: 9, 38, 41-42, 73, 94

Chronology, problems of: 3, 101-102
Christianity: 19, 103
Classicism: 17, 22, 45-46, 93, 117, 119
Coiffure: see hairstyle, female
Copies: see replicas
Costume: 3, 38-39, 41-42, 58, 70, 79, 80, 109, 114-115

Death masks: 7
Drill, use of: 13, 17, 51, 54, 61, 64, 68, 111, 114

Flavian style: 7, 16, 117
Folk-art: 18, 20, 77, 117
Funerary sculpture: 7, 8, 9, 54, 68-70, 73, 92, 114

Geometric pattern: 23, 24, 28-29, 32, 33-34, 35, 38, 40, 45, 47, 77, 88-91, 94, 98, 99, 118
Greek sculptural prototypes: 9, 19, 29, 44-45, 58, 79-80, 92-93, 109

Hairstyle, female: 3, 51-52, 61, 64, 69, 74, 76, 83, 87, 92, 98, 114
Hairstyle, male: 3, 15, 28, 30, 32, 34, 46, 50-51, 54-55, 56, 61, 68, 94, 98, 106, 108
Hellenistic art: 16, 17, 20, 24

Imitation of nature, theory of: 21-22
Impressionism: 23, 40, 43, 82-84, 85, 88, 110, 118
Italic style: 16, 17, 20, 24

Medieval art: 12, 16, 102
"Militaristic" style: 12
Millenial games: 42
Movement, portrayal of: 40, 43, 77-78, 80, 81, 83, 87, 104, 110, 118

Naturalism: see realism
Numismatics: 4, 30, 42, 50, 52, 92, 107, 122

Patrician style: 20, 24
Personality, artistic: 9-10, 55, 69, 89-91, 95-96, 97-98, 99, 112, 119
Plebeian style: 17, 19, 20, 24, 117-118
Popular style: see folk-art
Propaganda: 5-6, 8, 14, 16, 24, 29, 70, 116-117, 119, 121
Provincial styles: 18-20, 24, 31

Realism: x, 14, 16, 22, 38, 40, 59, 85, 87, 97, 100
Replicas: 4-5, 6, 29-30, 89, 103, 105, 109, 122
Republican style: 13, 14, 16
Revivals: 14, 15-16, 24, 101, 116, 119

Sarcophagi: 8, 11, 17, 35-36, 68-70, 74, 77, 85-86, 107-108
Schisms in artistic style: 14, 16, 20, 24, 70, 116, 117
Senatorial style: 12-13
Spirituality, representation of: 16, 21-22, 58, 66, 88, 93, 102
Stilwandel: 16
Structural analysis: 3-4
Surface, treatment of: 58, 66, 72, 105
Symmetry: 21-22, 38, 89-91, 97, 99, 106, 118

Tetrarchy: 20, 114
Trajanic style: 15, 108

Verism: x, 13, 16, 17, 18, 20, 22, 23, 62-63, 87

Workshop tradition: 24, 77, 116, 121

# PHOTO CREDITS

Fig. 1. Photo courtesy of the museum
Fig. 2. Photo museum
Fig. 3a. Photo museum
Fig. 3b. Photo museum
Fig. 4. Photo Deutsches Archaeologisches Institut, Rom.Inst. Neg. 686
Fig. 5. Photo Deutsches Archaeologisches Institut, Rom.Inst. Neg. 38.667
Fig. 6. Photo Deutsches Archaeologisches Institut, Rom.Inst. Neg. 72.485
Fig. 7. Photo museum
Fig. 8. Photo Alinari
Fig. 9. Photo Alinari
Fig. 10. Photo Deutsches Archaeologisches Institut, Rom.Inst. Neg. 55.13
Fig. 11a. Photo museum
Fig. 11b. Photo museum
Fig. 12a. Photo museum
Fig. 12b. Photo museum
Fig. 13. Photo Deutsches Archaeologisches Institut, Rom.Inst. Neg. 67.500
Fig. 14. Photo Deutsches Archaeologisches Institut, Rom.Inst. Neg. 4256
Fig. 15. Photo Anderson
Fig. 16. Photo museum
Fig. 17. Photo courtesy of the Trustees of the British Museum
Fig. 18. Photo Hartwig Koppermann
Fig. 19. Photo Hartwig Koppermann
Fig. 20. Photo museum
Fig. 21. Photo Gisela Fittschen-Badura, reproduced courtesy of Prof. Dr. Klaus Fittschen, Archäologisches Institut, Göttingen
Fig. 22. Photo Gisela Fittschen-Badura, reproduced courtesy of Prof. Dr. Klaus Fittschen, Archäologisches Institut, Göttingen
Fig. 23. Photo Alinari
Fig. 24. Photo museum, reproduced courtesy of the Trustees of the British Museum
Fig. 25. Photo Deutsches Archaeologisches Institut, Rom.Inst. Neg. 57.743
Fig. 26. Photo Deutsches Archaeologisches Institut, Rom.Inst. Neg. 37.1767
Fig. 27. Photo Deutsches Archaeologisches Institut, Rom.Inst. Neg. 68.5066
Fig. 28. Photo Deutsches Archaeologisches Institut, Rom.Inst. Neg. 32.1758
Fig. 29. Photo author
Fig. 30. Photo museum
Fig. 31. Photo courtesy of the Museum of Fine Arts, Boston
Fig. 32. Photo Deutsches Archaeologisches Institut, Rom.Inst. Neg. 41.994
Fig. 33. Photo museum
Fig. 34. Photo Deutsches Archaeologisches Institut, Rom.Inst. Neg. 38.668
Fig. 35. Photo Deutsches Archaeologisches Institut, Rom.Inst. Neg. 68.954
Fig. 36. Photo Deutsches Archaeologisches Institut, Rom.Inst. Neg. 69.2168
Fig. 37. Photo museum
Fig. 38. Photo Deutsches Archaeologisches Institut, Rom.Inst. Neg. 55.10
Fig. 39. Photo Deutsches Archaeologisches Institut, Rom.Inst. Neg. 68.5068
Fig. 40a. Photo Anderson

Fig. 40b. Photo author
Fig. 41. Photo museum
Fig. 42a. Photo museum
Fig. 42b. Photo museum
Fig. 43. Photo museum
Fig. 44. Photo Deutsches Archaeologisches Institut, Rom.Inst. Neg. 8098
Fig. 45. Photo museum
Fig. 46. Photo Deutsches Archaeologisches Institut, Rom.Inst. Neg. 57.356
Fig. 47. Photo Deutsches Archaeologisches Institut, Rom.Inst. Neg. 67.37
Fig. 48. Photo courtesy of the Deutsches Archaeologisches Institut (after a Faraglia photograph)
Fig. 49a. Photo Deutsches Archaeologisches Institut, Rom.Inst. Neg. 67.56
Fig. 49b. Photo Deutsches Archaeologisches Institut, Rom.Inst. Neg. 34.1692
Fig. 50. Photo Deutsches Archaeologisches Institut, Rom.Inst. Neg. 81.4578, courtesy of the Fototeca Unione, American Academy in Rome
Fig. 51. Photo Deutsches Archaeologisches Institut, Rom.Inst. Neg. 69.2161
Fig. 52. Photo museum
Fig. 53a. Photo Ampliaciones y Reproducciones MAS, neg. C-44661
Fig. 53b. Photo Ampliaciones y Reproducciones MAS, neg. C-44665
Fig. 54. Photo Deutsches Archaeologisches Institut, Rom.Inst. Neg. 78.1150, after an earlier photograph
Fig. 55. Photo museum
Fig. 56. Photo museum
Fig. 57a. Photo courtesy of the Trustees of the British Museum
Fig. 57b. Photo courtesy of the Trustees of the British Museum
Fig. 58. Photo courtesy of the Soprintendenza alle Antichità dell'Etruria Meridionale
Fig. 59. Photo courtesy of the Soprintendenza alle Antichità dell'Etruria Meridionale
Fig. 60. Photo museum
Fig. 61. Photo Barbara Malter, Musei Capitolini, Archivio Fotographico 6876
Fig. 62. Photo Alinari
Fig. 63. Photo courtesy of the Soprintendenza Archeologica per il Veneto
Fig. 64a. Photo courtesy of the Trustees of the British Museum
Fig. 64b. Photo courtesy of the Trustees of the British Museum
Fig. 65a. Photo Hartwig Koppermann
Fig. 65b. Photo Hartwig Koppermann
Fig. 66. Photo Anderson
Fig. 67a. Photo Deutsches Archaeologisches Institut, Rom.Inst. Neg. 30.895
Fig. 67b. Photo Deutsches Archaeologisches Institut, Rom.Inst. Neg. 30.921
Fig. 68. Photo museum
Fig. 69. Photo Barbara Malter, Musei Capitolini, Archivio Fotografico 6871
Fig. 70. Photo Hartwig Koppermann
Fig. 71a. Photo museum
Fig. 71b. Photo museum
Fig. 72a. Photo Deutsches Archaeologisches Institut, Rom.Inst. Neg. 8094
Fig. 72b. Photo Deutsches Archaeologisches Institut, Rom.Inst. Neg. 8095
Fig. 73. Photo museum
Fig. 74. Photo Deutsches Archaeologisches Institut, Rom.Inst. Neg. 29.199
Fig. 75. Photo Deutsches Archaeologisches Institut, Rom.Inst. Neg. 8158
Fig. 76. Photo Deutsches Archaeologisches Institut, Rom.Inst. Neg. 8153A
Fig. 77. Photo Deutsches Archaeologisches Institut, Rom.Inst. Neg. 8162A

Fig. 78. Photo Istituto Centrale per il Catalogo e la Documentazione F-5694, after Himmelmann-Wildschutz, Festschrift *Matz*, pl. 35

Fig. 79. Photo Deutsches Archaeologisches Institut, Rom.Inst. Neg. 66.732

Fig. 80. Photo Deutsches Archaeologisches Institut, Rom.Inst. Neg. 57.379

Fig. 81. Photo Deutsches Archaeologisches Institut, Rom.Inst. Neg. 36.478

Fig. 82. Photo museum

Fig. 83. Photo Udo F. Sitzenfray, courtesy of the Museum

Fig. 84. Photo museum

Fig. 85. Photo museum

Fig. 86. Photo Barbara Malter, Musei Capitolini, Archivio Fotografico 6868

Fig. 87. Photo museum

PLATE I

Fig. 2. Caracalla, New York, Metropolitan Museum of Art, Samuel D. Lee Fund, 1940, inv. 40.11.1.

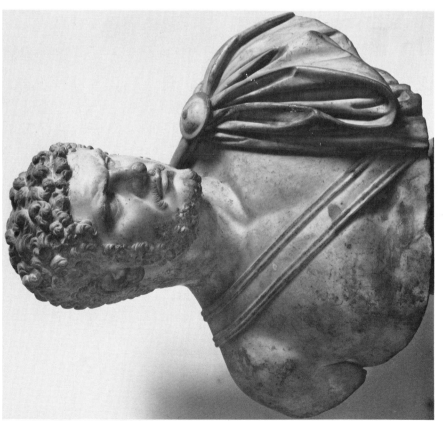

Fig. 1. Caracalla, Berlin, Staatliche Museen, Antiken-Sammlung, Cat. R96.

PLATE II

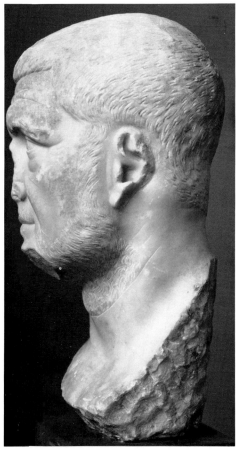

Fig. 3a. Maximinus Thrax, Copenhagen, Ny Carlsberg Glyptotek, cat. 744.

Fig. 3b. Maximinus Thrax, Copenhagen, Ny Carlsberg Glyptotek, cat. 744, profile.

PLATE III

Fig. 4. Pupienus, bust in Vatican, Braccio Nuovo.

PLATE IV

Fig. 6. Sarcophagus of Balbinus, detail of portrait of Balbinus on relief. Rome,

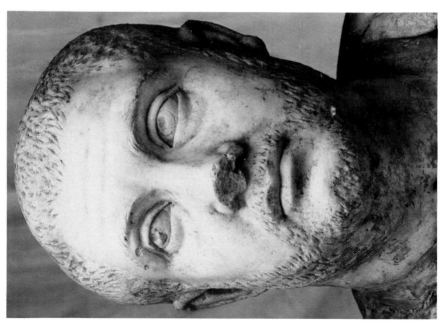

Fig. 5. Sarcophagus of Balbinus, detail: face of figure of

PLATE V

Fig. 8. Gordian III, Rome, Museo Nazionale Romano, inv. 326.

Fig. 7. Gordian III, type 1, Berlin, Staatliche Museen, Antikensammlung, cat. R102.

PLATE VI

Fig. 9. Philip the Arab, Rome, Vatican, Braccio Nuovo, inv. 2216.

PLATE VII

Fig. 10. Trajan Decius, Rome, Museo Capitolino.

PLATE VIII

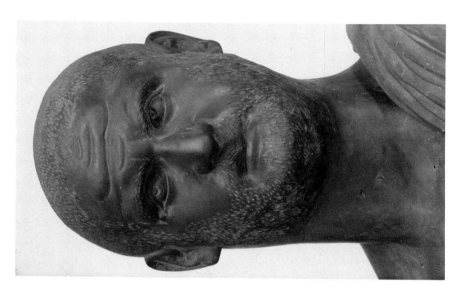

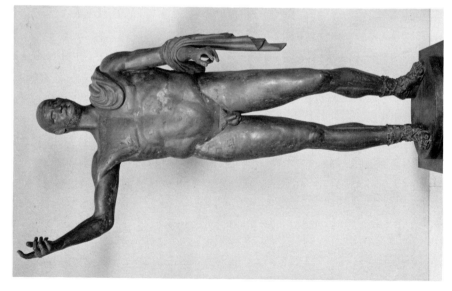

Fig. 11a. Trebonianus Gallus? Bronze statue, New

Fig. 11b. Trebonianus Gallus? Bronze statue,

PLATE IX

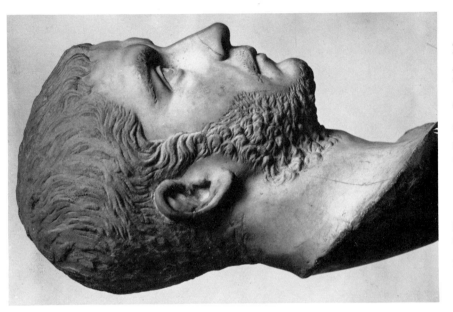

Fig. 12b. Gallienus, type 1. Berlin, Staatliche Museen, Antiken-Sammlung, cat. R114, profile.

Fig. 12a. Gallienus, type 1. Berlin, Staatliche Museen, cat. R114.

PLATE X

Fig. 13. Gallienus, type 2. Rome, Museo Nazionale Romano, inv. 644.

PLATE XI

Fig. 14. Elagabalus, Rome, Museo Capitolino.

PLATE XII

Fig. 15. Naples, Museo Nazionale, bust of a woman.

Fig. 16. Julia Paula? Copenhagen, Ny Carlsberg Glyptotek, cat. 755.

Fig. 17. British Museum, cat. 2009, bust of a woman.

PLATE XIII

Fig. 19. Munich Glyptothek, cat. 386.

Fig. 18. Munich Glyptothek, cat. 396.

PLATE XIV

Fig. 20. Fogg Art Museum, Harvard University, 1949.83. Grace Nichols Strong Memorial Fund.

PLATE XV

Fig. 21. Rome, Museo Nazionale Romano, cat. 300, inv. 124486.

PLATE XVI

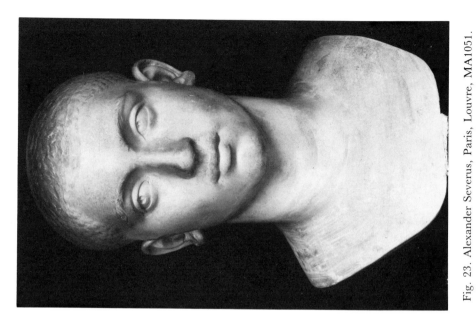

Fig. 23. Alexander Severus, Paris, Louvre, MA1051.

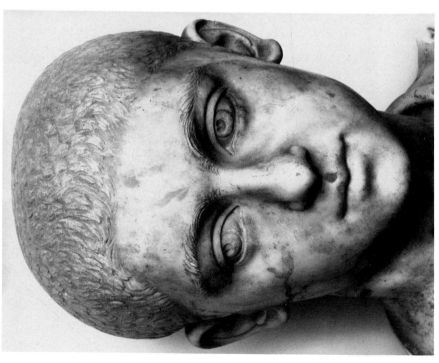

Fig. 22. Alexander Severus, Museo Capitolino.

PLATE XVII

Fig. 25. Julia Mammaea, Rome, Museo Capitolino, inv. 457.

Fig. 24. Julia Mammaea, British Museum, cat. 1920.

PLATE XVIII

Fig. 26. Alexander Severus, Vatican, Sala dei Busti, No. 361, inv. 632.

PLATE XIX

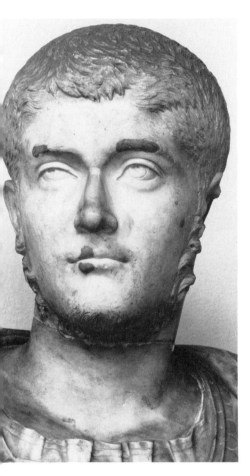

Fig. 27. Venice, Museo Archeologico, inv. 148.

Fig. 28. Florence, Uffizi Gallery, inv. 1914-280.

PLATE XX

Fig. 29. Rome, Museo Capitolino, inv. 708.

PLATE XXI

Fig. 30. Copenhagen, Ny Carlsberg Glyptotek, cat. 750.

PLATE XXII

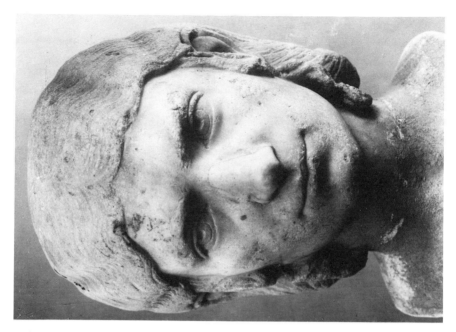

Fig. 32. Vatican, Galleria dei Candelabri, No. 22.

Fig. 31. Boston, Museum of Fine Arts, 1970.325.

PLATE XXIII

Fig. 33. Maximus, Copenhagen, Ny Carlsberg Glyptotek, cat. 745.

PLATE XXIV

Fig. 35. Sarcophagus of Balbinus, detail of portrait of
wife from the relief

Fig. 34. Sarcophagus of Balbinus, detail of face of wife from
figure on lid. Rome, Museum of the Catacomb of the Praetextatus.

PLATE XXV

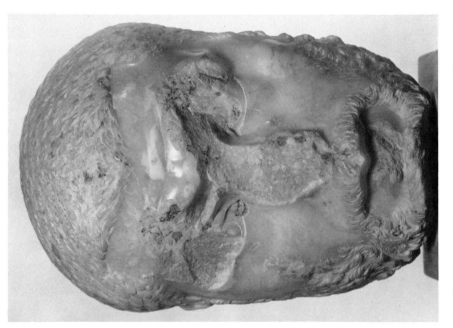

Fig. 37. Macrinus? Fogg Art Museum, Harvard University, inv. 1949.47.138, Alpheus Hyatt Fund.

Fig. 36. Macrinus? Palazzo dei Conservatori inv. 1757.

PLATE XXVI

Fig. 38. Rome, Palazzo Braschi, inv. 478.

PLATE XXVII

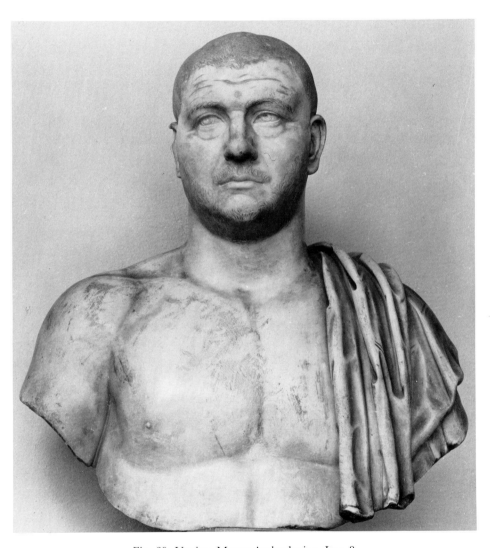

Fig. 39. Venice, Museo Archeologico, Inv. 8.

PLATE XXVIII

Fig. 40a. Rome, Museo Capitolino, Stanza degli Imperatori, No. 42.

Fig. 40b. Rome, Museo Capitolino,
Stanza degli Imperatori, No. 42, profile.

PLATE XXIX

Fig. 41. New York, Metropolitan Museum of Art, Rogers Fund, 1918 (inv. 18.145.39).

PLATE xxx

Fig. 42b. Copenhagen, Ny Carlsberg Glyptotek, cat. 738, pro-

Fig. 42a. Copenhagen, Ny Carlsberg Glyptotek, cat. 738.

PLATE XXXI

Fig. 43. Berlin, Staatliche Museen, Antiken-Sammlung, inv. SK 1764. Face.

PLATE XXXII

Fig. 44. Rome, Museo Nazionale Romano, inv. 8652, cat. 296.

PLATE XXXIII

Fig. 45. Berlin, Staatliche Museen, Antiken-Sammlung, inv. SK 1764. Statue of an official presiding at a contest.

Fig. 46. Rome, Palazzo dei Conservatori, Sala dei Magistrati 6, inv. 778. Statue of an emperor (Trajan Decius?) as Mars.

PLATE XXXIV

Fig. 47. Rome, Museo Capitolino, Stanza del Fauno 2, inv. 356.

PLATE XXXV

Fig. 48. Rome, Museo Capitolino, Sala delle Colombe 12.

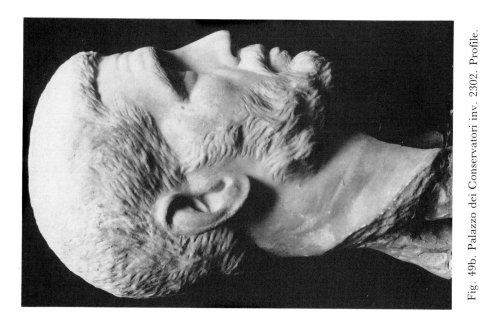

Fig. 49b. Palazzo dei Conservatori inv. 2302. Profile.

Fig. 49a. Palazzo dei Conservatori inv. 2302.

PLATE XXXVII

Fig. 50. Portrait head of philosopher (Plotinus?), Ostia Antica, inv. 436.

PLATE XXXVIII

Fig. 51. Otacilia Severa. Rome, Palazzo dei Conservatori, inv. 2765.

PLATE XXXIX

Fig. 52. Berlin, Staatliche Museen, Antiken-Sammlung, cat. R111, inv. SK441.

PLATE XL

Fig. 53a. Tarragona, Museo Paleocristiano. Marble sarcophagus.

Fig. 53b. Tarragona, Museo Paleocristiano. Marble sarcophagus, detail of bust of deceased.

PLATE XLI

Fig. 54. Ostia Antica, Museo Inv. 213-A.

Fig. 56. Copenhagen, Ny Carlsberg Glyptotek, cat. 752.

Fig. 55. Fragment from a sarcophagus, Berlin, Staatliche Mu-

PLATE XLIII

57a. Tranquillina, London, British Museum, cat. 1923.

Fig. 57b. Tranquillina, London, British Museum, cat. 1923, profile.

PLATE XLIV

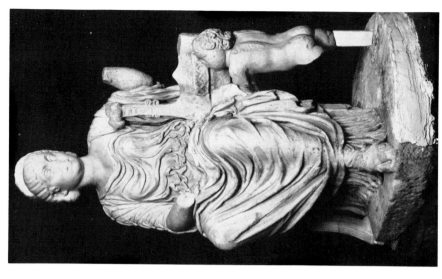

Fig. 59. Rome, Museo Nazionale della Villa

Fig. 58. Rome, Museo Nazionale della Villa Giulia, provisional deposit.

PLATE XLV

Fig. 61. Rome, Museo Capitolino, Sala Terrena a Destra 1, No. 21.

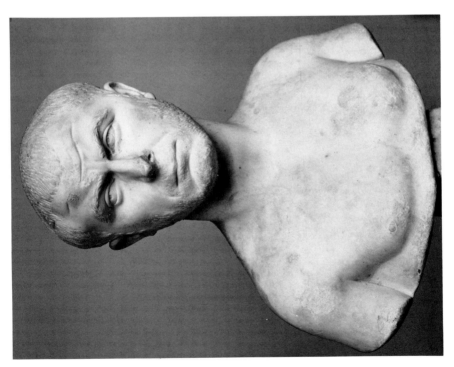

Fig. 60. Copenhagen, Ny Carlsberg Glyptotek, cat. 761, inv. 827.

PLATE XLVI

Fig. 62. Museo Capitolino, Stanza degli Imperatori, No. 49.

PLATE XLVII

Fig. 63. Venice, Museo Archeologico inv. 203, currently in the Biblioteca Marciana.

PLATE XLVIII

Fig. 64a. London, British Museum, cat. 1924.

Fig. 64b. London, British Museum, cat. 1924, profile.

PLATE XLIX

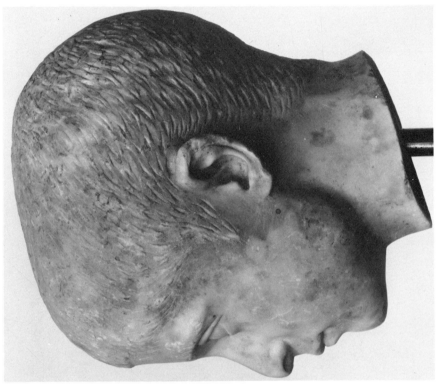

Fig. 65b. Philip II? Munich Glyptothek, cat. 360, inv. KH150. Profile.

Fig. 65a. Philip II? Munich Glyptothek, cat. 360, inv. KH150.

PLATE L

Fig. 66. Palazzo dei Conservatori, inv. 428.

PLATE LI

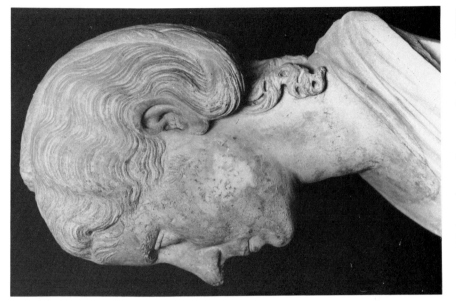

Fig. 67b. Vatican, former Lateran collection, inv. 10206.

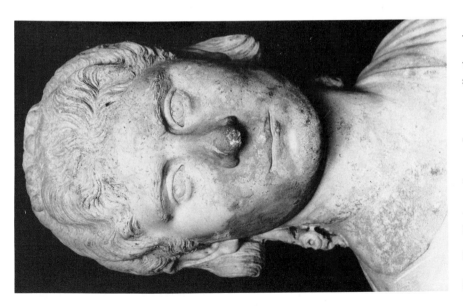

Fig. 67a. Vatican, former Lateran collection, inv. 10206.

PLATE LII

Fig. 68. Frankfurt-am-Main, Liebighaus Museum, inv. 87.

PLATE LIII

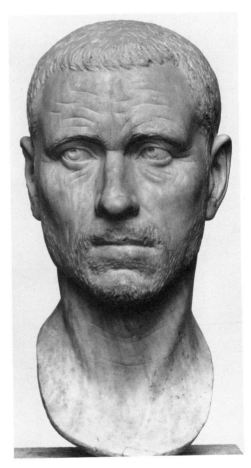

Fig. 69. Palazzo dei Conservatori, inv. 184.

Fig. 70. Munich Glyptothek, cat. 362.

PLATE LIV

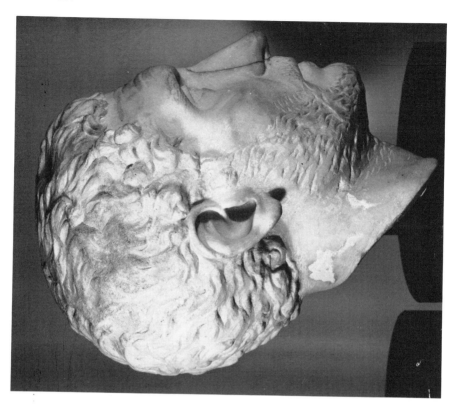

Fig. 71b. Vatican, former Lateran collection, inv. 10205, profile.

Fig. 71a. Vatican, former Lateran collection, inv. 10205.

PLATE LV

Fig. 72b. Rome, Museo Nazionale Romano, cat. 301, inv. 108607, profile.

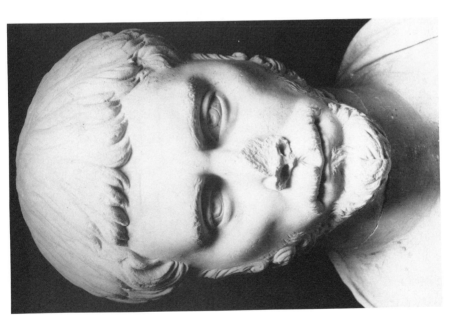

Fig. 72a. Rome, Museo Nazionale Romano, cat. 301, inv. 108607.

PLATE LVI

Fig. 73. New York, Metropolitan Museum of Art, Rogers Fund 1906 (08.258.46).

PLATE LVII

Fig. 74. Museo Capitolino, inv. 430.

PLATE LVIII

Fig. 77. Rome, Villa Doria Pam-

Fig. 76. Rome, Villa Doria Pamfili,

Fig. 75. Rome, Villa Doria Pam-

PLATE LIX

Fig. 78. Ostia Antica, Museum, inv. 62, bust of a young man.

PLATE LX

Fig. 80. Museo Capitolino, inv. 645, Salone, No. 27

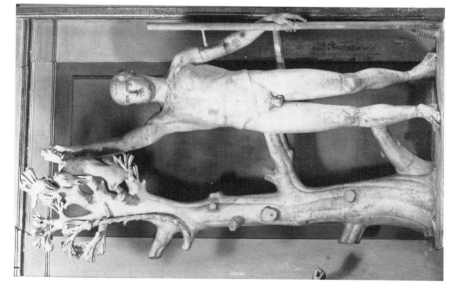

Fig. 79. Museo Capitolino, inv. 645, Salone, No. 27

PLATE LXI

Fig. 81. Rome, Palazzo dei Conservatori, inv. 1794.

PLATE LXII

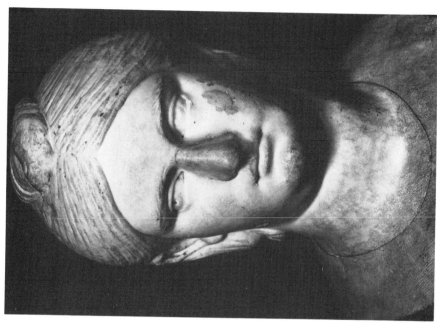

Fig. 83. Vienna, Kunsthistorisches Museum, inv. 257.

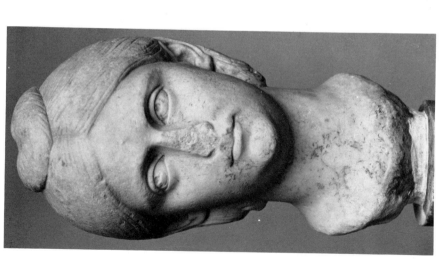

Fig. 82. Copenhagen, Ny Carlsberg Glyp-

PLATE LXIII

Fig. 85. Copenhagen, Ny Carlsberg Glyptotek, inv. 824, cat. 751.

Fig. 84. Malibu, J. Paul Getty Museum, inv. 73.AA.47.

PLATE LXIV

Fig. 87. Bust of Aurelia Monina. Berlin, Staatliche

Fig. 86. Palazzo dei Conservatori, inv. 2767.